Level 1
BRICKWORK

NVQ/SVQ and CAA Diploma

D1421711

C333028389

Part of Pearson

Heinemann is an imprint of Pearson Education Limited, a company incorporated in England and Wales, having its registered office at Edinburgh Gate, Harlow, Essex, CM20 2JE. Registered company number: 872828

www.pearsonschoolsandfecolleges.co.uk

Heinemann is a registered trademark of Pearson Education Limited

Text © Carillion Construction Ltd 2008 and 2010

First published 2010

14 13 12 11 10
10 9 8 7 6 5 4 3 2 1

British Library Cataloguing in Publication Data is available from the British Library on request.

ISBN 978 0 435027 07 0

Copyright notice

Designed by Wooden Ark
Typeset by Tek-Art
Original illustrations © Pearson Education 2010
Illustrated by Oxford Designers & Illustrators Ltd
Cover design by Wooden Ark
Cover photo/illustration © Construction Photography/Phil Starling
Printed in the UK by Scotprint, Haddington

Acknowledgements

Every effort has been made to contact copyright holders of material reproduced in this book. Any omissions will be rectified in subsequent printings if notice is given to the publishers.

Websites

The websites used in this book were correct and up-to-date at the time of publication. It is essential for tutors to preview each website before using it in class so as to ensure that the URL is still accurate, relevant and appropriate. We suggest that tutors bookmark useful websites and consider enabling students to access them through the school/college intranet.

The information and activities in this book have been prepared according to the standards reasonably to be expected of a competent trainer in the relevant subject matter. However, you should be aware that errors and omissions can be made and that different employers may adopt different standards and practices over time. Before doing any practical activity, you should always carry out your own Risk Assessment and make your own enquires and investigations into appropriate standards and practices to be observed.

Contents

Acknowledgements

Carillion would like to thank the following people for their contribution to this book: Ralph Need, Kevin Jarvis, David Whitten and John Harvie McLaughlin.

Pearson Education Limited would like to thank the following for providing technical feedback: Rob Harrison from Stoke College and Jim Neil from North Glasgow College.

Photo acknowledgements
The author and publisher would like to thank the following individuals and organisations for permission to reproduce photographs:

(Key: b-bottom; c-centre; l-left; r-right; t-top)

Alamy Images: Geoff du Feu 83, David J Green 61, Nic Hamilton 3, Imagebroker 213 (7.12), Judith Collins 140 (4.3), Justin Kase 28, 129 (3.41), 164, David Lawrence 129 (3.38), Image Source Pink 22 (1.10), The Photolibrary Wales 24; **Construction Photography:** Buildpix 15, 129 (3.37), 181, Xavier de Canto 12, Jean-Francois Condella 146 (4.13), Chris Henderson 7, 118, Sally-Ann Norman 50 (1.34), David Potter 52 (1.40), 127 (3.29), Ken Price 50 (1.35), Adrian Sherratt 127 (3.31), David Stewart-Smith 128; **Corbis:** 52 (1.38), Samos Images / Steve Hix 133; **CSCS:** 14; **Getty Images:** PhotoDIsc 25, 51, 110, Photonica 155; **Image Source Ltd:** 115, 176; **iStockphoto:** Leigh Schindler 66 (1.60); **Martyn F. Chillmaid:** 141 (4.7); **Pearson Education Ltd:** Gareth Boden 22 (1.9), 33tl, 33tr, 33bl, 33bc, 33br, 39 (1.17), 39 (1.18), 39 (1.19), 44, 46, 47, 67 (1.62), 68 (1.64), 68 (1.65), 120, 124, 145 (4.11), 145 (4.12), 146 (4.14), 148 (4.17), 148 (4.18), 148 (4.19), 148l (4.20), 148r (4.20), 149 (4.21), 149 (4.22), 149 (4.23), 169 (5.19), 169 (5.20), 169 (5.21), 169 (5.23), 169l (5.22), 169r (5.22), 170 (5.24), 170 (5.25), 170 (5.26), 177 (5.37), 177 (5.38), 212, 213 (7.13), Chris Honeywell 64 (1.52), David Sanderson 65 (1.58), 66 (1.59), 67 (1.63), Jules Selmes 19; **Pearson Education Ltd:** Clark Wiseman, Studio 8 144tl, 144tr, 144cl, 144cr, 144b, 158tl, 158tr, 158cl, 158cr, 158b; **Robert Down Photography:** 150; **Science Photo Library Ltd:** Scott Camazine 23, Garry Watson 29l; **Shutterstock:** Yuri Arcurs 14 (inset), Andrey Bayda 29c, Kevin Britland 129 (3.39), Rob Byron 65 (1.55), Istvan Csak 203, Sebastian Duda 73, Guy Erwood 52 (1.39), FDIMEO 140 (4.5), IOFoto 65 (1.54), Stanislav Komogorov 1, Alex Kosev 64 (1.51), Latentlight 141 (4.6), Frances A. MIller 50 (1.33), Michael Shake 64 (1.53), StillFX 65 (1.57), Fekete Tibor 129 (3.40), Edd Westmacott 65 (1.56), Yobidaba 29r

Cover images: *Front:* **Construction Photography:** Phil Starling

All other images © Pearson Education

Picture Research by: Chrissie Martin

Every effort has been made to trace the copyright holders and we apologise in advance for any unintentional omissions. We would be pleased to insert the appropriate acknowledgement in any subsequent edition of this publication.

Introduction

Welcome to NVQ/SVQ CAA Diploma Level 1 Brickwork!

Brickwork combines many different practical and visual skills with a knowledge of specialised materials and techniques. This book will introduce you to the construction trade and in particular the knowledge and skills needed for laying bricks and blocks, basic cavity walling and setting out.

About this book

This book has been produced to help you build a sound knowledge and understanding of all aspects of the Diploma and NVQ requirements associated with brickwork.

The information in this book covers the information you will need to attain your Level 1 qualification in brickwork. Each unit of the book relates to a particular unit of the CAA Diploma and provides the information needed to form the required knowledge and understanding of that area. The book is also designed to support those undertaking the NVQ at Level 1.

This book has been written based on a concept used by Carillion Training Centres for many years. The concept is about providing learners with the necessary information they need to support their studies and at the same time ensuring it is presented in a style which is both manageable and relevant.

This book will also be a useful reference tool for you in your professional life once you have gained your qualifications and are a practising builder.

This introduction will introduce the construction industry and the different types of construction work, alongside the qualifications available.

About the construction industry

Construction means creating buildings and services. These might be houses, hospitals, schools, offices, roads, bridges, museums, prisons, train stations, airports, monuments – and anything else you can think of that needs designing and building! What about an Olympic stadium? The 2012 London games will bring a wealth of construction opportunities to the UK and so it is an exciting time to be getting involved.

In the UK, 2.2 million people work in the construction industry and it is constantly expanding and developing. There are more choices and opportunities than ever before. Your career doesn't have to end in the UK either – what about taking the skills and experience you are developing abroad? Construction is a career you can take with you wherever you go. There's always going to be something that needs building!

The construction industry is made up of countless companies and businesses that all provide different services and materials. An easy way to divide these companies into categories is according to their size.

- A small-sized company is defined as having between 1 and 49 members of staff.
- A medium-sized company consists of between 50 and 249 members of staff.
- A large-sized company has 250 or more people working for it.

A business might even consist of only a single member of staff (a sole trader).

Different types of construction work

There are four main types of construction work:

- **new work** – this refers to a building that is about to be or has just been built
- **maintenance work** – this is when an existing building is kept up to an acceptable standard by fixing anything that is damaged so that it does not fall into disrepair
- **refurbishment/renovation work** – this generally refers to an existing building that has fallen into a state of disrepair and is then brought up to standard by repair work being carried out; it also refers to an existing building that is to be used for a different purpose, for example changing an old bank into a pub
- **restoration work** – this refers to an existing building that has fallen into a state of disrepair and is then brought back to its original condition or use.

These four types of work can fall into one of two categories depending upon who is paying for the work:

- **public** – the government pays for the work, as is the case with most schools and hospitals, etc.
- **private** – work that is paid for by a private client and can range from extensions on existing houses to new houses or buildings.

Jobs and careers

Jobs and careers in the construction industry fall mainly into one of four categories:

- **building** – the physical construction (making) of a structure; it also involves the maintenance, restoration and refurbishment of structures
- **civil engineering** – the construction and maintenance of work such as roads, railways, bridges, etc.
- **electrical engineering** – the installation and maintenance of electrical systems and devices such as lights, power sockets and electrical appliances, etc.
- **mechanical engineering** – the installation and maintenance of services such as heating, ventilation and lifts.

The category that is the most relevant to your course is building.

What is a building?

There are, of course, lots of very different types of building, but the main types are:

- **residential** – houses, flats, etc.
- **commercial** – shops, supermarkets, etc.
- **industrial** – warehouses, factories, etc.

These types of building can be further broken down by the height or number of storeys that they have (one storey being the level from floor to ceiling):

- **low-rise** – a building with one to three storeys
- **medium-rise** – a building with four to seven storeys
- **high-rise** – a building with seven storeys or more.

Buildings can also be categorised according to the number of other buildings they are attached to:

- **detached** – a building that stands alone and is not connected to any other building
- **semi-detached** – a building that is joined to one other building and shares a dividing wall, called a party wall
- **terraced** – a row of three, or more, buildings that are joined together, of which the inner buildings share two party walls.

Building requirements

Every building must meet the minimum requirements of the 'HAVE' regulations, which were first introduced in 1961 and then updated in 1985. The purpose of building regulations is to ensure that safe and healthy buildings are constructed for the public and that conservation (the preservation of the environment and the wildlife) is taken into account when they are being constructed. Building regulations enforce a minimum standard of building work and ensure that the materials used are of a good standard and fit for purpose.

What makes a good building?

When a building is designed, there are certain things that need to be taken into consideration, such as:

- security
- warmth
- safety
- light
- privacy
- ventilation.

A well-designed building will meet the minimum standards for all of the considerations above and will also be built in line with building regulations.

Qualifications for the construction industry

There are many ways of entering the construction industry, but the most common method is as an apprentice.

Apprenticeships

You can become an apprentice by being employed:

- directly by a construction company who will send you to college
- by a training provider, such as Carillion, which combines construction training with practical work experience.

Construction Skills is the national training organisation for construction in the UK and is responsible for setting training standards.

The framework of an apprenticeship is based around an NVQ (or SVQ in Scotland). These qualifications are developed and approved by industry experts and will measure your practical skills and job knowledge on-site.

You will also need to achieve:

- a technical certificate
- the Construction Skills health and safety test
- the appropriate level of functional skills assessment
- an Employers' Rights and Responsibilities briefing.

You will also need to achieve the right qualifications to get on a construction site, including qualifying for the CSCS card scheme.

Construction Awards Alliance (CAA) Diploma

The Construction Awards Alliance (CAA) Diploma was launched on 1 August 2008 to replace Construction Awards. They aim to make you:

- more skilled and knowledgeable
- more confident with moving across projects, contracts and employers.

The CAA Diploma is a common testing strategy with knowledge tests for each unit, a practical assignment and the Global Online Assessment (GOLA) test.

The CAA Diploma meets the requirements of the new Qualifications and Credit Framework (QCF) which bases a qualification on the number of credits (with ten learning hours gaining one credit):

- Award (1 to 12 credits)
- Certificate (13 to 36 credits)
- Diploma (37+ credits)

As part of the CAA Diploma you will gain the skills needed for the NVQ as well as the functional skills knowledge you will need to complete your qualification.

National Vocational Qualifications

National Vocational Qualifications (NVQs) are available to anyone, with no restrictions on age or length or type of training, although learners below a certain age can only perform certain tasks. There are different levels of NVQ (for example 1, 2, 3), which in turn are broken down into units of competence. NVQs are not like traditional examinations in which someone sits an exam paper. An NVQ is a 'doing' qualification, which means it lets the industry know that you have the knowledge, skills and ability to actually 'do' something.

NVQs are made up of both mandatory and optional units and the number of units that you need to complete for an NVQ depends on the level and the occupation.

NVQs are assessed in the workplace, and several types of evidence are used:

- witness testimony provided by individuals who have first-hand knowledge of your work and performance relating to the NVQ
- your performance can be observed a number of times in the workplace
- historical evidence means that you can use evidence from past achievements or experience, if it is directly related to the NVQ
- assignments or projects can be used to assess your knowledge and understanding
- photographic evidence showing you performing various tasks in the workplace can be used, providing it is authenticated by your supervisor.

Functional skills

Functional skills are the skills needed to work independently in everyday life. The references are headed FM for mathematics and FE for English.

Features of this book

This book has been fully illustrated with artworks and photographs. These will help to give you more information about a concept or a procedure, as well as helping you to follow a step-by-step procedure or identify a particular tool or material.

This book also contains a number of different features to help your learning and development.

Key term

These are new or difficult words. They are picked out in **bold** in the text and then defined in the margin.

Remember

This highlights key facts or concepts, sometimes from earlier in the text, to remind you of important things you will need to think about.

Did you know?

This feature gives you interesting facts about the building trade.

Safety tip

This feature gives you guidance for working safely on the tasks in this book.

Find out

These are short activities and research opportunities, designed to help you gain further information about, and understanding of, a topic area.

Working life

This feature gives you a chance to read about and debate a real life work scenario or problem. Why has the situation occurred? What would you do?

FAQ

These are frequently asked questions appearing at the end of each unit to answer your questions with informative answers from the experts.

Check it out

A series of questions at the end of each unit to check your understanding. Some of these questions may support the collecting of evidence for the NVQ.

Getting ready for assessment

This feature provides guidance for preparing for the practical assessment. It will give you advice on using the theory you have learnt about in a practical way.

Knowledge check

This is a series of multiple choice questions at the end of each unit, in the style of the GOLA end of unit tests.

UNIT 1001

Safe working practices in construction

Health and safety is a vital part of all construction work. All work should be completed in a way that is safe, not only for the individual worker, but also for the other workers on the site, people near by and the final users of the building.

Therefore, learning as much as you can about health and safety is very important. This unit also supports NVQ Unit VR1 Conform to General Workplace Safety and VR03 Move and Handle Resources. This unit contains material that supports TAP Unit 1: Erect and Dismantle Working Platforms. It also contains material that supports the delivery of the five generic units.

This unit will cover the following learning outcomes:

- Health and safety regulations – roles and responsibilities
- Accident, first aid and emergency procedures and reporting
- Hazards on construction sites
- Health and hygiene
- Safe handling of materials and equipment
- Basic working platforms
- Working with electricity
- Using appropriate PPE
- Fire and emergency procedures
- Safety signs and notices.

Key terms

Legislation – a law or set of laws passed by Parliament, often called an Act

Hazardous – something or a situation that is dangerous or unsafe

Employer – the person or company you work for

Employee – the worker

Proactive – acting in advance, before something happens (such as an accident)

Reactive – acting after something has happened, in response to it

Functional skills

When reading and understanding the text in this unit, you are practising several functional skills:

FE 1.2.1 – Identifying how the main points and ideas are organised in different texts.

FE 1.2.2 – Understanding different texts in detail.

FE 1.2.3 – Read different texts and take appropriate action, e.g. respond to advice/instructions.

If there are any words or phrases you do not understand, use a dictionary, look them up using the internet or discuss with your tutor.

K1. Health and safety regulations

While at work, whatever your location or the type of work you are doing, there is important **legislation** that you must comply with. Health and safety legislation is there not just to protect you – it also states what you must and must not do to ensure that no workers are placed in a situation **hazardous** to themselves or others.

There are hundreds of Acts covering all manner of work from hairdressing to construction. Each Act states the duties of the **employer** and **employee** – and you should be aware of both. If an employer or employee does something they shouldn't – or doesn't do something they should – they can end up in court and be fined or even imprisoned.

Approved code of practice, guidance notes and safety policies

As well as Acts, there are two sorts of codes of practice and guidance notes: those produced by the Health and Safety Executive (HSE; see page 5), and those created by companies themselves. Most large construction companies – and many smaller ones – have their own guidance notes, which go further than health and safety law. For example, the law states that everyone must wear safety boots in a hazardous area, but a company's code may state that everyone must wear safety boots at all times. This is called taking a **proactive** approach, rather than a **reactive** one.

Most companies have some form of safety policy outlining the company's commitment and stating what they plan to do to ensure that all work is carried out as safely as possible. As an employee, you should make sure you understand the company's safety policy as well as its codes of practice. If you don't follow company policy you may not be prosecuted in court, but you could still be disciplined by the company or even fired.

Health and safety legislation you need to be aware of

There are some 20 pieces of legislation that you will need to be aware of, each of which sets out requirements for employers and often for employees.

Did you know?

The Health and Safety at Work Act 1974 states that an employer must 'so far as is reasonably practicable' ensure that a safe place of work is provided. But employers are not expected to do everything they can to protect their staff from lightning strikes, as there is only a 1 in 800,000 chance of this occurring – this would not be reasonable!

We will now look at the regulations that will affect you most.

The Health and Safety at Work Act 1974 (HASAW)

The Health and Safety at Work Act 1974 (HASAW) applies to all types and places of work and to employers, employees, self-employed people, **subcontractors** and even **suppliers**. The Act is there to protect not only the people at work but also the general public, who may be affected in some way by the work that has been or will be carried out.

Key terms

Subcontractors – workers who have been hired by the main contractor to carry out works, usually specialist works, e.g. a general builder may hire a plumber as a subcontractor as none of their staff can do plumbing work

Suppliers – a company that supplies goods, materials or services

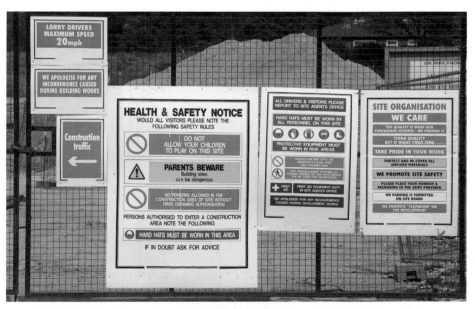

Figure 1.1 Legislation is there to protect employees and the public alike

Did you know?

One phrase that often comes up in legislation is 'so far as is resonably practicable'. This means that health and safety must be adhered to at all times, but must take a common sense, practical approach

The main objectives of the HASAW are to:

- ensure the health, safety and welfare of all persons at work
- protect the general public from all work activities
- control the use, handling, storage and transportation of explosives and highly **flammable** substances
- control the release of noxious or offensive substances into the atmosphere.

To ensure that these objectives are met, there are duties for all employers, employees and suppliers.

Key term

Flammable – something that is easily lit and burns rapidly

Key terms

Access – entrance, a way in

Egress – exit, a way out

PPE – personal protective equipment, such as gloves, a safety harness or goggles

Key terms

Omissions – something that has not been done or has been missed out

Obligations – something you have a duty or a responsibility to do

The employer's duties

Employers must:

- provide safe **access** and **egress** to and within the work area
- provide a safe place to work
- provide and maintain plant and machinery that is safe and without risks to health
- provide information, instruction, training and supervision to ensure the health and safety at work of all employees
- ensure safety and the absence of risks to health in connection with the handling, storage and transportation of articles and substances
- have a written safety policy that must be revised and updated regularly, and ensure that all employees are aware of it
- involve trade union safety representatives, where appointed, in all matters relating to health and safety
- carry out risk assessments (see page 24) and provide supervision where necessary
- provide, and not charge for, personal protective equipment (**PPE**).

The employee's duties

Employees must:

- take reasonable care for their own health and safety
- take reasonable care for the health and safety of anyone who may be affected by their acts or **omissions**
- co-operate with their employer or any other person to ensure the legal **obligations** are met
- not misuse or interfere with anything provided for their health and safety
- report hazards and accidents (see pages 15–18)
- use any equipment and safeguards provided by their employer.

Employers can't charge their employees for anything that has been done or provided for them to ensure that legal requirements on health and safety are met. Self-employed people and subcontractors have their duties as employees. But also, if they have employees of their own, they must obey the duties set down for employers.

The supplier's duties

Persons designing, manufacturing, importing or supplying articles or substances for use at work must ensure that:

- articles are designed and constructed so that they will be safe and without risk to health at all times while they are being used or constructed

- substances will be safe and without risk to health at all times when being used, handled, transported and stored
- tests on articles and substances are carried out as necessary
- adequate information is provided about the use, handling, transporting and storage of articles or substances.

Health and Safety Executive (HSE)

The HASAW, like most of the other Acts mentioned, is enforced by the Health and Safety Executive (HSE).

The HSE is the government body responsible for the encouragement, regulation and enforcement of health, safety and welfare in the workplace in the UK. It also has responsibility for research into occupational risks in England, Wales and Scotland. In Northern Ireland the responsibility lies with the Health and Safety Executive for Northern Ireland.

The HSE's duties are to:

- assist and encourage anyone who has any dealings with the objectives of HASAW
- produce and encourage research, publication, training and information on health and safety at work
- ensure that employers, employees, suppliers and other people are provided with an information and advisory service, and are kept informed and advised on any health and safety matters
- propose regulations
- enforce HASAW.

To aid in these duties the HSE has several resources, including a laboratory used for, among other things, research, development and **forensic investigation** into the causes of accidents. The enforcement of HASAW is usually delegated to local government bodies such as county or district councils.

Local government bodies can be **enforcing authorities** for several workplaces, including offices, shops, retail and wholesale distribution, hotel and catering establishments, petrol filling stations, residential care homes and the leisure industry.

An enforcing authority may appoint **inspectors**, who, under the authority, have the power to:

- enter any premises, which she or he has reason to believe it is necessary to enter, so as to enforce the Act, at any reasonable time, or in a dangerous situation
- bring a police constable if there is reasonable cause to fear any serious obstruction in carrying out their duty

Key terms

Forensic investigation – a branch of science that looks at how and why things happen

Enforcing authorities – an organisation or people who have the authority to enforce certain laws or Acts, as well as providing guidance or advice

Inspector – someone who is appointed or employed to inspect/ examine something in order to judge its quality or compliance with any laws

- bring any other person authorised by the enforcing authority, and any equipment or materials required
- examine and investigate any circumstance that is necessary for the purpose of enforcing the Act
- give orders that the premises, any part of them or anything therein, shall be left undisturbed for so long as is needed for the purpose of any examination or investigation
- take measurements and photographs and make any recordings considered necessary for the purpose of examination or investigation
- take samples of any articles or substances found and of the atmosphere in or in the vicinity of the premises
- have an article or substance which appears to be a danger to health or safety, dismantled, tested or even destroyed if necessary
- take possession of such an article and retain it for as long as is necessary in order to examine it and ensure that it is not tampered with and that it is available for use as evidence in any **prosecution**
- interview any person believed to have information, ask any questions the inspector thinks fit to ask and ensure that all statements are signed as a declaration of the truth of the answers
- require the production of, inspect and take copies of, any entry in any book or document as is necessary for the purposes of any examination or investigation
- use any other power which is necessary to enforce the Act.

Key term

Prosecution – accusing someone of committing a crime, which usually results in the accused being taken to court and, if found guilty, being punished

Contacting the Health and Safety Executive

Employers, self-employed people or those in control of work premises have legal duties to record and report to the HSE certain work-related accidents. The incidents that must be reported are:

- **death** – where someone is killed as a result of an accident related to work; this includes deaths resulting from physical violence
- **major injury** – including fractures, amputations, loss of sight and loss of consciousness
- **dangerous occurrence** – an event that may not have caused injury, but clearly could have done so; for example, some kinds of fire or explosion, collapse of buildings or scaffolding
- **over-three-day injury** – where someone suffers an injury at work that results in them being away from work or unable to do their full duties for more than three consecutive days
- **disease** – where a doctor notifies the person that they are suffering from some work-related disease.

Reporting of Injuries, Diseases and Dangerous Occurrences Regulations 1995 (RIDDOR)

Under RIDDOR, employers have a duty to report accidents, diseases or dangerous occurrences. The HSE use this information to identify where and how risk arises and to investigate serious accidents.

Control of Substances Hazardous to Health Regulations 2002 (COSHH)

The COSHH regulations state how employees and employers should work with, handle, store, transport and dispose of potentially hazardous substances (substances that might adversely affect your health) including:

- substances used directly in work activities (e.g. adhesives or paints)
- substances generated during work activities (e.g. dust from sanding wood)
- naturally occurring substances (e.g. sand dust)
- biological agents (e.g. germs such as bacteria).

These substances can be found in nearly all work environments.

The Control of Noise at Work Regulations 2005

At some point in your career in construction, you are likely to work in a noisy environment. These regulations help protect you against the consequences of being exposed to high levels of noise. High levels of noise can lead to permanent hearing loss. These regulations state that the employer must:

- assess the risks to the employee from noise at work
- take action to reduce the noise exposure that produces these risks
- provide employees with hearing protection or, if this is impossible, reduce the risk by other methods
- make sure the legal limits on noise exposure are not exceeded
- provide employees with information, instruction and training
- carry out **health surveillance** where there is a risk to health.

Remember

All hazardous substances are covered by COSHH regulations, except asbestos and lead paint, which have their own special regulations

Figure 1.2 Noise at work

Key term

Health surveillance – where a company will assess the risks of tasks that are to be done and see if these tasks will create risks to health

The Electricity at Work Regulations 1989

These regulations cover any work involving the use of electricity or electrical equipment. An employer has the duty to ensure that the electrical systems their employees come into contact with are safe and regularly maintained. They must also have done everything that the law states to reduce the risk of their employees coming into contact with live electrical conductors.

Construction (Design and Management) Regulations 2007

The Construction (Design and Management) Regulations 2007, often referred to as CDM, are important regulations in the construction industry. They were introduced by the HSE's Construction Division. The regulations deal mainly with the construction industry and aim to improve safety.

The duties for employers under the regulations are to:

- plan, manage and monitor own work and that of workers
- check competence of all their appointees and workers
- train their employees
- provide information to their workers
- comply with the specific requirements in Part 4 of the Regulations, which deals with lighting, excavations, traffic routes, etc.
- ensure there are adequate welfare facilities for their workers.

The duties for employees are to:

- check their own competence
- co-operate with others and co-ordinate work so as to ensure the health and safety of construction workers and others who may be affected by the work
- report obvious risks.

The CDM also requires certain duties from the clients (with the exception of domestic clients). These duties are to:

- check competence and resources of all appointees
- ensure that there are suitable management arrangements for the project welfare facilities
- allow sufficient time and resources for all stages
- provide pre-construction information to designers and contractors.

There is a general expectation by the HSE that all parties involved in a project will co-operate and co-ordinate with each other.

Remember

On large projects, a person is appointed as the CDM co-ordinator. This person has overall responsibility for compliance with CDM

Provision and Use of Work Equipment Regulations 1998 (PUWER)

These regulations cover all new or existing work equipment – leased, hired or second-hand. They apply in most working environments where the HASAW applies, including all industrial, offshore and service operations.

The regulations cover starting, stopping, regular use, transport, repair, modification, servicing and cleaning.

The general duties of PUWER require equipment to be:

* suitable for its intended purpose and only to be used in suitable conditions
* maintained in an efficient state, and maintenance records kept
* used, repaired and maintained only by a suitably trained person, when that equipment poses a particular risk
* able to be isolated from all its sources of energy
* constructed or adapted to ensure that maintenance can be carried out without risks to health and safety
* fitted with warnings or warning devices as appropriate.

In addition, PUWER requires:

* all those who use, supervise or manage work equipment to be suitably trained
* access to any dangerous parts of the machinery to be prevented or controlled
* injury to be prevented from any work equipment that may have a very high or low temperature
* suitable controls to be provided for starting and stopping the work equipment
* suitable emergency stopping systems and braking systems to be fitted to ensure the work equipment is brought to a safe condition as soon as reasonably practicable
* suitable and sufficient lighting to be provided for operating the work equipment.

Manual Handling Operations Regulations 1992

These regulations cover all work activities in which a person rather than a machine does the lifting. The regulations state that, wherever possible, manual handling should be avoided, but where this is unavoidable, a risk assessment should be done.

In a risk assessment, there are four considerations:

* **load** – is it heavy, sharp-edged or difficult to hold?

> **Did you know?**
>
> 'Work equipment' includes any machinery, appliance, apparatus or tool, and any assembly of components that is used in non-domestic premises. Dumper trucks, circular saws, ladders, overhead projectors and chisels would all be included, but substances, private cars and structural items fall outside this definition

- **individual** – is the individual small, pregnant or in need of training?
- **task** – does the task require holding goods away from the body or repetitive twisting?
- **environment** – is the floor uneven, are there stairs or is it raining?

After the assessment, the situation must be monitored constantly and updated or changed if necessary.

Personal Protective Equipment at Work Regulations 1992 (PPER)

These regulations cover all types of personal protection equipment (PPE), from gloves to breathing apparatus. After doing a risk assessment and once the potential hazards are known, suitable types of PPE can be selected. PPE should be checked prior to issue by a trained and competent person and in line with the manufacturer's instructions. Where required, the employer must provide PPE free of charge along with a suitable and secure place to store it.

The employer must ensure that the employee knows:

- the risks the PPE will avoid or reduce
- its purpose and use
- how to maintain and look after it
- its limitations.

The employee must:

- ensure that they are trained in the use of the PPE prior to use
- use it in line with the employer's instructions
- return it to storage after use
- take care of it and report any loss or defect to their employer.

Work at Height Regulations 2005

Construction workers often work high off the ground, on scaffolding, ladders or roofs. These regulations make sure that employers do all that they can to reduce the risk of injury or death from working at height.

The employer has a duty to:

- avoid work at height where possible
- use any equipment or safeguards that will prevent falls
- use equipment and any other methods that will minimise the distance and consequences of a fall.

As an employee, you must follow any training given to you, report any hazards to your supervisor and use any safety equipment provided to you.

Remember

PPE must only be used as a last line of defence

Other Acts to be aware of

You should also be aware of the following pieces of legislation:

- The Fire Precautions (Workplace) Regulations 1997
- The Fire Precautions Act 1991
- The Highly Flammable Liquids and Liquid Petroleum Gases Regulations 1972
- The Lifting Operations and Lifting Equipment Regulations 1998
- The Construction (Health, Safety and Welfare) Regulations 1996
- The Environmental Protection Act 1990
- Controlled Waste Regulations 1992
- Hazardous Waste (England and Wales) Regulations
- The Confined Spaces Regulations 1997
- The Working Time Regulations 1998
- The Health and Safety (First Aid) Regulations 1981
- The Management of Health and Safety at Work Regulations 1999.

You can find out more at the library or online.

Sources of health and safety information

Health and safety is a large and varied subject that changes regularly. The introduction of new regulations or updates to current legislation means that it's often hard to remember or keep up to date. Your tutor will be able to give you information on current legislation.

Your employer should also keep you updated on any changes to legislation that will affect you. You can also access other sources of information to keep you informed.

Health and Safety Executive (HSE)

The HSE has a wide range of information ranging from the actual legislation documents to helpful guides to working safely. Videos, leaflets and documents are available to download free from its website. Specific sections of the website are dedicated to different industries ranging from agriculture to hairdressing. The specific construction website address is www.hse.gov.uk/construction.

ConstructionSkills

ConstructionSkills mainly offers advice on qualifications in construction. However, it also has advice on health and safety matters and on sitting the CSCS (Construction Skills Certification Scheme) health and safety test as well as providing a way of booking the test. The website address is www.cskills.org.

Find out

Look into the other regulations listed here via the HSE website (www.hse.gov.uk)

Remember

Legislation can change or be updated. New legislation can be created as well – this could even supersede all pieces of legislation

Did you know?

The HSE now also includes the Health and Safety Commission (HSC), with which they merged in 2008

Royal Society for the Prevention of Accidents (RoSPA)

The Royal Society for the Prevention of Accidents (RoSPA) provides information, advice, resources and training and is actively involved in the promotion of safety and the prevention of accidents in all areas of life – at work, in the home, on the roads, in schools, at leisure and on (or near) water. Their website address is www.rospa.com.

Royal Society for the Promotion of Health (RSPH)

The Royal Society for the Promotion of Health (RSPH) aims to promote and protect health and well-being. It uses **advocacy**, mediation, knowledge and practice to advise on policy development. It also provides education and training services, encourages research, communicates information and provides certification for products, training centres and processes.

The RSPH's main focus is people working in healthcare, for example doctors. It publishes two journals:

- Public Health
- Perspectives on Public Health

Site inductions

> **Key term**
>
> **Advocacy** – actively supporting or arguing for

Figure 1.3 A site induction talk

> **Key term**
>
> **Induction** – a formal introduction you will receive when you start any new job, where you will be shown around, shown where the toilets and canteen etc. are, and told what to do if there is a fire

Site **induction** is the process that an individual undergoes in order to accelerate their awareness of the potential health and safety hazards and risks they may face in their working environment. Site induction doesn't include job-related skills training.

Different site inductions will include different topics, depending on the work that is being carried out. The basic information that should be included in inductions will cover:

- the scope of operations carried out at the site, project, etc.
- the activities that have health and safety hazards and risks
- the control measures in place
- emergency arrangements
- local organisation and management structure
- consultation procedures, including 'Don't walk by. Take action now' and Safety Action Groups
- the resource for health and safety advice
- the welfare arrangements
- a zero-tolerance approach to health and safety risks at work
- the process for reporting near misses (see pages 17–18).

Inductions are also vital for informing all people working on the site of amenities, restricted areas, dress code (PPE) and evacuation procedures. Inductions must be carried out by a competent person. Records of all inductions must be kept to ensure that all workers have received an induction. Some sites will even hand out cards to those who have been inducted and people without cards will not be admitted to the site.

Visitors to the site who may not be actually doing any work should still receive an induction of sorts as they also need to be aware of amenities, restricted areas and procedures etc.

Toolbox talks

Toolbox talks are used by management, supervisors and employees to deliver basic training and/or to inform all workers of any updates to policy, hazardous activities/areas or any other information.

Toolbox talk topics should be relevant to the people it is being delivered to (there is no point delivering a talk on plumbing systems to bricklayers unless it directly affects them!). The topics can vary from simply being informative, such as letting everyone know about the reclassification of a PPE area, to basic training on the use of a certain tool.

They should be delivered by a competent person and a record of all attendees should be kept.

Remember

A site induction must take place *before* you start work on that site

Did you know?

Toolbox talks don't need to be formal meetings but can be held in a canteen at break time, but a list of all attendees must be kept to ensure that everyone who needs to receive the talk does so

Safe working pratices in construction **Unit 1001**

Unit 1001 Safe working practices in construction

Working life

Alex and Molly have been asked to attend a toolbox talk on scaffolding safety. They had both attended a toolbox talk on the same subject just over a week ago. Molly thinks they should attend this talk too as it could be important. However, Alex thinks it's a mistake and that it will be the same as the last one. Molly agrees that they are very busy and that if they don't attend they can get the job they are doing finished on time, but she is still concerned about missing the talk.

- Why could Alex and Molly be asked to attend if they had a similar titled toolbox talk recently?
- What could the outcome be if they do/don't attend?
- What things might be discussed in a toolbox talk on scaffolding?

Construction Skills Certification Scheme (CSCS)

The Construction Skills Certification Scheme (CSCS) was introduced to help improve the quality of work and to reduce accidents. It requires all workers to obtain a CSCS card before they are allowed to carry out work on a building site. There are various levels of card that indicate your competence and skill background. This ensures that only skilled and safe tradespeople can carry out the required work on site.

To get a CSCS card the applicant must sit a health and safety test. The aim of the test is to examine knowledge across a wide range of topics to improve safety and productivity on site. You usually take it as a PC-based touch-screen test, either at a mobile testing unit or at an accredited test centre. The type of card you apply for will determine the level of test that you need to take.

As a trainee, once you pass the health and safety test you will qualify for a trainee card. Once you have achieved a Level 2 qualification you can then upgrade your card to an experienced worker card. Achieving a Level 3 qualification allows you to apply for a gold card. People who make regular visits to site can apply for a visitor card.

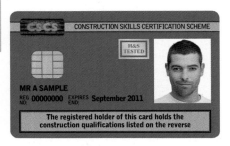

Figure 1.4 A CSCS card

K2. Accident, first aid and emergency procedures and reporting

Major types of emergency

There are several types of major emergency that could occur on site. These include not only accidents but also:

- fires
- security alerts
- bomb scares.

At your site induction, it should be made perfectly clear to you what you should do in an emergency. You should also be aware of any sirens or warning noises that accompany each and every type of emergency, such as bomb scares or fire alarms. Some sites may have different variations on sirens or emergency procedures, so it is vital that you pay attention and listen to all the instructions. If you are unsure always ask.

The key legislation that controls the reporting of accidents is RIDDOR.

Health and welfare in the construction industry

Jobs in the construction industry have one of the highest injury and accident rates. As a worker you will be at constant risk unless you adopt a good health and safety attitude. By following the rules and regulations set out to protect you, and by taking reasonable care of yourself and others, you will become a safe worker and thus reduce the chance of any injuries or accidents.

Accidents

We often hear the saying 'accidents will happen', but when working in the construction industry, we should not accept that accidents just happen sometimes. When we think of an accident, we quite often think about it as being no one's fault and something that could not have been avoided. The truth is that most accidents are caused by human error, which means that someone has done something they shouldn't have done or, just as importantly, not done something they should have done.

Accidents often happen when someone:

- is hurrying
- is not paying enough attention to what they are doing
- has not received the correct training.

Reporting accidents

When an accident occurs, there are certain things that must be done. All accidents need to be reported and recorded in the accident book. The injured person

> **Remember**
>
> Health and safety laws are there to protect you and other people. If you take shortcuts or ignore the rules, you are placing yourself and others at serious risk

Figure 1.5 Accidents can happen if your work area is untidy

must report to a trained first-aider to receive treatment. Serious accidents must be reported under RIDDOR.

Accidents and emergencies must be reported to the relevant authorised persons. These can be:

- **first-aiders** – all accidents need to be reported to a first-aider; if you are unsure who the first-aiders are or have no direct way of contacting them, you must report it to your supervisor
- **supervisors** – you must inform your supervisor of any accident as it is vital that they can act immediately to inform the relevant first-aider or their manager and stop the work if necessary to prevent any further accidents
- **safety officers** – your supervisor or the site manager will alert the safety officer who will assess the area to check if it is safe, investigate what might have caused the accident and prepare reports for the HSE (if needed)
- **HSE** – if death or major injury occurs to a member of staff, or a member of the public is killed or taken to hospital, the accident must be reported to the HSE immediately and followed up by a written report within ten days. The written report is made on form F2508. If an employee suffers an 'over-three-day' injury it must be reported on the F2508 form within ten days
- **managers** – managers should be informed by either the supervisor or safety officer as it may need to be reported to head office; they may also be the one tasked with contacting the HSE
- **emergency services** – the emergency services should be called as soon as possible; usually the first-aiders will call the ambulance and the supervisors will call the fire brigade, but if in doubt you should also call.

Under RIDDOR your employer must report to the HSE any accident that results in:

- death
- major injury
- an injury that means that the injured person is not at work for more than three consecutive days
- disease.

Diseases that can be caused in the workplace include:

- certain poisonings
- some skin diseases – such as occupational dermatitis, skin cancer, chrome ulcer, oil folliculitis/acne
- lung diseases – including occupational asthma, farmer's lung, pneumoconiosis, asbestosis, mesothelioma

> **Remember**
>
> An accident that falls under RIDDOR should be reported by the safety officer or site manager. It can be reported to the HSE by phone (0845 3009923) or via the RIDDOR website (www.riddor.gov.uk)

> **Safety tip**
>
> The emergency services would rather be called twice than not at all

- infections – such as leptospirosis (see page 30), hepatitis, tuberculosis, anthrax, legionellosis and tetanus
- other conditions – such as occupational cancer, certain musculoskeletal disorders, decompression illness and hand–arm vibration syndrome (see page 31).

The nature and seriousness of the accident will decide who it needs to be reported to. There are several types of documentation used to record accidents and emergencies.

The accident book

The accident book is completed by the person who had the accident or, if this is not possible, someone who is representing the injured person. The accident book will ask for some basic details about the accident, including:

- who was involved
- what happened
- where it happened
- the day and time of the accident
- any witnesses to the accident
- the address of the injured person
- what PPE was being worn
- what first aid treatment was given.

Major and minor accidents

If an accident happens, you or the person it happened to may be lucky and will not be injured. More often, an accident will result in an injury which may be minor (e.g. a cut or a bruise) or possibly major (e.g. loss of a limb). Accidents can also be fatal. The most common causes of fatal accidents in the construction industry are:

- falling from scaffolding
- being hit by falling objects and materials
- falling through fragile roofs
- being hit by forklifts or lorries
- cuts
- infections
- burns
- electrocution.

Near misses

As well as reporting accidents, 'near misses' must also be reported. A 'near miss' is when an accident nearly happened, but did not actually occur. Reporting near misses might identify

Find out

Visit the NHS Choices website (www.nhs.uk) to find out more about these diseases, and others that can be caused in the workplace

Safety tip

Near misses must be recorded because they are often the accidents of the future a problem and could prevent accidents from happening in the future. This allows a company to be proactive rather than reactive.

Work-related injuries in the construction industry

Construction has the largest number of fatal injuries of all the main industry groups. In 2007–2008 there were 72 fatal injuries. This gave a rate of 3.4 people injured per 100,000 workers. The rate of fatal injuries in construction over the past decade has shown a downward trend, but the rate has shown little change in the most recent years.

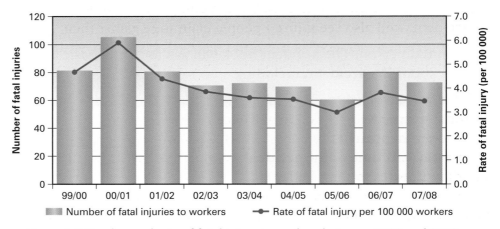

Figure 1.6 Number and rate of fatal injury to workers between 1999 and 2008

- Between 1999 and 2007 the rate of reported major injuries in construction fell. It is unclear whether the rise in 2007–2008 means an end to this trend. Despite this falling tend, the rate of major injury in construction is the highest of any main industry group (599.2 per 100 000 employees in 2007–2008).
- A higher proportion of the reported injuries in construction were caused by falls from height, falling objects and contact with moving machinery.
- The THOR-GP surveillance scheme data (2006–2007) indicates a higher rate of work-related illness in construction than across all industries. The rate of self-reported work-related ill health in construction is similar to other industries.

The cost of accidents

As well as the tragedy, pain and suffering that accidents cause, they can also have a negative financial and business impact.

Small accidents will affect profits as sick pay may need to be paid. Production may also slow down or stop if the injured person is a specialist. Replacement or temporary workers may need to be used to keep the job going. This can cost small companies with a handful of employees hundreds of pounds for every day

Remember

Clients don't want to hire companies that are not deemed safe that an injured person can't work. Larger companies with many employees may have several people off work at once, which can cost thousands of pounds per day.

More serious accidents will increase the financial loss as the injured person will be off work for longer. This can cause jobs to fall seriously behind and, in extreme cases, may even cause the contractor to lose the job and possibly have to close the site.

Companies that have a lot of accidents will have a poor company image for health and safety. They will also find it increasingly difficult to gain future contracts. Unsafe companies with lots of accidents will also see injured people claiming against their insurance, which will see their premiums rise. This will eventually make them uninsurable, meaning that they will not get any work.

First aid

In the unfortunate event of an accident on site, first aid may have to be administered. If there are more than five people on a site, then a qualified first-aider must be present at all times. On large building sites there must be several first-aiders. During your site induction you will be made aware of who the first-aiders are and where the first-aid points are situated. A first aid point must have the relevant first-aid equipment to deal with the types of injury that are likely to occur. However, first aid is only the first step and, in the case of major injuries, the emergency services should be called.

A good first aid box should have plasters, bandages, antiseptic wipes, latex gloves, eye patches, slings, wound dressings and safety pins. Other equipment, such as eye wash stations, must also be available if the work being carried out requires it.

Remember

Health and safety is everyone's duty. If you receive first aid treatment and notice that there are only two plasters left, you should report it to your line manager

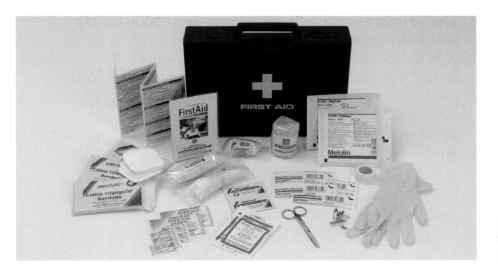

Figure 1.7 A first aid box provides the supplies to deal with minor injuries

Actions for an unsafe area

On discovering an accident the first thing to do is to ensure that the victim is in no further danger. This will require you to do tasks such as switching off the electrical supply. Tasks like this must only be done if there is no danger to yourself.

Turning off the electricity is just one possible example. There will be specific safety issues for individual jobs that the injured person may have been working on.

You must next contact the first-aider. Unless you have been trained in first aid you must not attempt to move the injured person as you may cause more damage. If necessary, the first-aider will then call the emergency services.

Safety tip

After an accident, always make sure the area is safe before you continue work – otherwise you could become a casualty as well

K3. Hazards on construction sites

A major part of health and safety at work is being able to identify hazards and to help prevent them in the first place, therefore avoiding the risk of injury.

Housekeeping

Housekeeping is the simple term used for cleaning up after yourself to ensure that your work area is clear and tidy. Good housekeeping is vital on a construction site, as an unclean work area is dangerous.

To maintain good housekeeping it is important that you:

- work tidily to reduce the chances of you or somebody getting hurt
- don't overfill skips as this can lead to fire hazards
- ensure that fire exits and emergency escape routes are clear
- correctly dispose of food waste as this can attract cockroaches, rats and other vermin
- only get as many nails and screws as you need – loose nails and screws can puncture tyres and even cause injury to feet
- clean and sweep up at the end of each day
- avoid blocking exits and walkways
- be aware while you are working – how might your mess affect you or others?

Remember

Learning to work tidily is part of your apprenticeship

Storing combustibles and chemicals

It is vital to store combustibles and chemicals on site correctly.

Chemicals

Certain chemicals such as brick cleaner or some types of adhesive are classified as dangerous chemicals. All chemicals should be stored in a locked area to prevent misuse or cross-contamination.

Highly flammable liquids

Liquefied petroleum gas (LPG), petrol, cellulose thinners, methylated spirits, chlorinated rubber paint and white spirit are all highly flammable liquids. These materials require special storage to ensure that they do not risk injuring workers.

- Containers should only be kept in a special storeroom built of concrete, brick or some other fireproof material.
- The floor should also be made of concrete and should slope away from the storage area. This is to prevent leaked materials from collecting under the containers.
- The roof should be made from an easily shattered material to minimise the effect of any explosion.
- Doors should be at least 50 mm thick and open outwards.
- Any glass used in the structure should be wired and not less than 6 mm thick.
- The standing area should have a sill surrounding it that is deep enough to contain the contents of the largest container stored.
- Containers should always be stored upright.
- The area should not be heated.
- Electric lights should be safe.
- Light switches should be flameproof and should be on the outside of the store.
- The building should be ventilated at high and low levels and have at least two exits.
- Naked flames and spark-producing materials should be clearly prohibited from the area, including smoking.
- The storeroom should be clearly marked with red and white squares and 'Highly Flammable' signage.

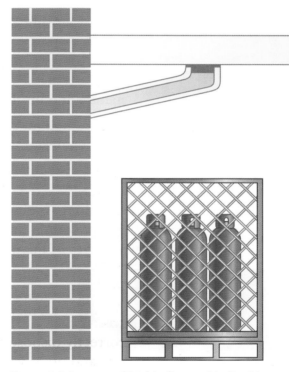

Figure 1.8 Storage of highly flammable liquids

Find out

Check out the storage details for any chemicals that you come across – look at the manufacturer's instructions or the COSHH regulations

Did you know?

'Inflammable' means the same thing as flammable, that it is easily lit and capable of burning rapidly

Unit 1001 Safe working practices in construction

Safety tips

- Never expose materials such as LPG, white spirit, methylated spirit and turps to a naked flame (including cigarettes) – they are highly flammable
- Make sure when working with potentially hazardous materials that you take the appropriate precautions, for example wear gloves and eye protection, work in a ventilated area, etc.

Figure 1.9 Vertical storage of glass

In addition to these requirements, there are storage regulations specifically for LPG:

- LPG must be stored in the open and usually in a locked cage.
- It should be stored off the floor and protected from direct sunlight and from frost or snow.
- The storage of LPG is governed by the Highly Flammable Liquids and Liquefied Petroleum Gases Regulations 1972. Note that these regulations apply when 50 or more litres are stored, and permission must be obtained from the District Inspector of Factories.

Glass

Glass should be stored vertically in racks. The conditions for glass storage should be:

- clean – storing glass in dirty or dusty locations can cause discoloration
- dry – if moisture is allowed between the sheets of glass it can make them stick together, which will make them difficult to handle and more likely to break.

If only a small number of sheets of glass are to be stored, they can be leant against a stable surface, as shown in Figure 1.9.

Hazards on the construction site

The building industry can be a very dangerous place to work and there are certain hazards that all workers need to be aware of. The main types of hazard that you will face are:

- falling from height
- tripping
- chemical spills
- burns
- electrical
- fires.

Falling from height

When working in the construction industry a lot of the work that you do will be at height. The main hazard of working at height is falling. A fall from a scaffold, even if it is at low level, can cause serious injuries such as broken bones. A worker may also suffer permanent damage from the fall. This could leave them wheelchair-bound for life, or even kill them.

Figure 1.10 An untidy work site can present many trip hazards

Tripping

The main cause of tripping is poor housekeeping. Whether working on scaffolding or at ground level, an untidy workplace is an accident waiting to happen. All workplaces should be kept tidy and free of debris. All off-cuts should be put either in a wheelbarrow (if you aren't near a skip) or straight into the skip.

Chemical spills

Chemical spillages can range from minor inconvenience to major disaster. Most spillages are small and create minimal or no risk. If the material involved is not hazardous, it can simply be cleaned up by normal operations such as brushing or mopping up the spill. Occasionally, the spill may be on a larger scale and may involve a hazardous material. It is important to know what to do before the spillage happens so that remedial action can be prompt, and harmful effects minimised. Of course, when a hazardous substance is being used a COSHH or risk assessment will have been made, and it should include a plan for dealing with a spillage. This in turn should mean that the materials required for dealing with the spillage should be readily available.

Burns

Burns can occur not only from the obvious source of fire and heat but also from materials containing chemicals such as cement or painter's solvents. Even electricity can cause burns. It is vital when working with materials, that you are aware of the hazards, that they may present and take the necessary precautions.

Electricity

Electricity is a killer. Around 30 workers a year die from electricity-related accidents, with over 1000 more being seriously injured (source: HSE). One of the main problems with electricity is that it is invisible. You don't even have to be working with an electrical tool to be electrocuted. Working too close to live overhead cables, plastering a wall with electric sockets, carrying out maintenance work on a floor, or drilling into a wall can all lead to an electric shock.

Electric shocks may not always be fatal, but electricity can cause burns, muscular problems and cardiac (heart) problems.

Fires

The obvious main risk from fires is burns. However, during fires, the actual flames are not often the cause of injury or death. Smoke inhalation is a very serious hazard and this is what mainly causes death.

Fires will be covered in greater depth later in this unit (pages 66–68).

Remember

Good housekeeping will not only prevent trip hazards, but will also prevent costly clean-up operations at the end of the job and will promote a good professional image

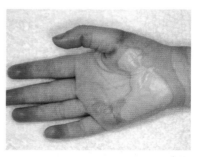

Figure 1.11 Fire, heat, chemicals and electricity can cause burns

Figure 1.12 Even an everyday task like cutting the grass has its own dangers

Key term

Carry out a risk assessment – this means measuring the dangers of an activity against the likelihood of accidents taking place

Key term

Residual current device (RCD) – a device that will shut the power down on a piece of electrical equipment if it detects a change in the current, thus preventing electrocution

Risk assessments

You will have noticed that most of the legislation we have looked at requires risk assessments to be carried out. The Management of Health and Safety at Work Regulations 1999 requires every employer to make suitable and sufficient assessment of:

- the risks to the health and safety of their employees to which the employees are exposed to while at work
- the risks to the health and safety of persons not in their employment, arising out of or in connection with their work activities.

It is vital that you know how to **carry out a risk assessment**. Often you may be in a position where you are given direct responsibility for this, and the care and attention you take over it may have a direct impact on the safety of others. You must be aware of the dangers or hazards of any task, and know what can be done to prevent or reduce the risk.

There are five steps in a risk assessment – here we use cutting the grass as an example.

- **Step 1 Identify the hazards** – when cutting the grass the main hazards are from the blades or cutting the wire, electrocution and any stones that may be thrown up.

- **Step 2 Identify who will be at risk** – the main person at risk is the user, but passers-by may be struck by flying debris.

- **Step 3 Calculate the risk from the hazard against the likelihood of an accident taking place** – the risks from the hazard are quite high – the blade or wire can remove a finger, electrocution can kill and the flying debris can blind or even kill. The likelihood of an accident happening is medium – you are unlikely to cut yourself on the blades, but the chance of cutting through the cable is medium, and the chance of hitting a stone high.

- **Step 4 Introduce measures to reduce the risk** – training can reduce the risks of cutting yourself. Training and the use of a **residual current device (RCD)** can reduce the risk of electrocution. Raking the lawn first can reduce the risk of sending up stones.

- **Step 5 Monitor the risk** – constantly changing factors mean that any risk assessment may have to be modified or even changed completely. In our example, one such factor could be rain.

Working life

Ralph and Vijay are working on the second level of some scaffolding clearing debris. Ralph suggests that, to speed up the task, they should throw the debris over the edge of the scaffolding into a skip below. The building that Ralph and Vijay are working on is on a main road and the skip is not in a closed off area.

- What do you think of Ralph's idea? What are your reasons for this answer?

Method statements

A method statements is a key safety document that takes the information about significant risks from your risk assessment, and combines them with the job specification, to produce a practical and safe working method for the workers to follow on site.

Method statements should be specific and relevant to the job in hand and should detail what work is to be done, how the work should be done and what safety precautions need to be taken.

Hazard books

The hazard book is a tool used on some sites to identify hazards within certain tasks. It can also help to produce risk assessments. The book will list tasks, and what hazards are associated with those tasks. Different working environments can create different types of hazard so risk assessments must always look at the specific task separately.

K4. Health and hygiene

As well as keeping an eye out for hazards, you must also make sure that you look after yourself and stay healthy. This is a responsibility that lies with both the employer and the employee.

Staying healthy

One of the easiest ways to stay healthy is to wash your hands regularly. By washing your hands you are preventing hazardous substances from entering your body through ingestion (swallowing). You should always wash your hands after going to the toilet and before eating or drinking. Personal hygiene is vital to ensure good health.

Remember that some health problems do not show symptoms straight away and what you do now can affect you much later in life.

Figure 1.13 Always wash your hands to prevent ingesting hazardous substances

Remember

This is covered by the Construction (Design and Management) Regulations

Key terms

Corrosive – a substance that can damage things it comes into contact with (e.g. material, skin)

Toxic – a substance which is poisonous

Contamination – when harmful chemicals, or substances, pollute something (e.g. water)

Safety tips

When placing clothes in a drying room, do not place them directly on heaters as this can lead to fire

When working in an occupied house, you can make arrangements with the client to use the facilities in their house

Welfare facilities

Welfare facilities are things such as toilets, which must be provided by your employer to ensure a safe and healthy workplace. There are several things that your employer must provide to meet welfare standards.

- **Toilets** – the number of toilets provided depends on the number of people who are intended to use them. Males and females can use the same toilets provided that there is a lock on the inside of the door. Toilets should be flushable with water or, if this is not possible, with chemicals.
- **Washing facilities** – employers must provide a basin large enough to allow people to wash their hands, face and forearms. Washing facilities must have hot and cold running water as well as soap and a means of drying your hands. Showers may be needed if the work is very dirty or if workers are exposed to **corrosive** and **toxic** substances.
- **Drinking water** – there should be a supply of clean drinking water available, either from a tap connected to the mains or from bottled water. Taps connected to the mains need to be clearly labelled as drinking water, and bottled drinking water must be stored in a separate area to prevent **contamination**.
- **Storage or dry room** – every building site must have an area where workers can store the clothes that they do not wear on site, such as coats and motorcycle helmets. If this area is to be used as a drying room then adequate heating must also be provided in order to allow clothes to dry.
- **Lunch area** – every site must have facilities that can be used for taking breaks and lunch well away from the work area. These facilities must provide shelter from the wind and rain and be heated as required. There should be access to tables and chairs, a kettle or urn for boiling water and a means of heating food, such as a microwave.

Substance abuse

Substance abuse is a general term that refers to the harmful, or hazardous, use of substances such as alcohol and drugs.

Taking drugs or inhaling solvents at work is not only illegal, but is also highly dangerous to you and everyone around you. These acts result in reduced concentration problems and can lead to accidents. Drinking alcohol is also dangerous at work; going to the pub for lunch and having just one drink can slow down your reflexes and reduce your concentration.

Although not a form of abuse as such, drugs prescribed by your doctor as well as over-the-counter painkillers can be dangerous. Many of these medicines carry warnings such as 'may cause drowsiness' or 'do not operate heavy machinery'. It is better to be safe than sorry, so always ensure that you follow any instructions on prescriptions and, if you feel drowsy or unsteady, then stop work immediately.

Health effects of noise

Hearing can be damaged by a range of causes, from ear infections to loud noises. Hearing loss can result from one very loud noise lasting only a few seconds, or from relatively loud noise lasting for hours, such as a drill.

The effects of noise damage

To appreciate the damage caused by noise, it helps to first understand how the human ear works.

- When the hairs contained within the ear vibrate they move like grass blowing in the wind. Very loud noises have the same effect on the hairs that a hurricane would have on a field.
- The hairs get blown away and can *never* be replaced.
- The fewer of these hairs you have, the worse is your hearing. This is called 'noise induced hearing loss'.

> **Did you know?**
>
> Substance abuse in a workplace doesn't just endanger yourself – it puts everyone you are working with in danger as well

> **Did you know?**
>
> Noise is measured in decibels (dB). The average person may notice a rise of 3 dB, but with every 3 dB rise, the noise is doubled. What may seem like a small rise is actually very significant

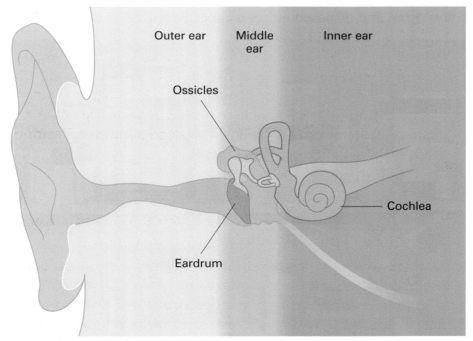

Figure 1.14 Inner workings of the human ear

Outer ear
Middle ear
Inner ear
Ossicles
Cochlea
Eardrum

Unit 1001 Safe working pratices in construction

> **Remember**
>
> Hearing loss affects the young as well as the old

The damage to hearing can be caused by one of two things:

- **intensity of the noise** – your hearing can be hurt in an instant from an explosive or very loud noise that can burst your ear drum
- **duration of the noise** – noise does not have to be deafening to harm you, a quieter noise over a long period, for example a 12-hour shift, can also damage your hearing.

Reducing the risks

This can be done in a number of ways:

- **remove** – get rid of whatever is creating the noise
- **move** – locate the noisy equipment away from people
- **enclose** – surround noisy equipment, for example with sound-proof material
- **isolation** – move the workers to protected areas.

Even after all of these are considered, PPE may still be required.

Hearing protection

The two most common types of hearing protection aids are earplugs and ear defenders. See page 65 for more details.

Hazardous substances

Hazardous substances are a major health and safety risk on a construction site. To this end, they need to be handled, stored, transported and disposed of in very specific ways.

Figure 1.15 Hazardous substances

To comply with COSHH regulations, eight steps must be followed by the employer:

- **Step 1** – assess the risks to health from hazardous substances used or created by employees' activities.
- **Step 2** – decide what precautions are needed.
- **Step 3** – prevent employees from being exposed to any hazardous substances. If prevention is impossible, the risk must be adequately controlled.
- **Step 4** – ensure that control methods are used and maintained properly.
- **Step 5** – monitor the exposure of employees to hazardous substances.
- **Step 6** – carry out health surveillance to ascertain if any health problems are occurring.
- **Step 7** – prepare plans and procedures to deal with accidents such as spillages.
- **Step 8** – ensure that all employees are properly informed, trained and supervised.

Identifying a substance that may fall under the COSHH regulations is not always easy, but you can ask the supplier or manufacturer for a COSHH data sheet, outlining the risks involved with a substance. Most substance containers carry a warning sign stating whether the contents are corrosive, harmful, toxic or bad for the environment.

Figure 1.16 Common safety signs for corrosive, toxic and explosive materials

Waste

Many different types of waste material are produced in construction work. It is your responsibility to identify the type of waste you have created and the best way of disposing it. There are several pieces of legislation that dictate the disposal of waste materials. They include:

- Environmental Protection Act 1990
- Controlled Waste Regulations 1992
- Waste Management Licensing Regulations 1994
- Hazardous Waste (England and Wales) Regulations

Safety tip

Not all substances are labelled, and sometimes the label may not match the contents. If you are in any doubt, don't use or touch the substance

Remember

Always read the manufacturer's label and remember to wear the relevant safety equipment when dealing with hazardous substances

Remember

If you leave material on site when your work is completed you may be discarding them. You are still responsible for this waste material!

Several different types of waste are defined by these regulations:

- household waste – normal household rubbish
- commercial waste – for example, from shops or offices
- industrial waste – from factories and industrial sites.

All waste must be handled properly and disposed of safely. The Controlled Waste Regulations state that only those authorised to do so may dispose of waste and that a record is kept of all waste disposal.

Hazardous waste

Some types of waste, such as chemicals or material that is toxic or explosive, are too dangerous for normal disposal and must be disposed of with special care. The Hazardous Waste (England and Wales) Regulations cover this disposal. Examples include:

- asbestos
- used engine oils and filters
- solvents
- pesticides
- lead-based batteries
- oily sludges
- chemical wastes
- fluorescent tubes.

If hazardous material is inside a container, the container must be clearly marked and a consignment note completed for its disposal.

Health risks in the workplace

While working in the construction industry, you will be exposed to substances or situations that may be harmful to your health. Some of these health risks may not be noticeable straight away. It may take years for **symptoms** to be noticed and recognised.

Ill health can result from:

- exposure to dust (such as asbestos), which can cause eye injuries, breathing problems and cancer
- exposure to solvents or chemicals, which can cause **dermatitis** and other skin problems
- lifting heavy or difficult loads, which can cause back injury and pulled muscles
- exposure to loud noise, which can cause hearing problems and deafness
- bacterial infections, such as **leptospirosis**, caused by coming into contact with germs

Key terms

Symptom – a sign of illness or disease (e.g. difficulty breathing, a sore hand or a lump under the skin)

Dermatitis – a skin condition where the affected area is red, itchy and sore

Leptospirosis – an infectious disease that affects humans and animals. The human form is commonly called Weil's disease. The disease can cause fever, muscle pain and jaundice. In severe cases it can affect the liver and kidneys. Leptospirosis is a germ that is spread by the urine of the infected person. It can often be caught from contaminated soil or water that has been urinated on

- exposure to sunlight, which can cause skin cancer
- using vibrating tools, which can cause **vibration white finger** and other problems with the hands
- head injuries, which can lead to blackouts and epilepsy
- cuts, which if infected can lead to disease.

Everyone has a responsibility for health and safety in the construction industry but accidents and health problems still happen too often. Make sure you do what you can to prevent them.

K5. Safe handling of materials and equipment

Manual handling

Manual handling means lifting and moving a piece of equipment or material from one place to another without using machinery. Lifting and moving loads by hand is one of the most common causes of injury at work. Most injuries caused by manual handling result from years of lifting items that are too heavy, are awkward shapes or sizes, or from using the wrong technique. However, it is also possible to cause a lifetime of back pain with just one single lift.

Poor manual handling can cause injuries such as muscle strain, pulled ligaments and hernias. The most common injury by far is spinal injury. Spinal injuries are very serious because there is very little that doctors can do to correct them and, in extreme cases, workers have been left paralysed.

The Manual Handling Operations Regulations 1992 is the key piece of legislation related to manual handling.

What you can do to avoid injury

The first and most important thing you can do to avoid injury from lifting is to receive proper manual handling training. **Kinetic lifting** is a way of lifting objects that reduces the chance of injury and is covered in more detail in the next section.

Before you lift anything you should ask yourself some simple questions:

- Does the object need to be moved?
- Can I use something to help me lift the object? A mechanical aid such as a forklift or crane, or a manual aid such as a wheelbarrow may be more appropriate than a person.

Key term

Vibration white finger – a condition that can be caused by using vibrating machinery (usually for very long periods of time). The blood supply to the fingers is reduced which causes pain, tingling and sometimes spasms (shaking)

Remember

Activities on site can also damage your body. You could have eye damage, head injury and burns along with other physical wounds

Key term

Kinetic lifting – a way of lifting objects that reduces the risk of injury to the lifter

- Can I reduce the weight by breaking down the load? Breaking down a load into smaller and more manageable weights may mean that more journeys are needed, but it will also reduce the risk of injury.
- Do I need help? Asking for help to lift a load is not a sign of weakness, and team lifting will greatly reduce the risk of injury.
- How much can I lift safely? The recommended maximum weight a person can lift is 25 kg, but this is only an average weight and each person is different. The amount that a person can lift will depend on their physique, age and experience.
- Where is the object going? Make sure that any obstacles in your path are out of the way before you lift. You also need to make sure there is somewhere to put the object when you get there.
- Am I trained to lift? The quickest way to receive a manual handling injury is to use the wrong lifting technique.

Lifting correctly (kinetic lifting)

When lifting any load it is important to keep the correct posture and to use the correct technique.

Get into the correct posture before lifting as follows:

- feet shoulder width apart with one foot slightly in front of the other
- knees should be bent
- back must be straight
- arms should be as close to the body as possible
- grip must be firm using the whole hand and not just the finger tips.

The correct technique when lifting is as follows:

Step 1 – approach the load squarely facing the direction of travel.

Step 2 – adopt the correct posture (as above).

Step 3 – place hands under the load and pull the load close to your body.

Step 4 – lift the load using your legs and not your back.

When lowering a load, you must also adopt the correct posture and technique:

- bend at the knees, not the back
- adjust the load to avoid trapping fingers
- release the load.

Remember

Even light loads can cause back problems so when lifting anything, always take care to avoid twisting or stretching

Think before lifting

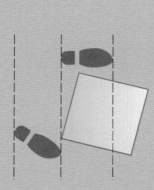

Adopt the correct posture before lifting

Get a good grip on the load

Adopt the correct posture when lifting

Move smoothly with the load

Adopt the correct posture and technique when lowering

Safe handling

When handling any materials or equipment, always think about the health and safety issues involved and remember the manual handling practices explained to you during your induction.

You aren't expected to remember everything, but basic common sense will help you to work safely:

- always wear your safety helmet and boots at work
- wear gloves and ear defenders when necessary
- keep your work areas free from debris and materials, tools and equipment not being used
- wash your hands before eating
- use barrier cream before starting work
- always use correct lifting techniques.

Ensure that you follow instructions given to you at all times when moving any materials or equipment. The main points to remember are:

- always try to avoid manual handling (or use mechanical means to aid the process)
- always assess the situation first to decide on the best method of handling the load
- always reduce any risks as much as possible (for example split a very heavy load, move obstacles from your path before lifting)
- tell others around you what you are doing
- if you need help with a load, get it. Don't try to lift something beyond what you can manage.

> **Did you know?**
>
> In 2004–2005 there were over 50 000 injuries while handling, lifting or carrying in the UK (Source: HSE)

> **Working life**
>
> Ahmed and Glynn are unloading bags of plaster from a wheelbarrow. While handling a bag of plaster. Glynn gets a sudden sharp pain in his back and drops the bag. Ahmed goes and tells their supervisor, who comes over to where Glynn is sitting in a great deal of pain.
>
> What do you think should happen next? Glynn will not want to continue working and possibly doing further damage to his back. What should his supervisor do straight away to look after Glynn's well-being?
>
> Could the accident have been prevented? Glynn may not have been working in a safe manner, and there are several important health and safety issues that both Ahmed and Glynn should be made aware of before they carry out another lifting task.
>
> What should their supervisor do in the long term to stop this happening again? The supervisor will want to make sure that he prevents another accident happening across the whole site. What risk assessments and hazard checks will he need to carry out?

Basic health and safety for tools

All tools are potentially dangerous. You, as an operator of tools, must make sure that all health and safety requirements relating to the tools are always carried out. This will help ensure that you do not cause injury to yourself and, equally important, to others who may be working around you, and to the general public. Make sure that you follow any instructions and demonstrations you are given on the use of tools, as well as any manufacturer's instructions provided on purchasing the tools.

Basic rules for handling tools:

- always make sure you use the correct PPE required to use the tool and do the job you are carrying out
- never 'make do' with tools; using the wrong tool for the job usually breaks health and safety laws
- never play or mess around with a tool regardless of the type, whether it is a hand tool or power tool
- never use a tool you have not been trained to use, especially a power tool.

Power tools

Always treat power tools with respect: they have the potential to cause harm either to the person using them or to others around. All power tools used on site should be regularly tested (PAT tested) by a qualified person. There are several health and safety regulations governing the use of power tools. Make sure that you wear suitable PPE at all times and that power tools are operated safely. In some cases, you must be qualified to use them. Refer to Provision and Use of Work Equipment Regulations 1998 (PUWER) if needed.

On-site transformers are used to reduce the mains voltage from 230 volts to 110 volts. All power tools used should be designed for 110 volts.

As well as the traditional powered tools there are also tools powered by gas or compressed air. Gas powered tools, such as nail guns, also require batteries to operate them. They must be handled carefully similar to other power tools.

Compressed air powered tools such as spray paint systems require an electric powered compressor to operate them. Care must be taken when dealing with these tools. As well as electrical hazards there is the additional danger of working with compressed air. If the air supply is held against the skin it can create air bubbles in your blood stream. This can lead to death.

Remember

- Follow the basic health and safety rules regarding use of tools and you (and others) will be safe
- Tools are expensive and very important for work so they need to be looked after

Did you know?

PAT stands for 'portable appliance testing'

Safety tip

When using power tools, always read the manufacturer's instructions and safety guidelines before use. This will ensure that they are being operated correctly and for the correct purpose

Special care should be taken with electrical tools.

Always:

- check plugs and connections (make sure that you have the correct fuse rating in the plug)
- inspect all leads to ensure no damage
- check that the power is off when connecting leads
- unwind extension leads completely from the reel to prevent the cable from overheating.

Never:

- use a tool in a way not recommended by the manufacturer
- use a tool with loose, damaged or makeshift parts
- lay a driver down while it is still switched on
- use a drill unless the chuck (the part in which the drill bit is held) is tight
- throw the tool onto the ground
- pass the tool down by its lead
- use a drill where it is difficult to see what you are doing or to hold the tool tightly
- allow leads to trail in water.

Safe storage and handling of tools and equipment

Hand tools

Hand tools need to be stored safely and securely. Tools such as chisels, saws, craft knives must be stored either in a roll or with a cover over the blade. This is because accidents could happen when people put their hands into tool bags to get something and cut their fingers on a sharp edge.

All tools must be stored in a suitable bag/box that will protect the tools from the elements. With a lot of tools being made from metal components, rust can affect them.

When not in use tools should be securely locked away – theft of tools can occur. It is your responsibility to look after your tools.

Power tools

Power tools should be handled with care. The manufacturer's guidance within the tool's manual will explain the safe handling and storage of the tool. You must follow this guidance.

Power tools should be carried by the handle and not the cable. When not in use, the tool should be stored away safely. Most power tools come in a plastic carry case. They should be kept in this case when not in use, and stored in a safe location to protect from damage and theft. Power tools that have gas powered cartridges must be stored in an area that is safe and away from sources of ignition, to prevent explosion. Used cartridges must be disposed of safely. Pneumatic, hydraulic and air powered tools must also be carried correctly and stored in a way that prevents damage.

Power tools include pressurised painting vessels and equipment, and compressed air and hydraulic powered equipment.

Safety tips

Never:

- store equipment, cables and plugs in wet areas/outdoors
- store equipment where leads may be damaged (near blades etc.)
- store equipment at height where it may fall on you

Always:

- store power tools away from children
- allow hot equipment to cool before storing
- unplug and coil lead before storing

Wheelbarrows

Wheelbarrows are generally used where large amounts of material need to be transported over a distance. The best type of wheelbarrow is one specially designed to go through narrow door openings.

Always clean the wheelbarrow out after use. Do not hit the body of the wheelbarrow with a heavy object. Keep tyres inflated, as this will allow for ease of movement. Check that all metal stays are in place.

Do not overload the wheelbarrow as it will put strain on your back and arms. Approach the barrow between the lifting arms and hold the arms at the end, bend your knees and lift. The weight of the material should be as much over the wheel as possible.

Bricks

Most bricks delivered to sites are now pre-packed and banded using either plastic or metal bands to stop the bricks from separating until ready for use. The edges are also protected by plastic strips to help stop damage during moving, usually by forklift or crane. They are then usually covered in shrink-wrapped plastic to protect them from the elements.

Safety tip

Take care and stand well clear of a crane used for offloading bricks on delivery

On arrival on site bricks should be stored on level ground and stacked no more than two packs high. This is done to prevent over-reaching or collapse, which could result in injury to workers. The bricks should be stored close to where they are required so that further movement is kept to a minimum. On large sites they may be stored further away and moved by telescopic lifting vehicles to the position required for use.

If bricks are unloaded by hand they should be stacked on edge in rows, on firm, level and well-drained ground. The ends of the stacks should be bonded and no higher than 1.8 m. To protect the bricks from rain and frost, all stacks should be covered with a tarpaulin or polythene sheets.

Using bricks

Great care should be taken when using the bricks from the packs. Once the banding is cut, the bricks can collapse, which can damage the bricks, especially on uneven ground.

Bricks should be taken from a minimum of three packs and mixed to give variations of colour and size. This is because the positioning of the bricks in the kiln can cause slight colour differences:

- the nearer the centre of the kiln, the lighter the colour
- the nearer the edge of the kiln, the darker the colour as the heat is stronger.

If the bricks are not mixed, you could get sections of brickwork in slightly different shades. This is called banding and this can be clearly made out even by people not working in construction.

Blocks

Blocks are made from concrete, which may be dense or lightweight. Lightweight blocks could be made from a fine aggregate that contains lots of air bubbles. The storage of blocks is the same as for bricks.

Paving slabs

Paving slabs are made from concrete or stone and are available in a variety of sizes, shapes and colours. They are used for pavements and patios, with some slabs given a textured top to improve appearance.

Paving slabs are normally delivered to sites by lorry and then crane offloaded, some in wooden crates covered with shrink-wrapped plastic, or banded and covered on pallets. They should not be stacked more than two packs high for safety reasons and to prevent damage to the slabs due to weight pressure.

Did you know?

The temperature must be taken into account when laying bricks and blocks as, if it is too cold, this will prevent the cement going off properly

Safety tip

When working with blocks, make sure that you always wear appropriate PPE, that is, boots, safety hat, gloves, goggles and facemask (see pages 64–66 for details)

Safety tip

It is good practice to put an intermediate flat stack in long rows to prevent rows from toppling

Paving slabs unloaded by hand are stored outside and stacked on edge to prevent the lower ones, if stored flat, from being damaged by the weight of the stack. The stack is started by laying about 10–12 slabs flat with the others leaning against these. If only a small number of slabs are to be stored, they can be stored flat (since the weight will be less).

Slabs should be stored on firm, level ground with timber bearers below to prevent the edges from getting damaged. This can happen if the slabs are placed on a solid surface.

Kerbs

Kerbs are concrete units laid at the edges of roads and footpaths to give straight lines or curves and retain the finished surfaces. The size of a common kerb is 100 mm wide, 300 mm high and 600 mm long. Path edgings are 50 mm wide, 150 mm high and 600 mm long.

Kerbs should be stacked on timber bearers or with overhanging ends, which provides a space for hands, or lifting slings if machine lifting is to be used. When they are stacked on top of each other, the stack must not be more than three kerbs high. To protect the kerbs from rain and frost it is advisable to cover them with a tarpaulin or sheet.

Roofing tiles

Roofing tiles are made from either clay or concrete. They may be machine-made or handmade and are available in a variety of shapes and colours. Many roofing tiles are able to interlock to prevent rain from entering the building. Ridge tiles are usually half round but sometimes they may be angled.

Storage of roofing tiles

Roofing tiles are stacked on edge to protect their 'nibs' and in rows on level, firm, well-drained ground. See Figure 1.21. They should not be stacked any higher than six rows high. The stack should be tapered to prevent them from toppling. The tiles at the end of the rows should be stacked flat to provide support for the rows.

Figure 1.17 Paving slabs stacked flat

Figure 1.18 Paving slabs on pallet

Figure 1.19 Stacked kerbs

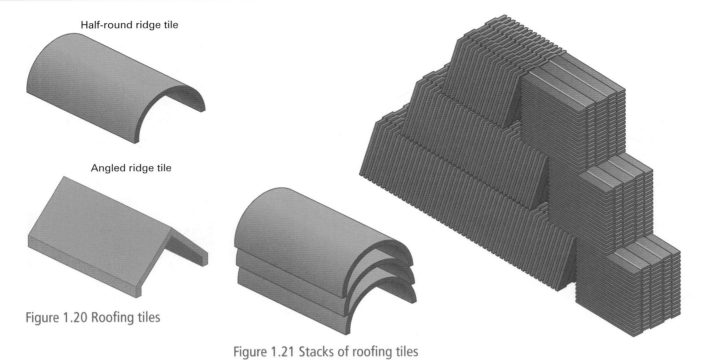

Half-round ridge tile

Angled ridge tile

Figure 1.20 Roofing tiles

Figure 1.21 Stacks of roofing tiles

100mm DPC

150mm DPC

ROOFING FELT

LEAD

Figure 1.22 Rolled materials stored on end

Ridge tiles may be stacked on top of each other, but not any higher than ten tiles.

To protect roofing tiles from rain and frost before use, they should be covered with a tarpaulin or plastic sheeting.

Storage of rolled materials

Rolled materials, for example damp proof course or roofing felt, should be stored in a shed on a level, dry surface. Narrower rolls may be best stored on shelves but in all cases they should be stacked on end to prevent them from rolling and to reduce the possibility of them being damaged by compression. See Figure 1.22. In the case of bitumen, the layers can melt together under pressure.

Aggregates

Aggregates are granules or particles that are mixed with cement and water to make mortar and concrete. Aggregates should be hard and durable. They should not contain any form of plant life or anything that can be dissolved in water.

Aggregates are classed in two groups:

- fine aggregates are granules that pass through a 5 mm sieve
- coarse aggregates are particles that are retained by a 5 mm sieve.

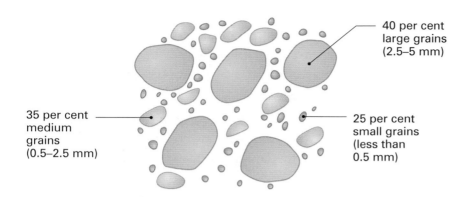

40 per cent large grains (2.5–5 mm)

35 per cent medium grains (0.5–2.5 mm)

25 per cent small grains (less than 0.5 mm)

Figure 1.23 Sand particles

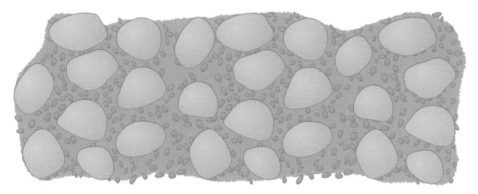

Figure 1.24 Mortar particles

Sand and mortar

The most commonly used fine aggregate is sand. Sand may be dug from pits and riverbeds, or dredged from the sea.

Good mortar should be mixed using 'soft' or 'building' sand. It should be well graded, which means having an equal quantity of fine, medium and large grains.

Concrete

Concrete should be made using 'sharp' sand, which is more angular and has a coarser feel than soft sand, which has more rounded grains.

When concreting, you also need 'coarse aggregate'. The most common coarse aggregate is usually limestone chippings, which are quarried and crushed to graded sizes, 10 mm, 20 mm or even larger.

Figure 1.25 Concrete particles

Storage of aggregates

Aggregates are usually delivered in tipper lorries, although nowadays 1-ton bags are available and may be crane handled. The aggregates should be stored on a concrete base, with a fall to allow for any water to drain away.

To protect aggregates from becoming contaminated with leaves and litter it is a good idea to situate stores away from trees and cover aggregates with a tarpaulin or plastic sheets.

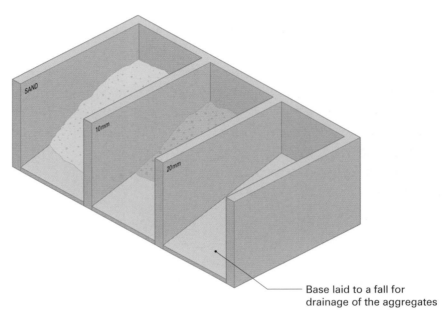

Base laid to a fall for drainage of the aggregates

Figure 1.26 Bays for aggregates

Plaster

Plaster is made from gypsum, water, and cement or lime. Aggregates can also be added depending on the finish desired. Plaster provides a jointless, smooth, easily decorated surface for internal walls and ceilings.

Gypsum plaster

Gypsum plaster is for internal use and contains different grades of gypsum, depending on the background finish. Browning is usually used as an undercoat on brickwork, but in most cases, a one-coat plaster is used. On plasterboard board finish is used.

Cement–sand plaster

This is used for external rendering, internal undercoats and waterproofing finishing coats.

Lime–sand plaster

This is mostly used as an undercoat, but may sometimes be used as a finishing coat.

Storage of cement and plaster

Both cement and plaster are usually available in 25 kg bags. The bags are made from multi-wall layers of paper with a polythene liner. Care must be taken not to puncture the bags before use. Each bag, if off-loaded manually, should be stored in a ventilated, waterproof shed, on a dry floor on pallets. If off-loaded by crane, the bags should be transferred to the shed and the same storage method used.

The bags should be kept clear of the walls, and piled no higher than five bags. It is most important that the bags are used in the same order as they were delivered. This minimises the length of time that the bags are in storage, preventing the contents from setting in the bags, which would require extra materials and cause added cost to the company.

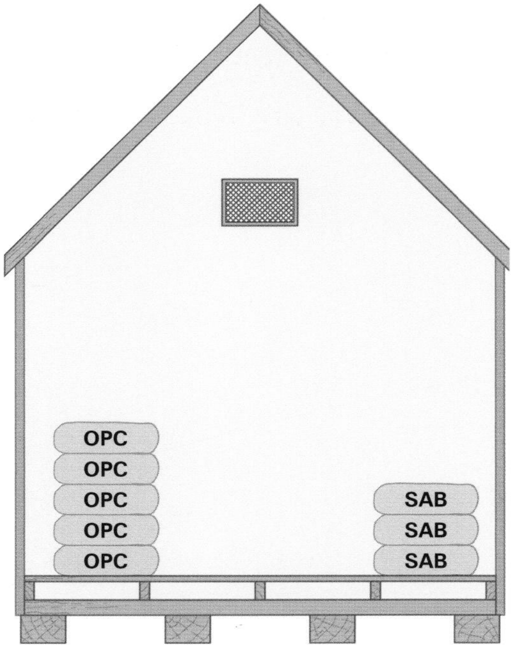

Plasterboard

Plasterboard is a sheet material that comes in various sizes. Some of the larger size sheets can be very awkward to carry. Special care must be taken when there is a strong wind as this can catch hold of the sheet and make the handling difficult and dangerous. Ideally two people should be used to transport larger plasterboard sheets.

Plasterboard is a gypsum-based product, so it must be stored in a waterproof area. As it is a sheet material it must also be stored flat and not leant up against a wall. Storing it against a wall will cause the sheet to bow.

Wood and sheet materials

Various types of wood and sheet materials are available. The most common are described below.

Carcassing timber

Carcassing timber is wood used for non-load-bearing jobs such as ceiling and floorboard supports, stud wall partitions and other types of framework. It should normally be stored outside under a covered framework. It should be placed on timber bearers clear of the ground. The ground should be free of vegetation and ideally covered over with concrete. This reduces the risk of

- Dry, ventilated shed
- Stock must be rotated so that old stock is used before new
- Not more than five bags high
- Clear of walls
- Off floor

Figure 1.27 Storage of cement and plaster bags in a shed

Remember
- The storage racks used to store wood must take account of the weight of the load
- Access to the materials being stored is another important consideration

absorption of ground moisture, which can damage the timber and cause wet rot.

Piling sticks or cross-bearers should be placed between each layer of timber, about 600 mm apart, to provide support and allow air circulation. Tarpaulins or plastic covers can be used to protect the timber from the elements, but care must be taken to allow air to flow freely through the stack. See Figure 1.28.

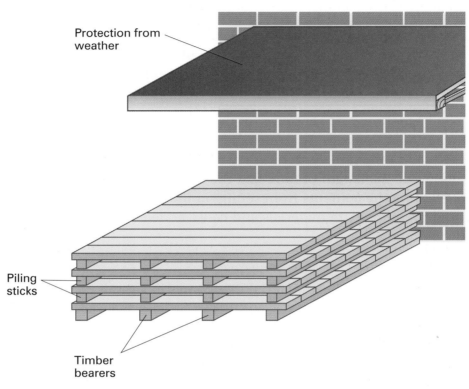

Protection from weather

Piling sticks

Timber bearers

Figure 1.28 Storage of carcassing timber

Joinery grade and hardwoods

These timbers should be stored under full cover wherever possible, preferably in a storage shed. Good ventilation is needed to avoid build-up of moisture through absorption. This type of timber should also be stored on bearers on a well-prepared base.

Plywood and other sheet materials

All sheet materials should be stored in a dry, well-ventilated environment. Specialised covers are readily available to give added protection for most sheet materials. This helps prevent condensation that is caused when non-specialised types of sheeting are used.

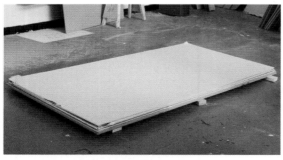

Figure 1.29 Storage of sheet materials

Sheet materials should be stacked flat on timber cross-bearers, spaced close enough together to prevent sagging. Alternatively, where space is limited, sheet materials can be stored on edge in purpose-made racks that allow the sheets to rest against the backboard. There should be sufficient space around the plywood for easy loading and removal. The rack should be designed to allow sheets to be removed from either the front or the ends.

Leaning sheets against walls is not recommended, as this makes them bow. This is then difficult to correct.

For sheet materials with faces or decorative sides, the face sides should be placed against each other. This is done to minimise the risk of damage due to friction of the sheets when they are moved. Different sizes, grades and qualities of sheet materials should be kept separate with off-cuts stacked separately from the main stack.

Sheet materials are awkward, heavy and prone to damage so extra care is essential when transporting them. Always ensure that the correct PPE is worn.

Joinery components

Joinery components, such as doors or kitchen units, must be stored safely and securely to prevent damage. Doors, windows, frames, etc. should ideally be stored flat on timber bearers under cover, to protect them from exposure to the weather. Where space is limited, they can be stored upright using a rack system (similar to the way sheet materials are stored). However, they must never be leant against a wall. This will bow the door/frame and make it very hard to fit.

Figure 1.30 Doors should be stacked on a flat surface

Wall and floor units – whether they be kitchen, bedroom or bathroom units – must be stacked on a flat surface, and no more than two units high. Units can be made from porous materials such as chipboard. Therefore, it is vital that they are stored inside, preferably in the room where they are to be fitted, to avoid double handling. Protective sheeting should be used to cover units to prevent damage or staining from paints, etc.

Safety tip

Due to the size, shape and weight of sheet materials, always get help to lift and carry them. If possible, use a purpose-made plywood trolley to transport the load

Find out

What are the PPE requirements when moving sheet materials?

Did you know?

- Wood and wood-based materials are susceptible to rot if the moisture content is too high, to insect attack and to many other defects such as bowing or warping
- Proper seasoning and chemical sprays can prevent defects

Unit 1001 Safe working practices in construction

Figure 1.31 Adhesives should be stored according to the manufacturer's instructions

Ideally all components and timber products, such as architrave, should be stored in the room where they are to be fitted. This will allow them to acclimatise to the room and prevent shrinkage or distortion after being fitted. This process is known as 'second seasoning'.

Adhesives

Adhesives are substances used to bond (stick) surfaces together. Because of their chemical nature, there are potentially serious risks connected with adhesives if they are not stored, used and handled correctly.

All adhesives should be stored and used in line with the manufacturer's instructions. This usually involves storing them on shelving, with labels facing outward, in a safe, secure area (preferably a lockable storeroom).

The level of risk when using an adhesive depends on the type of adhesive. Some of the risks include:

- explosion
- poisoning
- skin irritation
- disease.

As explained on page 7, these types of material are closely controlled by COSHH, which aims to minimise the risks involved with their storage and use.

All adhesives have a recommended **shelf life**. This must be taken into account when storing adhesives to ensure that the oldest stock is stored at the front and used first. Remember to check the manufacturer's guidelines as to how long the adhesive will remain fit for purpose once opened. Poor storage can affect the quality of the adhesives, such as loss in adhesive strength and prolongation of the setting time.

Paint and decorating equipment

Oil-based products

Oil-based products, such as gloss and varnish, should be stored on clearly marked shelves, with their labels turned to the front. They should always be used in date order. So new stock should be stored at the back with old stock at the front.

Figure 1.32 Correct storage of paints

Remember

Heavy materials should be stored at low levels to aid manual handling and should never be stacked more than two levels high

Oil-based products should be **inverted** at regular intervals to stop settlement and separation of the ingredients. They must also be kept in tightly sealed containers to stop the product **skinning**. Storage at a constant temperature will ensure that the product retains its desired consistency.

Water-based products

Water-based products, such as emulsions and acrylics, should also be stored on shelves with labels to the front and in date order.

Some water-based products have a very limited shelf life and must be used before their use-by date. As with oil-based products, water-based products keep best if stored at a constant temperature. It is also important to protect them from frost to prevent the water component of the product from freezing.

Powdered materials

Powdered materials that a decorator might use include Artex®, fillers, paste and sugar soap.

Large items such as heavy bags should be stored at ground or platform level. Smaller items can be stored on shelves. Sealed containers, such as a bin, are ideal for loose materials.

Powdered materials can have a limited shelf life and can set in high **humidity** conditions. They must also be protected from frost and exposure to any moisture, including condensation. These types of material must not be stored in the open air.

Key terms

Inverted – tipped and turned upside down

Skinning – formation of a skin on the product when the top layer dries out

Remember

Don't leave emulsions in a garage or shed over the winter. They are water based and will freeze, and when they thaw it will affect the finish

Key term

Humidity – dampness or moisture in the air

Key term

Volatile – a substance that is quick to evaporate (turn into a gas)

Substances hazardous to health

Some substances that the decorator will work with are potentially hazardous to health, as they can be **volatile** and highly flammable. COSHH applies to such materials and describe how they must be stored and handled (see page 7 for general information about COSHH).

Some larger bags of powdered material are heavier than they first appear. Make sure that you use the correct manual handling techniques (see pages 31–33).

Decorating materials that might be hazardous to health include spirits (i.e. methylated and white), turpentine (turps), paint thinners and varnish removers. These should be stored out of the way on shelves, preferably in a suitable locker or similar room that meets the requirements of COSHH. The temperatures must be kept below 15°C. A warmer environment may cause storage containers to expand and blow up.

The storage of LPG and other highly flammable liquids is covered on pages 21–22.

K6. Basic working platforms

Working at height

General safety considerations

You should be able to identify potential hazards associated with working at height, as well as hazards associated with equipment. It is essential that access equipment is well maintained and checked regularly for any deterioration or faults. These could compromise the safety of someone using the equipment and anyone else in the work area.

Although obviously not as important as people, equipment can also be damaged by the use of faulty access equipment. When maintenance checks are carried out they should be properly recorded. This provides very important information that helps to prevent accidents.

Risk assessment

Before any work is carried out at height, a thorough risk assessment needs to be completed. Your supervisor or someone else more experienced will do this while you are still training. But it is important that you understand what is involved so that you can carry out risk assessments in the future.

For doing a working-at-height risk assessment properly a number of questions must be answered:

- How will access to and egress from the work area be achieved?
- What type of work is to be carried out?
- How long is the work likely to take?
- How many people will be carrying out the task?
- How often will this work be carried out?
- What is the condition of the existing structure (if any) and the surroundings?
- Is adverse weather likely to affect the work and workers?
- How competent are the workforce and their supervisors?
- Is there a risk to the public and to work colleagues?

Duties

Your employer has a duty to provide and maintain safe plant and equipment. This includes scaffold access equipment and systems of work.

You have a duty:

- to comply with safety rules and procedures relating to access equipment
- to understand the hazards in the workplace and report things that you consider likely to lead to danger, for example a missing handrail on a working platform
- not to tamper with or modify equipment.

Fall protection

With any task that involves working at height, the main danger to workers is falling. Although scaffolding, etc. should have edge protection to prevent falls, there are certain tasks where edge protection or scaffolding simply can't be used. In these instances some form of fall protection must be in place to:

- prevent the worker falling
- keep the fall distance to a minimum
- ensure that the landing point is cushioned.

A variety of fall protection devices are available. The most commonly used ones are:

- harness and **lanyards**
- safety netting
- airbags.

Did you know?

Only a fully trained and competent person is allowed to erect any kind of working platform or access equipment. You should therefore not attempt to erect this type of equipment unless this describes you!

Key term

Lanyard – a rope that is used to support a weight

Fall-arrest system – this means that in the event of a slip or fall, the worker will only fall a few feet at most

Harness and lanyards

Harness and lanyards are a type of **fall-arrest system**. The system works with a harness that is attached to the worker and a lanyard attached to a secure beam/eyebolt. If the worker slips, they will only fall as far as the length of the lanyard and will be left hanging, rather than falling to the ground.

Safety netting

Safety netting is also a type of fall-arrest system. It's used mainly on the top floor where there is no higher point to attach a lanyard.

Figure 1.33 A harness and lanyard can prevent a worker from falling to the ground

Figure 1.34 Safety netting is used when working at the highest point

Figure 1.35 Safety netting can be used under fragile roofs

Safety nets are primarily used when decking a roof. They are attached to the joists/beams and are used to catch any worker who may slip or fall. Safety netting is also used on completed buildings where there is a fragile roof.

Airbags

An airbag safety system is a form of soft fall-arrest. It consists of interlinked modular air mattresses. The modules are connected by push connectors and/or flexible couplings and are inflated by a pump-driven fan, which can be electric, petrol, or butane gas powered. As the individual airbags fill with low-pressure air, they expand together to form a continuous protective safety surface, giving a cushioned soft fall and preventing serious injury.

The system must be kept inflated. If it is run on petrol or gas, it should be checked regularly to ensure that it is still functioning. This system is ideal for short fall jobs, but should not be used where a large fall could occur.

Stepladders and ladders

Stepladders

A stepladder has a prop that, when folded out allows the ladder to be used without having to lean it against anything. Stepladders are one of the most frequently used pieces of access equipment in the construction industry and are often used every day. This means that they are not always treated with the respect they deserve.

Stepladders are often misused. They should only be used for work that will take no more than a few minutes to complete. When work is likely to take longer, use a sturdier alternative.

When stepladders are used, the following safety points should be observed:

- ensure that the ground on which the stepladder is to be placed is firm and level; if the ladder rocks or sinks into the ground it should not be used for the work
- always open the steps fully
- never work off the top tread of the stepladder
- always keep your knees below the top tread
- never use stepladders to gain additional height on another working platform
- always look for the BSI Kitemark (Figure 1.36), which shows that the ladder has been made to BSI standards.

Figure 1.36 BSI Kitemark

A number of other safety points need to be observed depending on the type of stepladder being used.

Wooden stepladder

Before using a wooden stepladder, you should check:

- for loose screws, nuts, bolts and hinges
- that the tie ropes between the two sets of **stiles** are in good condition and not frayed
- for splits or cracks in the stiles
- that the treads are not loose or split.

Never paint any part of a wooden stepladder as this can hide defects, which may cause the ladder to fail during use, causing injury.

Safety tip

If any faults are revealed when checking a stepladder, it should be taken out of use, reported to the person in charge, and a warning notice attached to it to stop anyone using it

Figure 1.37 A wooden stepladder

Key term

Stiles – the side pieces of a stepladder into which the steps are set

Figure 1.39 A pole ladder

Figure 1.40 An aluminium extension ladder

Aluminium stepladder

Before using an aluminium stepladder check for damage to stiles and treads to see whether they are twisted, badly dented or loose.

Avoid working close to live electricity supplies as aluminium will conduct electricity.

Fibreglass stepladder

Before using a fibreglass stepladder, check for damage to stiles and treads. Once damaged, fibreglass stepladders cannot be repaired and must be disposed of.

Ladders

A ladder, unlike a stepladder, does not have a prop and so has to be leant against something in order for it to be used. Together with stepladders, ladders are one of the most common pieces of equipment used to carry out work at height and to gain access to the work area.

Ladders are also made of timber, aluminium or fibreglass, and require similar checks to stepladders before use.

Pole ladder

These are single ladders and are available in a range of lengths. They are most commonly used for access to scaffolding platforms. Pole ladders are made from timber. They must be stored under cover and flat, supported evenly along their length to prevent them sagging and twisting. They should be checked for damage or defects every time before being used.

Extension ladder

Extension ladders have two or more interlocking lengths. The lengths can be slid together for convenient storage or slid apart to the desired length when in use.

Extension ladders are available in timber, aluminium and fibreglass. Aluminium types are the most favoured as they are lightweight yet strong and available in double and triple extension types. Although also very strong, fibreglass versions are heavy, making them difficult to manoeuvre.

Figure 1.38 An aluminium stepladder

Erecting and using a ladder

The following points should be noted when considering the use of a ladder:

- as with stepladders, ladders are not designed for work of long duration; alternative working platforms (see pages 55–60) should be considered if the work will take longer than a few minutes
- the work should not require the use of both hands; one hand should be free to hold the ladder
- you should be able to do the work without stretching
- you should make sure that the ladder can be adequately secured to prevent it slipping on the surface it is leaning against.

Pre-use checks

Before using a ladder, check its general condition. Make sure that:

- no rungs are damaged or missing
- the stiles are not damaged
- no **tie-rods** are missing
- no repairs have been made to the ladder.

In addition, for wooden ladders ensure that:

- they have not been painted, which may hide defects or damage
- there is no decay or rot
- the ladder is not twisted or warped.

Erecting a ladder

Observe the following guidelines when erecting a ladder:

- ensure that you have a solid, level base
- do not pack anything under either (or both) of the stiles to level it
- if the ladder is too heavy to put it in position on your own, get someone to help
- ensure that there is at least a four rung overlap on each extension section
- never rest the ladder on plastic guttering as it may break, causing the ladder to slip and the user to fall
- where the base of the ladder is in an exposed position, ensure that it is adequately guarded so that no one knocks it or walks into it
- the ladder should be secured at both the top and the bottom; the bottom of the ladder can be secured by a second person, however, this person must not leave the base of the ladder while it is in use.

Safety tip

Ladders must *never* be repaired once damaged and must be disposed of

Key term

Tie-rods – metal rods underneath the rungs of a ladder that give extra support to the rungs

Did you know?

On average in the UK, every year 14 people die at work falling from ladders, and nearly 1200 suffer major injuries (source: HSE)

Remember

You must carry out a thorough risk assessment before working from a ladder. Ask yourself, 'Would I be safer using an alternative method?'

Unit 1001

Safe working pratices in construction

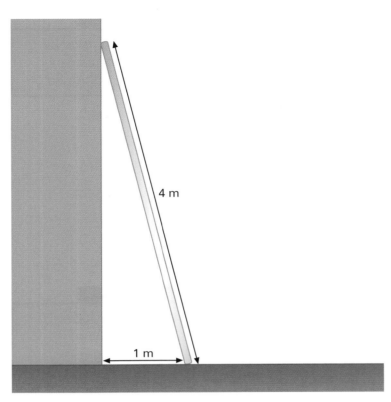

Figure 1.41 Correct angle for a ladder

4 m

1 m

- The angle of the ladder should be a ratio of 1:4 (or 75°). This means that the bottom of the ladder is 1 m away from the wall for every 4 m in height (see Figure 1.41).
- The top of the ladder must extend at least 1 m, or five rungs, above its landing point.

Roof work

When carrying out any work on a roof, a roof ladder or **crawling board** must be used. Roof work also requires the use of edge protection or, where this is not possible, a safety harness.

The roof ladder is rolled up the surface of the roof and over the ridge tiles, just enough to allow the ladder to be turned over and the ladder hook allowed to bear on the tiles on the other side of the roof. This hook prevents the roof ladder sliding down the roof once it is accessed.

Key term

Crawling board – a board or platform placed on roof joists that spreads the weight of the worker allowing the work to be carried out safely

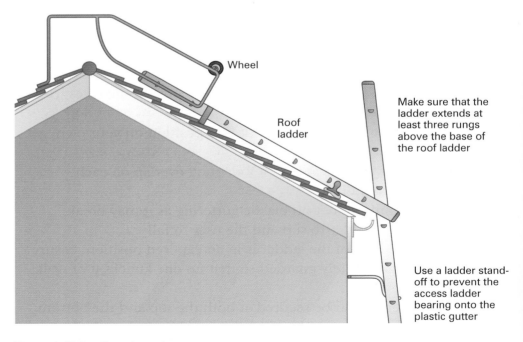

Wheel

Roof ladder

Make sure that the ladder extends at least three rungs above the base of the roof ladder

Use a ladder stand-off to prevent the access ladder bearing onto the plastic gutter

Figure 1.42 Roof work equipment

Trestle platforms

Frames

A-frames

These are most commonly used by carpenters and painters. As the name suggests, the frame is in the shape of a capital A and can be made from timber, aluminium or fibreglass. Two are used together to support a platform (a scaffold or staging board). See Figure 1.43.

Figure 1.43 A-frame trestles with scaffold board

When using A-frames:

- they should always be opened fully and, in the same way as stepladders, must be placed on firm, level ground
- the platform width should be no less than 450 mm
- the overhang of the board at each end of the platform should be not more than four times its thickness
- a risk assessment should be carried out before using.

Steel trestles

These are sturdier than A-frame trestles and are adjustable in height. They are also capable of providing a wider platform than timber trestles – see Figure 1.44. As with the A-frame type, they must be used only on firm and level ground but the trestle itself should be placed on a flat scaffold board on top of the ground. Trestles should not be placed more than 1.2 m apart.

> **Safety tip**
>
> A-frame trestles should never be used as a stepladder as they are not designed for this purpose. Newer types of trestles have handrail attachments to help prevent falls

Figure 1.44 Steel trestle with staging board

Platforms

Scaffold boards

To ensure that scaffold boards provide a safe working platform, before using them check that they:

- are not split
- are not twisted or warped
- have no large knots, which cause weakness
- it should be a minimum of four boards wide.

Care should be taken when handling scaffold boards as they can be long and unwieldy. Ideally two people should be used when carrying them. It is important to store scaffold boards correctly – that is flat and level – otherwise they will twist or bow. They also need to be kept covered to prevent damage from rain, which could lead to rot.

Staging boards

These are designed to span a greater distance than scaffold boards and can offer a 600 mm wide working platform. They are ideal for use with trestles.

Hop-ups

Also known as step-ups, hop-ups are ideal for reaching low-level work that can be carried out in a relatively short period of time. A hop-up needs to be of sturdy construction and have a base of not less than 600 mm by 500 mm. Hop-ups have the disadvantage that they are heavy and awkward to move around.

Safety tip

The thickness of boards determines the distance between supports:

- 32 mm boards can span 1 m
- 38 mm boards can span 1.5 m
- 50 mm boards can span 2.5 m

If boards are spaced over this they will sag or break during use

Safety tip

Do not use items as hop-ups that are not designed for the purpose (e.g. milk crates, stools or chairs). They are usually not very sturdy and can't take the weight of someone standing on them. This may result in falls and injury

Scaffolding

Tubular scaffold is the most commonly used type of scaffolding within the construction industry. There are two types of tubular scaffold:

- **Independent scaffold** – free-standing scaffold that does not rely on any part of the building to support it (although it must be tied to the building to provide additional stability).
- **Putlog scaffold** – scaffolding that is attached to the building via the entry of some of the poles into holes left in the brickwork by the bricklayer. The poles stay in position until the construction is complete and give the scaffold extra support.

No one other than a qualified **carded scaffolder** is allowed to erect or alter scaffolding. Although you are not allowed to erect or alter this type of scaffold, you must be sure that it is safe before you work on it. Ask yourself the following questions to assess the condition and suitability of the scaffold before you use it:

- Are there any signs, attached to the scaffold, that state that it is incomplete or unsafe?
- Is the scaffold overloaded with materials such as bricks?
- Are the platforms cluttered with waste materials?
- Are there adequate guard rails and scaffold boards in place?
- Does the scaffold actually 'look' safe?
- Is there correct access to and from the scaffold?
- Are the various scaffold components in the correct place (see Figure 1.45 below)?
- Have the correct types of fittings been used (see Figure 1.46)?

Key term

Carded scaffolder – someone who holds a recognised certificate showing competence in scaffold erection

Did you know?

It took 14 years to finally settle on 48 mm as the diameter of most tubular scaffolding poles

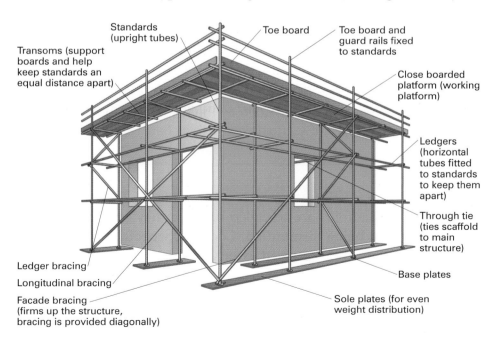

Standards (upright tubes)
Toe board
Toe board and guard rails fixed to standards
Transoms (support boards and help keep standards an equal distance apart)
Close boarded platform (working platform)
Ledgers (horizontal tubes fitted to standards to keep them apart)
Through tie (ties scaffold to main structure)
Ledger bracing
Longitudinal bracing
Facade bracing (firms up the structure, bracing is provided diagonally)
Base plates
Sole plates (for even weight distribution)

Figure 1.45 Components of a tubular scaffolding structure

Right angle coupler – load-bearing; used to join tubes at right angles

Universal coupler – load-bearing; also used to join tubes at right

Swivel coupler – load-bearing; used to join tubes at various angles, e.g. diagonal braces

Adjustable base plate or base plate used at the base of standards to allow even weight distribution

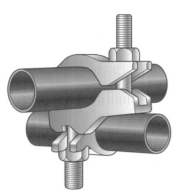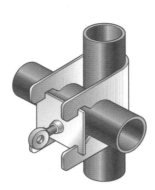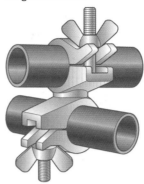

Figure 1.46 Types of scaffold fittings

If you have any doubts about the safety of scaffolding, report them. You could very well prevent serious injury or even someone's death.

Working life

Sanjit has been asked by a client to take a look at all the fascia boards on a two-storey building. Depending on the condition of the fascia boards, they will need either repairing or replacing. The job will probably take Sanjit between two and six hours, depending on what he has to do.

- What types of scaffolding do you think might be suitable for Sanjit's job?
- Can you think of anything that Sanjit will need to consider while he prepares for and carries out this task?

He will need to think about things such as access and egress points, whether the area will be closed off to the public, how long he will need to work at height, etc.

Take a look through the information on the following pages on types of scaffold. What type of scaffold do you think Sanjit should use for this task?

Mobile tower scaffolds

Figure 1.47 Mobile tower scaffold

Mobile tower scaffolds are so called because they can be moved around without being dismantled. Lockable wheels make this possible, and they are used extensively throughout the construction industry by many different trades. A tower can be made from either traditional steel tubes and fittings or aluminium, which is lightweight and easy to move. The aluminium type of tower is normally specially designed and is referred to as a 'proprietary tower'.

Low towers

These are a smaller version of the standard mobile tower scaffold and are designed specifically for use by one person. They have a recommended working height of no more than 2.5 m and a safe working load of 150 kg. They are lightweight and easily transported and stored.

These towers require no assembly other than the locking into place of the platform and handrails. However, you still require training before you use one and you must ensure that the manufacturer's instructions are followed when setting up and working from this type of platform.

Erecting a tower scaffold

It is essential that tower scaffolds are situated on a firm and level base. The stability of any tower depends on the height in relation the size of the base:

*   for use inside a building, the height should be no more than three and a half times the smallest base length
*   for outside use, the height should be no more than three times the smallest base length.

The height of a tower can be increased, provided that the area of the base is increased **proportionately**. The base area can be increased by fitting outriggers to each corner of the tower.

For mobile towers, the wheels must be in the locked position while they are in use and unlocked only while they are being repositioned.

There are several important points you should observe when working from a scaffold tower:

*   Any working platform above 2 m high must be fitted with guardrails and toe boards. Guard rails may also be required at heights of less than 2 m if there is a risk of falling onto potential hazards below, for example reinforcing rods. Guard rails must be fitted at a minimum height of 950 mm.
*   If guard rails and toe boards are needed, they must be positioned on all four sides of the platform.
*   Any tower higher than 9 m must be secured to the structure.
*   Towers must not exceed 12 m in height, unless they have been specifically designed for that purpose.
*   The working platform of any tower must be fully boarded and be at least 600 mm wide.

Figure 1.48 Low tower scaffold

Key term

Proportionately – in relation to the size of something else

Safety tip

*   Mobile towers must *only* be moved when they are free of people, tools and materials
*   Never climb a scaffold tower on the outside as this can cause it to tip over

- If the working platform is to be used for materials, then the minimum width must be 800 mm.
- All towers must have their own access and this should be by an internal ladder.

The dangers of working at height

While working at height there are a number of dangers that need to be identified. The obvious danger is falling from the height, which can result in serious injury, but there are also additional dangers in working at height that are not present when working at ground level.

Although good housekeeping (page 20) is important while working at ground level to prevent slips and trips, it is *vital* when working at height. Not only are you at added risk, but materials and tools that are left on a working platform can be knocked off the platform onto people working below. There is a risk of causing serious head injuries to those below and not just the workforce, as in some instances the working platform may be in an area that involves the general public.

When working in a public area, the public must be protected from hazards by way of barriers around the work area. You must also ensure that the sides of the working platform are sealed off to prevent any materials or other objects from falling.

K7. Working with electricity

Electricity is a killer. One of the main problems with electricity is that it is invisible. You don't even have to be working with an electric tool to be electrocuted. You can get an electric shock:

- working too close to live overhead cables
- plastering a wall with electric sockets
- carrying out maintenance work on a floor
- drilling into a wall.

However, not all electric shocks are fatal – they can also cause injuries such as burns and problems with your muscles and heart.

A common error is to think that the level of voltage is directly related to the level of injury or danger of death. However, a small shock from static electricity may contain thousands of volts but has very little current behind it.

Voltages

There are two main types of voltage in use in the UK – 230 V and 110 V. The standard UK power supply is 230 V and this is what all the sockets in your house are. On construction sites, 230 V has been deemed as unsafe and 110 V must be used here. The 110 V is identified by a yellow casement and a different style plug. It works from a transformer which converts the 230 V to 110 V.

When working within domestic dwellings where 230V is the standard power source, ideally a portable transformer should be used. If this is not possible then residual current devices (RCD) should be used.

Contained within the wiring there should be three wires: the live and neutral, which carry the alternating current, and the earth wire, which acts as a safety device. The three wires are colour-coded with standard European colours so that all electrical installations are standardised and any person needing to do work can easily identify which wire is which.

Precautions to take to prevent electric shocks

Never:

- carry electrical equipment by the cable
- remove plugs by pulling on the lead
- allow tools to get wet; if they do, get them checked before use.

Always:

- check equipment, leads and plugs before use; if you find a fault don't use the equipment and tell your supervisor immediately
- keep cable off the ground where possible to avoid damage/trips
- avoid damage to the cable by keeping it away from sharp edges
- keep the equipment locked away and labelled to prevent it being used by accident
- use cordless tools where possible
- follow instructions on extension leads.

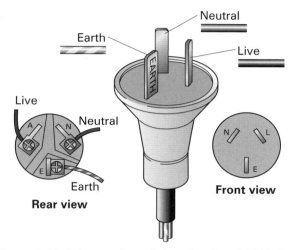

Figure 1.49 Colour coding of the wires in a 230 V plug

Figure 1.50 A 110 V plug

Remember

Current coding:

- live – brown
- neutral – blue
- earth – yellow and green

Some older properties may have older colour-coding:

- live – red
- neutral – black
- earth – yellow and green

Dealing with electric shocks

In helping the victim of an electric shock, the first thing you must do is disconnect the power supply if it is safe to do so and will not take long to find. Touching the power source may put you in danger.

- If the victim is in contact with something portable, such as a drill, attempt to move it away using a non-conductive object such as a wooden broom.
- Time is precious, and separating the victim from the source can prove an effective way to speed the process.
- Do not attempt to touch the affected person until they are free and clear of the supplied power. Be especially careful in wet areas, such as bathrooms – most water will conduct electricity and electrocuting yourself is also possible.

People 'hung up' in a live current flow may think they are calling out for help, but most likely no sound will be heard from them. When the muscles contract under household current (most electrocutions happen from house current at home), the person affected will appear in 'locked-up' state, unable to move or react to you.

- Using a wooden object, swiftly and strongly knock the person free, trying not to injure them, and land them clear of the source.
- The source may also be lifted or removed, if possible, with the same wooden item. This is not recommended on voltages that exceed 500 V.

First aid procedures for an electric shock victim

- Check to see if you are alone. If there are other people around, instruct them to call an ambulance immediately.
- Check for a response and breathing.
- If the area is safe for you to be in, and you have removed the object or have cut off its power supply, shout to the person to see if they are conscious. At this stage, do not touch the victim.
- Check once again to see if the area is safe. If you are satisfied that it is safe, start resuscitating the victim. If you have no first aid knowledge, call 999 for an ambulance.

Safety tip

Don't attempt going near a victim of an electric shock without wearing rubber or some form of insulated sole shoes; bare or socked feet will allow the current to flow to ground through your body as well

Working life

Tyrone and Macy are knocking down a small wall in an old block of flats. The wall has an electric socket in it. Tyrone says that they should switch off the power at the mains, disconnect the socket and put some tape over the wires. Macy isn't sure, but they find the mains switch in the flat and switch off the power. Tyrone removes the socket cover and suddenly there is a bang. Tyrone is thrown backwards.

- What do you think has happened?
- How could this have happened?
- What should have been done?
- What should Macy do now?

K8. Using appropriate PPE

Personal protective equipment (PPE) is the name for clothes and other wearable items that form a line of defence against accidents or injury. PPE is not the only way of preventing accidents or injury. It should be used with all the other methods of staying healthy and safe in the workplace (equipment, training, regulations and laws etc.).

Maintaining and storing PPE

It is important that PPE is well maintained. The effectiveness of the protection it offers will be affected if the PPE is damaged in any way. Maintenance may include:

- cleaning
- examination
- replacement
- repair and testing.

The wearer may be able to carry out simple maintenance (such as cleaning), but more intricate repairs must only be carried out by a competent person. The costs associated with the maintenance of PPE are the responsibility of the employer.

Where PPE is provided, adequate storage facilities for PPE must also be provided for when it is not in use, unless the employee can take PPE away from the workplace (for example, footwear or clothing).

Accommodation may be simple (for example, pegs for waterproof clothing or safety helmets) and it need not be fixed (for example, a case for safety glasses or a container in a vehicle). Storage should be adequate to protect the PPE from contamination, loss, damage, damp or sunlight. Where PPE may become contaminated during use, storage should be separate from any storage provided for ordinary clothing.

Remember

PPE only works properly if it is being used – and used correctly!

The main pieces of legislation that govern the use of PPE are:

- Control of Substances Hazardous to Health 2002
- Provision and Use of Work Equipment Regulations (1992 and 1998)
- Personal Protective Equipment at Work Regulations 1992

All PPE must be maintained regularly and should be 'CE' marked. This will indicate that is complies with the requirements of the Personal Protective Equipment Regulations 2002. The CE marking shows that the PPE satisfies safety requirements. In some cases it may have been tested and certified by an independent body.

PPE must be supplied by your employer free of charge. You have responsibility as an employee to look after it and use it whenever it is required. See page 10 for the conditions laid down for the protection and maintenance of PPE by the regulations. The HSE website (www.hse.gov.uk) also gives information on maintenance and use of PPE.

The possible consequences of not using PPE can be serious and cause long-term health problems. The health problems and their consequences are described on pages 30–31.

Types of PPE

Different jobs require different types of PPE – the protection needed while using a circular saw is different from the protection needed for building a gable end. Some body parts need more protection than others. Each piece of PPE must be suitable for the job and used properly.

Head protection

There are several different types of head protection; the one most commonly used in construction is the safety helmet (or hard hat). This is used to protect the head from falling objects and knocks, and has an adjustable strap to ensure a snug fit. Some safety helmets come with attachments for ear defenders or eye protection. Safety helmets are meant to be worn directly on the head and must not be worn over any other type of hat.

Eye protection

Eye protection is used to protect the eyes from dust and flying debris. The three main types are:

- **safety goggles** – made of a durable plastic and used when there is a danger of dust getting into the eyes or a chance of impact injury.
- **safety spectacles** – these are also made from a durable plastic but give less protection than goggles. This is because they don't fully enclose the eyes and so only protect from flying debris.

Figure 1.51 A safety helmet

Figure 1.52 Safety goggles

Figure 1.53 Safety spectacles

- **facemasks** – again made of durable plastic, these protect the entire face from flying debris. They do not, however, protect the eyes from dust.

Foot protection

Safety boots or shoes are used to protect the feet from falling objects and to prevent sharp objects such as nails from injuring the foot. Safety boots should have a steel toe-cap and steel mid-sole.

Figure 1.54 Safety boots

Hearing protection

Hearing protection is used to prevent damage to the ears caused by very loud noise. There are several types of hearing protection available, but the two most common types are ear-plugs and ear defenders.

- **Ear-plugs** – these are small fibre plugs that are inserted into the ear and used when the noise is not too severe. Before inserting ear-plugs, make sure that you have clean hands. Never use plugs that have been used by somebody else.

Figure 1.55 Ear-plugs

- **Ear defenders** – these are worn to cover the entire ear and are connected to a band that fits over the top of the head. They are used when there is excessive noise and must be cleaned regularly.

Respiratory protection

Respiratory protection is used to prevent the worker from breathing in any dust or fumes that may be hazardous. The main type of respiratory protection is the dust mask.

Dust masks are used when working in a dusty environment and are lightweight, comfortable and easy to fit. They should be worn by only one person and must be disposed of at the end of the working day.

Figure 1.57 A respiratory system

Figure 1.56 Ear defenders

Safety tip

Dust masks only offer protection from non-toxic dust, so if the worker is to be exposed to toxic dust or fumes, a full respiratory system should be used

Example

- Wearing lightweight rubber gloves to move glass will not offer much protection, so leather gauntlets must be used
- Plastic-coated gloves will protect you from certain chemicals
- Kevlar® gloves offer cut resistance

Hand protection

There are several types of hand protection and the correct type must be used for the task at hand. To make sure you are wearing the most suitable type of gloves for the task, you need to look first at what is going to be done and then match the type of gloves to that task.

Figure 1.58 Safety gloves

Figure 1.59 High-visibility jacket

Figure 1.60 Overalls

Figure 1.61 The triangle of fire

Skin and sun protection

Another precaution you can take is ensuring that you wear barrier cream. This is a cream used to protect the skin from damage and infection. Don't forget to ensure that your skin is protected from the sun with a good sunscreen, and make sure your back, arms and legs are covered by suitable clothing.

Whole body protection

The rest of the body also needs protecting when working on site. This will usually involve wearing either overalls or a high-visibility jacket.

High-visibility jackets are essential whenever you are on site or working near traffic. They ensure that the person wearing them is clearly visible at all times. This helps to avoid accidents by making the wearer easier to avoid.

Overalls provide protection from dirt and the possibility of minor cuts. In wet conditions you may also need to use waterproof or thermal clothing. Some circumstances will require chemical-resistant clothing.

Knee pads can be worn by workers who will spend a lot of time kneeling, such as carpet fitters. Paper overalls or paper boiler suits can be worn for such tasks as insulating a loft where irritant fibres may be a problem.

K9. Fire and emergency procedures

Fires can start almost anywhere and at any time, but a fire needs three things to burn:

- fuel
- heat
- oxygen.

Together these elements are known as 'the triangle of fire'. If any one of the three ingredients is missing, fire cannot burn. Remove one side of the triangle and the fire will be extinguished.

If it has all three ingredients in the triangle, a fire will spread. Cutting off the fire's access to fuel, heat or oxygen will stop the spread of the fire.

Fire moves from area to area either by burning the fuel along the way – paper or wood shavings, for example – or through the direct transfer of heat. If a burning piece of plywood is leaning against another piece of plywood, both pieces of plywood will eventually go up in flames, causing the fire to spread.

Fires are classified according to the type of material that is involved:

- Class A – wood, paper, textiles, etc.
- Class B – flammable liquids: petrol, oil, etc.
- Class C – flammable gases: LPG, propane, etc.
- Class D – metal, metal powder, etc.
- Class E – electrical equipment.

Firefighting equipment

There are several types of firefighting equipment, such as fire blankets and fire extinguishers. Each type is designed to be the most effective at putting out a particular class of fire. Some should never be used in certain types of fire.

Fire extinguishers

A fire extinguisher is a metal canister containing a substance that can put out a fire. There are several different types and it is important that you learn which type should be used on specific classes of fires. This is because if you use the wrong type, you may make the fire worse or risk severely injuring yourself.

Fire extinguishers are now all one colour (red), but they have a band of colour which shows what substance is inside.

Water

The coloured band is red and this type of extinguisher can be used on Class A fires. Water extinguishers can also be used on Class C fires to cool the area down.

Figure 1.62 Water fire extinguisher

> **Safety tip**
>
> A water fire extinguisher should *never* be used to put out an electrical or burning fat/oil fire. This is because electrical current can carry along the jet of water back to the person holding the extinguisher, electrocuting them. Putting water on to burning fat or oil will make the fire worse as the fire will 'explode', potentially causing serious injury

Foam

The coloured band is cream and this type of extinguisher can be used on Class A fires. A foam extinguisher can also be used on a Class B fire if the liquid is not flowing.

> **Remember**
>
> - Remove the fuel – without anything to burn, the fire will go out
> - Remove the heat and the fire will go out
> - Remove the oxygen and the fire will go out – without oxygen, a fire won't even ignite

Figure 1.63 Foam fire extinguisher

Figure 1.64 Carbon dioxide (CO₂) extinguisher

Figure 1.65 Dry powder extinguisher

Find out

What fire risks are there in the construction industry? Think about some of the materials (fuel) and heat sources that could make up two sides of the triangle of fire

Carbon dioxide (CO$_2$)

The coloured band is black and the extinguisher can be used primarily on electrical fires. However, as well as Class E, it can also be used on Class A, B and C fires.

Dry powder

The coloured band is blue and this type of extinguisher can be used on all classes of fire, but most commonly on electrical and liquid fires. The powder puts out the fire by smothering the flames.

Fire blankets

Fire blankets are normally found in kitchens or canteens as they are good at putting out cooking fires. They are made of a fireproof material and work by smothering the fire and stopping any more oxygen from getting to it, thus putting it out. A fire blanket can also be used if a person is on fire.

It is important to remember that when you put out a fire with a fire blanket, you must take extra care as you will have to get quite close to the fire.

What to do in the event of a fire

During your induction to any workplace, you will be made aware of the fire procedure as well as where the fire assembly points (also known as 'muster points') are and what the alarm sounds like.

All muster points should be clearly indicated by signs, and a map of their location clearly displayed in the building. On hearing the alarm you must stop what you are doing and make your way to the nearest muster point. This is so that everyone can be accounted for. If you do not go to the muster point, or if you leave the muster point before someone has taken your name, someone may risk their life to go back into the fire to get you.

When you hear the alarm, you should not stop to gather any belongings and you must not run. If you discover a fire, you must only try to fight the fire if it is blocking your exit or if it is small. Only re-enter the site or building when you have been given the all-clear.

Every building and organisation will have its own unique fire evacuation procedures and practices. Make sure that you are familiar with the procedures in your workplace so that you will know what to do in the event of an evacuation. Fire drills should be part of every organisation's routine, to ensure that the procedures and practices required in the case of a fire are well known to everyone in the building.

- Fire and smoke can kill in seconds, so think and act clearly, quickly and sensibly
- Evacuation procedures are not just to protect your safety, but everyone's safety. If you do not follow the correct procedures and go to the correct assembly areas, other people may risk their own lives trying to find you

Figure 1.66 A prohibition sign

K10. Safety signs and notices

You will see safety signs in many parts of the workplace.

Uses of safety signs

Safety signs are used to:

- warn of any hazards
- prevent accidents
- explain where things are
- tell you what to do – or not do – in certain areas.

Figure 1.67 A mandatory sign

Types of safety sign

There are several different types of safety sign, and they have different purposes.

- Prohibition signs – these tell you that something *must not* be done. They always have a white background and a red circle with a red line through it.
- Mandatory signs – these tell you that something *must* be done. They are also circular, but have a white symbol on a blue background.
- Warning signs – these signs are there to alert you to a specific hazard. They are triangular and have a yellow background and a black border.
- Safe condition signs (often called information signs) – these give you useful information like the location of things (for example a first aid point). They can be square or rectangular and are green with a white symbol.

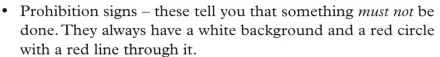

Figure 1.68 A warning sign

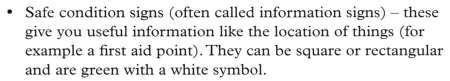

Figure 1.69 An information sign

Figure 1.70 A safety sign with symbol and words

Most signs consist of only the symbols that let you know what they are saying. Others have some words as well. For example, a no smoking sign might have a cigarette in a red circle with a red line crossing through the cigarette and the words 'No smoking' underneath.

FAQ

How do I find out what safety legislation is relevant to my job?

Ask your employer or manager, or contact the HSE at www.hse.gov.uk.

When do I need to do a risk assessment?

A risk assessment should be carried out if there is any chance of an accident happening as a direct result of the work being done. To be on the safe side, you should make a risk assessment before starting each task.

Do I need to read and understand every regulation?

No. It is part of your employer's duty to ensure that you are aware of what you need to know.

Do I have to attend every toolbox talk?

No, you only need to attend the toolbox talks relevant to you, but if you are unsure or think that you have missed a toolbox talk discuss it with your supervisor.

What do I need to do if my PPE is damaged?

You need to inform your employer immediately so that you can have the PPE replaced. Damaged PPE will not offer sufficient protection.

Check it out

1. Name five pieces of health and safety legislation that affect the construction industry and give a brief explanation of what they do.
2. What is the HSE? Give a brief explanation of its role.
3. Sketch the triangle of fire and explain how each part of the triangle relates to the others.
4. Describe, with sketches, the major warning signs and explain what they do.
5. Name six different types of PPE and give an example of each.
6. Describe the key items that should be included in a first aid kit.
7. Describe the purpose of a toolbox talk.
8. Describe three key things you should never do with a portable power tool.
9. Using a material that is familiar to you explain, with the aid of sketches if necessary, how that material should be stored.
10. Describe how a wooden stepladder should be checked before use.
11. When should a trestle platform be used? What two types of board can be used as a platform with a trestle frame?

Getting ready for assessment

The information contained in this unit, as well as continued health and safety good practice throughout your training, will help you with preparing for both your end of unit test and the diploma multiple-choice test. It will also help you to understand the dangers of working in the construction industry. Wherever you work in the construction industry, you will need to understand the dangers of working there. You will also need to know the safe working practices for the work required for your practical assignments.

Your college or training centre should provide you with the opportunity to practise these skills, as part of preparing for the test.

You will need to know about and understand the dangers that could arise and precautions that can be taken:

- the safety rules and regulations
- knowing accident and emergency procedures
- identifying hazards on-site
- health and hygiene
- safe handling of materials and equipment
- working at heights
- working with electricity
- using personal protective equipment (PPE)
- fire and emergency procedures
- safety signs

You will need to apply the things that you have learnt in this unit to the actual work you will be carrying out in the synoptic test and in your professional life. For example, with learning outcome 6 you have seen why basic working platforms are used and the good practice that you should use when working on these platforms. You have also seen the different parts of ladders and scaffolding and identified the dangers of working at height. You will now need to use this knowledge yourself when you are working, by using access equipment to the correct legislation and safeguarding your health, through using the correct PPE. You will also need to use your understanding of how PPE should be stored to maintain it in perfect condition.

Before you start work you should always think of a plan of action. You will need to know the clear sequences of operations for the practical work that is to be constructed, to be sure that you are not making mistakes as you work and that you are working safely at all times.

Your speed in carrying out these tasks in a practice setting will also help to prepare you for the time set for the test. However, you must never rush the test. This is particularly important with health and safety, as you must always make sure that you are working safely. Make sure throughout the test that you are wearing appropriate and correct PPE and using tools correctly.

This unit has explained the dangers that you may face when working. Understanding these dangers and the precautions that can be taken to help protect you from them, will not only aid you in your training, but will also help you to remain safe and healthy throughout your working life.

Good luck!

Unit 1001 Safe working practices in construction

Knowledge check

1 Legislation is:
  a) a law that must be complied with
  b) a guide to tell you what to do
  c) a code of practice
  d) not your responsibility.

2 Accidents are caused by:
  a) following all instructions carefully
  b) taking care of yourself and others
  c) hurrying and not paying attention
  d) nothing – accidents just happen.

3 Manual handling injuries can be caused by:
  a) lifting items that are too heavy
  b) lifting an item once
  c) lifting an item repetitively
  d) all of the above.

4 Which regulation deals with lifting components?
  a) The Work at Height Regulations 2005
  b) The Manual Handling Operations Regulations 1992
  c) The Personal Protective Equipment at Work Regulations 1992
  d) The Electricity at Work Regulations 1989

5 With regards to PPE, the employer must:
  a) supply you with it
  b) not charge you for it
  c) ensure that you wear it
  d) do all of the above.

6 A sign that is circular with a white background and a red circle around the edge with a red line through it is a:
  a) warning sign
  b) mandatory sign
  c) prohibition sign
  d) information sign.

7 Which of the following regulations deals with chemicals?
  a) Control of Substances Hazardous to Health 2002
  b) The Health and Safety at Work Act 1974
  c) Provision and Use of Work Equipment Regulations 1998
  d) Control of Noise at Work Regulations 2005

8 Who should carry out risk assessments?
  a) No one.
  b) Everyone.
  c) An untrained supervisor.
  d) A trained supervisor.

9 Welfare facilities must include a:
  a) bathing area
  b) sleeping area
  c) lunch area
  d) TV room.

10 Under current European electrical regulations what colour wire is live?
  a) Red
  b) Blue
  c) Brown
  d) Black

UNIT 1002

Information, quantities and communicating with others

The construction industry contains a great deal of information that you must fully understand to meet the needs of a project. Some of the most important information relates to the start of a project, and tells you the type of construction you will be working on, what it will be used for and what you will need in order to build it.

When working with information, you will also be working with other people. You will need to make sure that you use the correct method to communicate different types of information to other people. This unit contains material that supports the five generic units. It will also support your completion of scaled drawings throughout all TAP units.

This unit will cover the following learning outcomes:

- Interpreting building information
- Determining quantities of materials
- Communicating information in the workplace.

K1. Interpreting building information

Building information is often presented as written documents. These can be:

- paperwork
- forms
- plans
- diagrams.

To understand all of these documents you need to know what they are used for in a building project.

Diagrams and plans are not drawn to life size, but to scales. So to be able to use diagrams, you need to understand how scales work and what they tell you about the final building.

In this section you will learn about:

- document security
- how to use scales and symbols
- specifications, drawings and schedules.

Document security

A lot of the information we will be looking at in this unit is vitally important for smooth and safe working on a site. Therefore it is important to store documents safely, securely and correctly. You need to understand this before you begin to work with documents.

Some documents may contain sensitive information such as addresses, national insurance numbers, etc. The Data Protection Act (1998) states that any company that holds personal information must make sure that it is secure and is only used for the purpose that it was provided for. This means that your employer, who will have information such as your bank details, must ensure that all of this is kept secure.

Other documents such as drawings should also be kept secure, especially for the duration of the job. This is because these are a permanent record, both of what is happening and of what has yet to happen. It is also considered good practice to keep records even after a job has been completed. This is because these can be used for reference at a later date and can be invaluable when estimating the cost of other similar jobs.

One problem with record keeping is obviously storage and large companies have thousands of documents. However, storage is becoming a lot easier as we can now create and save documents on computers. We can even scan hard copies and save the original documents electronically.

Scales, symbols and abbreviations

All building plans are drawn to scales by using symbols and abbreviations. To draw a building on a drawing sheet, its size must be reduced. This is called a scale drawing.

Using scales

The scales that are preferred for use in building drawings are shown in Table 2.1.

Type of drawing	Scales
Block plans	1:2500, 1:1250
Site plans	1:500, 1:200
General location drawings	1:200, 1:100, 1:50
Range drawings	1:100, 1:50, 1:20
Detail drawings	1:10, 1:5, 1:1
Assembly drawings	1:20, 1:10, 1:5

Table 2.1 Preferred scales for building drawings

These scales mean that, for example, on a block plan drawn to 1:2500, 1 mm on the plan would represent 2500 mm (or 2.5 m) on the actual building. Some other examples are:

- on a scale of 1:50, 10 mm represents 500 mm
- on a scale of 1:100, 10 mm represents 1000 mm (1.0 m)
- on a scale of 1:200, 30 mm represents 6000 mm (6.0 m).

Accuracy of drawings

Printing or copying of drawings introduces variations that affect the accuracy of drawings. Hence, although measurements can be read from drawings using a rule with common scales marked (Figure 2.1), you should work to written instructions and measurements wherever possible.

Remember

A scale is merely a convenient way of reducing a drawing in size

Functional skills

In addition to your reading skills, you will be using and practising several functional skills:

FM 1.1.1 – Identifying and selecting mathematical procedures.

FM 1.2.1a – Using appropriate mathematical procedures.

FM 1.2.2b – Interpreting information from various sources – such as the diagrams, tables and charts throughout this unit.

Find out

With a little practice, you will easily master the use of scales. Try the following:

- On a scale of 1:50, 40 mm represents: _____
- On a scale of 1:200, 70 mm represents: _____
- On a scale of 1:500, 40 mm represents: _____

Unit 1002 Information, quantities and communicating with others

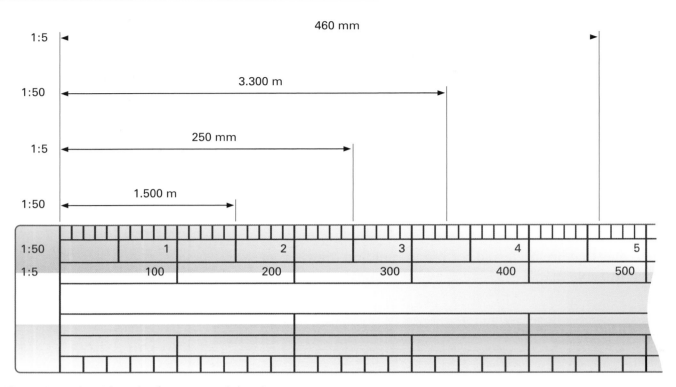

Figure 2.1 Rule with scales for maps and drawings

Remember

You can use a scale to:

- work out the actual measurement from a plan
- work out how long to draw a line on the plan to represent an actual measurement

Key term

Ratio – one value divided by the other

Scale drawings

Building plans are drawn to scale. Each length on the plan is in proportion to the real length. On a drawing that has been drawn to a scale of 1 cm representing 10 m:

- a length of 5 cm represents an actual length of 5 × 10 = 50 m
- a length of 12 cm represents an actual length of 12 × 10 = 120 m
- an actual length of 34 m is represented by a line 34 ÷ 10 = 3.4 cm long.

Scales are often given as **ratios**. For example:

- a scale of 1:100 means that 1 cm on the drawing represents an actual length of 100 cm (or 1 m)
- a scale of 1:20 000 means that 1 cm on the drawing represents an actual length of 20 000 cm (or 20 m).

Table 2.2 shows some common scales used in the construction industry.

1:5	1 cm represents 5 cm	5 times smaller than actual size
1:10	1 cm represents 10 cm	10 times smaller than actual size
1:20	1 cm represents 20 cm	20 times smaller than actual size
1:50	1 cm represents 50 cm	50 times smaller than actual size
1:100	1 cm represents 100 cm = 1 m	100 times smaller than actual size
1:1250	1 cm represents 1250 cm = 12.5 m	1250 times smaller than actual size

Table 2.2 Common scales used in the construction industry

Now look at the following examples.

Example

A plan is drawn to a scale of 1:20. On the plan, a window is 45 mm tall. How tall is the actual window?

   1 cm on the plan = actual length 20 cm

So 4.5 cm on the plan = actual length 4.5 × 20 = 90 cm or 0.9 m.

Example

A wall is 3 m long. How long is it on the plan?

   3 m = 300 cm

   an actual length of 20 cm is 1 cm on the plan

   an actual length of 5 × 20 = 100 cm is 5 × 1 cm on the plan

   an actual length of 3 × 100 cm is 3 × 5 cm on the plan.

Therefore, the wall is 15 cm long on the plan.

Did you know?

To make scale drawings, architects use a scale rule. The different scales on the ruler give the equivalent actual length measurements for different lengths in cm, for each scale

Symbols and abbreviations

The use of symbols and abbreviations allows the maximum amount of information to be included on a drawing sheet in a clear way.

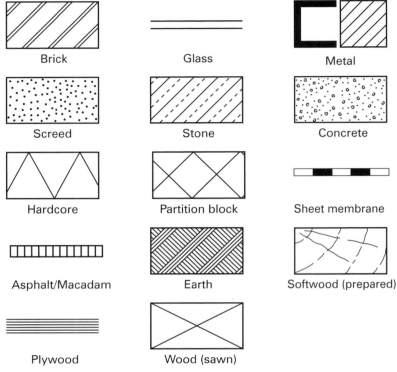

Figure 2.2 Building material symbols

Figure 2.2 shows some recommended drawing symbols for a range of building materials.

Figure 2.3 illustrates the recommended methods for indicating different types of doors and windows and their direction of opening.

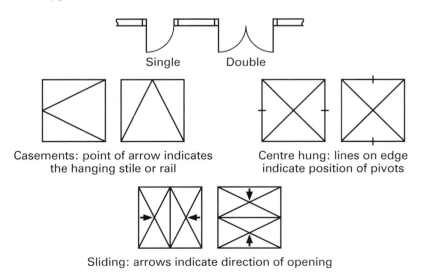

Figure 2.3 Doors and windows, type and direction of opening

Figure 2.4 shows some of the most frequently used graphical symbols, which are recommended in the British Standards Institute standard BS 1192.

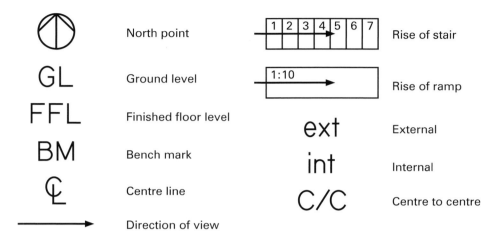

Figure 2.4 Graphical symbols used in the building industry

Table 2.3 lists some standard abbreviations used on drawings.

Item	Abbreviation	Item	Abbreviation
Airbrick	AB	Hardcore	hc
Asbestos	abs	Hardwood	hwd
Bitumen	bit	Insulation	insul
Boarding	bdg	Joist	jst
Brickwork	bwk	Mild steel	MS
Building	bldg	Plasterboard	pbd
Cast iron	ci	Polyvinyl acetate	PVA
Cement	ct	Polyvinyl chloride	PVC
Column	col	Reinforced concrete	RC
Concrete	conc	Satin anodised aluminium	SAA
Cupboard	cpd	Satin chrome	SC
Damp proof course	DPC	Softwood	swd
Damp proof membrane	DPM	Stainless steel	SS
Drawing	dwg	Tongue and groove	T&G
Foundation	fnd	Wrought iron	WI
Hardboard	hdbd		

Table 2.3 Standard abbreviations used on drawings

Location drawings, specifications and schedules

Specifications, drawings and schedules are the main reference documents for work on site and are used to plan all the work that takes place during the build. It is important that all these documents are accurate and correct, and that any changes made to them are clearly communicated to everyone working on the site.

Location drawings

Location drawings include block plans and site plans, and are used to show what the site will look like when it is completed. It is drawn to a chosen scale.

- **Block plans** – identify the proposed site by giving a bird's eye view of the site in relation to the surrounding area. An example is shown in Figure 2.5.
- **Site plans** – give the position of the proposed building and the general layout of the roads, services, drainage etc. on site. An example is shown in Figure 2.6.

> **Remember**
>
> It is important to check that the documents you are working with are the most recent. If they have changed in any way, and you haven't been told, what you will be doing will be wrong

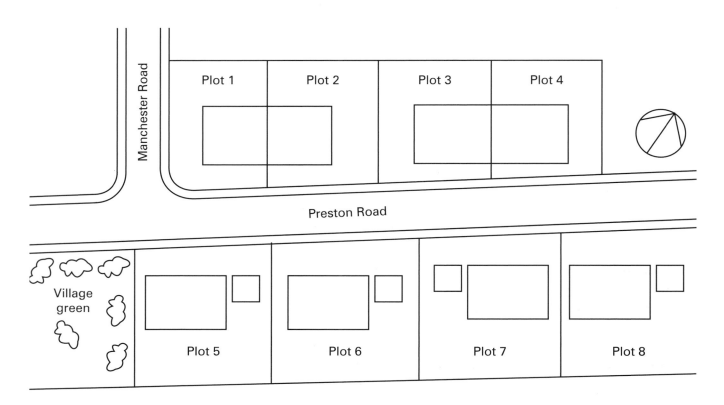

Figure 2.5 Block plan showing location

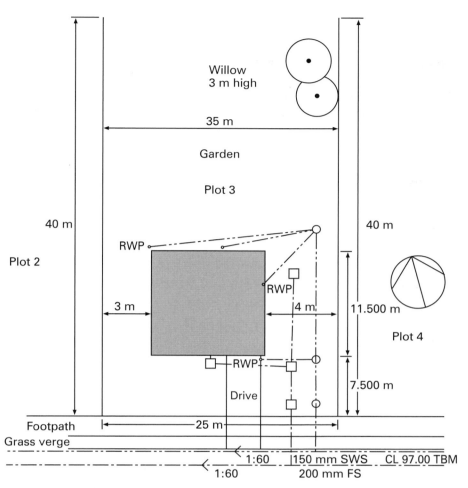

Figure 2.6 Site plan

Specifications

The specification or 'spec' is a document produced alongside the plans and drawings and is used to show information that can't be shown on the drawings. Specifications are almost always used, except in the case of very small contracts. A specification should contain:

- **materials description** – including type, sizes, quality, moisture content, etc.
- **restrictions** – what restrictions apply, such as working hours or limited access
- **services** – what services are available, what services need to be connected and what type of connection should be used
- **site description** – a brief description of the site, including the address
- **workmanship** – including methods of fixing, quality of work and finish.

Figure 2.7 A good 'spec' helps avoid confusion when dealing with subcontractors or suppliers

The specification may also name subcontractors or suppliers, or give details such as how the site should be cleared, and so on.

Schedules

A schedule is used to record repeated design information that applies to a range of components or fittings. Schedules are mainly used on bigger sites where there are multiples of several types of house (four-bedroom, three-bedroom, three-bedroom with dormers, etc.), each type having different components and fittings. Schedules avoid the wrong component or fitting being put in the wrong house. Schedules can also be used on smaller jobs such as a block of flats with 200 windows, where there are six different types of window.

The need for a schedule depends on the complexity of the job and the number of repeated designs that there are. Schedules are mainly used to record repeated design information for:

- doors
- sanitary components
- windows
- heating components and radiators
- ironmongery
- kitchens
- joinery fitments.

A schedule is usually used with a range drawing and a floor plan.

Figures 2.8–2.10 show basic examples of these documents, using a window as an example:

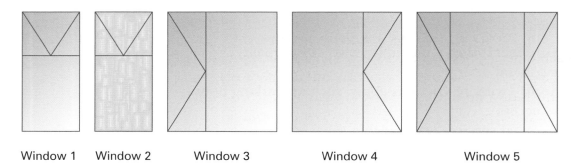

Window 1   Window 2   Window 3   Window 4   Window 5

Figure 2.8 Range drawing

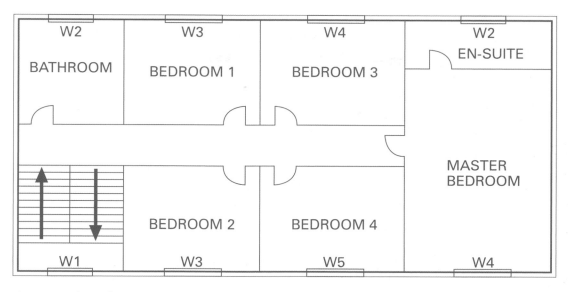

Figure 2.9 Floor plan

WINDOW SCHEDULE			
WINDOW	WINDOW SIZE	LOCATIONS	NOTES
Window 1	1200 x 600	Stairwell	
Window 2	1200 x 600	Bathroom En-suite	Obscure glass
Window 3	1600 x 800	Bedroom 1 Bedroom 2	
Window 4	1600 x 800	Bedroom 3 Master bedroom	
Window 5	1800 x 900	Bedroom 4	

Figure 2.10 Schedule for the windows

The schedule in Figure 2.10 shows that there are five types of window, each differing in size and appearance. The range drawing shows what each type of window looks like and the floor plan shows which window goes where. For example, the bathroom window is a type 2 window, which is 1200 × 600 cm with a top-opening sash and obscure glass.

Work programme

A work programme is a method of showing very easily what work is being carried out on a building and when. The most common form of work programme is a bar chart. Used by many site agents, or supervisors, a bar chart lists the tasks that need to be done down the left side and shows a timeline across the top. A work programme is used to make sure that the relevant trade is on site at the correct time and that materials are delivered when needed. A site agent or supervisor can quickly tell from looking at the chart if work is keeping to schedule or falling behind.

Bar charts

The bar, or Gantt, chart is the most popular work programme. It is simple to construct and easy to understand. Bar charts have tasks listed in a vertical column on the left and a horizontal timescale running along the top.

> **Did you know?**
>
> The Gantt chart is named after Henry Gantt, an American engineer, who, in 1910, was the first to design and use this chart

Activity	Time in days									
	1	2	3	4	5	6	7	8	9	10
Dig for foundation and service routes										
Lay foundations										
Run cabling, piping etc. to meet existing services										
Build up to damp proof course										
Lay concrete floor										

Figure 2.11 Basic bar chart

Each task is given a proposed time, which is shaded in along the horizontal timescale. Timescales often overlap as one task often overlaps another.

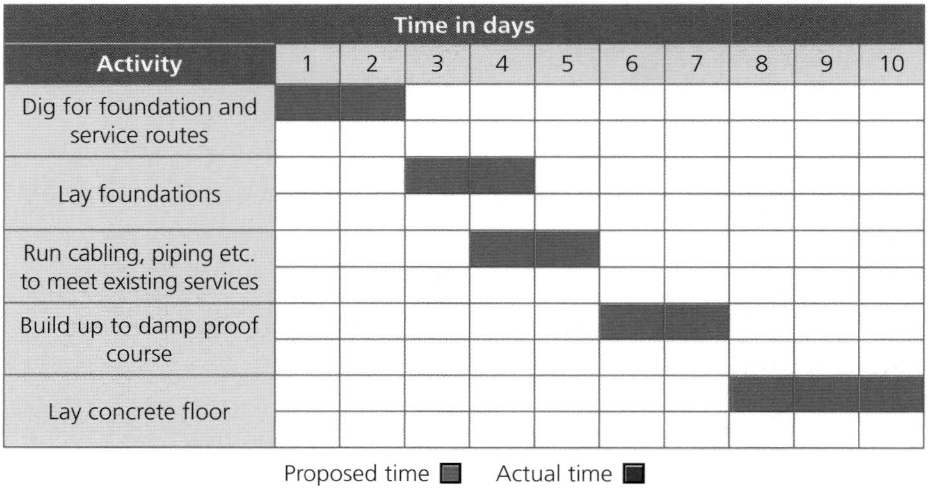

Activity	Time in days									
	1	2	3	4	5	6	7	8	9	10
Dig for foundation and service routes	▓	▓								
Lay foundations			▓	▓						
Run cabling, piping etc. to meet existing services				▓	▓					
Build up to damp proof course						▓	▓			
Lay concrete floor								▓	▓	

Proposed time ▓ Actual time ■

Figure 2.12 Bar chart showing proposed time for a contract

The bar chart can then be used to check progress. Often the actual time taken for a task is shaded in underneath the proposed time (in a different way or colour to avoid confusion). This shows how what *has* been done matches up to what *should* have been done.

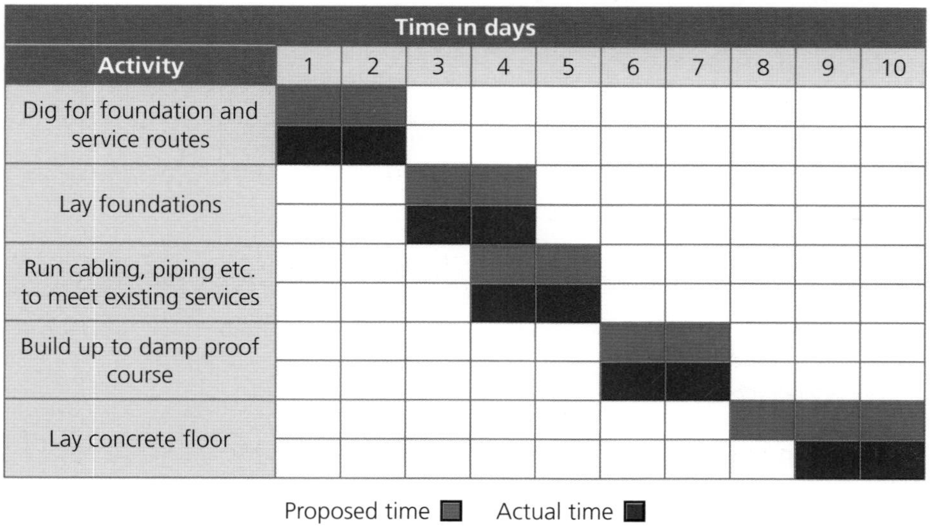

Activity	Time in days									
	1	2	3	4	5	6	7	8	9	10
Dig for foundation and service routes										
Lay foundations										
Run cabling, piping etc. to meet existing services										
Build up to damp proof course										
Lay concrete floor										

Proposed time ▨   Actual time ▨

Figure 2.13 Bar chart showing actual time half way through a contract

So a bar chart can help you plan when to order materials or plant, see what trade is due in and when, and so on. A bar chart can also tell you if you are behind on a job; this information is vital if your contract contains a **penalty clause**.

When creating a bar chart, you should build in some extra time to allow for things such as bad weather, labour shortages, delivery problems or illness. It is also advisable to have contingency plans to help solve or avoid problems, such as:

- capacity to work overtime to catch up time
- bonus scheme to increase productivity
- penalty clause on suppliers to try to avoid late or poor deliveries
- source of extra labour (for example from another site) if needed.

Good planning, with contingency plans in place, should allow a job to run smoothly and finish on time, leading to the contractor making a profit.

Key term

Penalty clause – a condition written into the contract that states that the work must be completed to the required quality by a certain date. If the job overruns, the contractor will not be paid the full amount for each day the job runs over

Did you know?

Bad weather is the main external factor responsible for delays on building sites in the UK. A Met Office survey showed that UK construction companies experience problems caused by the weather on average 26 times a year

Key term

Estimate – to assess something, such as a job to be done, and to state a likely price for it

Functional skills

FM 1.2.1 relates to using whole numbers. These may be positive or negative numbers. Think of a situation where these numbers would be used – e.g. attendance figures at a football match or the temperature in both winter and summer.

K2. Determining quantities of materials

The information contained in the drawings and specification for a project will tell you what materials you will need for the job. You will use this information to determine the quantity of each type of material you will need. To work this out you need to know the methods used to calculate basic **estimates** of material quantity.

When making calculations there are several resources you will find useful. These include:

- diagrams and plans
- calculators
- conversion tables
- scale rules.

Numbers

Place value

The ten digits we work with are 0, 1, 2, 3, 4, 5, 6, 7, 8 and 9. We can write any number you can think of, however huge, using any combination of these ten digits. In a number, the value of each digit depends on its 'place value'. Table 2.4 is a place value table and shows how the value of digit 2 is different, depending on its position.

Millions	Hundred thousands	Ten thousands	Thousands	Hundreds	Tens	Units	Value
2	9	4	1	3	7	8	2 million
	2	5	3	1	0	7	2 hundred thousand
	7	**2**	5	6	6	4	2 × ten thousand = 20 thousand
		6	**2**	4	9	2	2 thousands
		5	6	**2**	9	1	2 hundreds
			8	4	**2**	7	2 tens = 20
				1	6	**2**	2 units

Table 2.4 Place value table for the digit 2

Positive numbers

A positive number is a number that is greater than zero. If we make a number line, positive numbers are all the numbers to the right of zero.

$$0\ 1\ 2\ 3\ 4\ 5\ 6\ 7\ 8\ 9\ 10\ 11\ 12\ 13\ \ldots \longrightarrow$$
Positive numbers

Did you know?

Zero is neither positive nor negative

Negative numbers

A negative number is a number that is less than zero. If we make another number line, negative numbers are all the numbers to the left of zero.

$$\longleftarrow \ldots -13\ -12\ -11\ -10\ -9\ -8\ -7\ -6\ -5\ -4\ -3\ -2\ -1\ 0$$
Negative numbers

Functional skills

FM 1.2.1a relates to mathematical procedures such as addition and subtraction. You will need to organise numbers in units, tens, hundreds and thousands in order to carry out the task.

Making calculations

There are several calculation methods that are used to calculate the area of basic shapes. The main ones you will need to use are:

- addition
- subtraction
- multiplication
- division.

These methods are used to calculate the basic areas of a series of shapes that you will encounter on plans and diagrams.

Addition

When adding numbers using a written method, write digits with the same place value in the same column. For example, to work out what 26 + 896 + 1213 is, write the calculation:

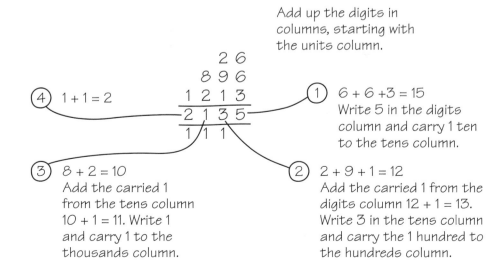

Add up the digits in columns, starting with the units column.

④ 1 + 1 = 2

① 6 + 6 + 3 = 15
Write 5 in the digits column and carry 1 ten to the tens column.

③ 8 + 2 = 10
Add the carried 1 from the tens column 10 + 1 = 11. Write 1 and carry 1 to the thousands column.

② 2 + 9 + 1 = 12
Add the carried 1 from the digits column 12 + 1 = 13. Write 3 in the tens column and carry the 1 hundred to the hundreds column.

To add numbers with decimals, write the numbers with the decimal points in line:

$$
\begin{array}{r}
4.56 \\
10.2 \\
0.32 \\
\hline
15.08 \\
\hline
\end{array}
$$

In a problem, the following words mean you need to add.

- **Total** – What is the total of 43 and 2457? (43 + 2457)
- **Sum** – What is the sum of 56 and 345? (56 + 345)
- **Increase** – Increase 3467 by 521 (3467 + 521)

Subtraction

When subtracting numbers using a written method, write digits with the same place value in the same column.

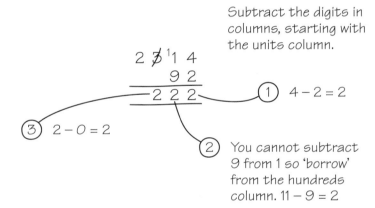

Subtract the digits in columns, starting with the units column.

① 4 – 2 = 2

② You cannot subtract 9 from 1 so 'borrow' from the hundreds column. 11 – 9 = 2

③ 2 – 0 = 2

In a problem, the following words and phrases mean you need to subtract.

- **Find the difference** – Find the difference between 200 and 45 (200 – 45)
- **Decrease** – Decrease 64 by 9 (64 – 9)
- **How much greater than?** – How much greater than 98 is 110? (110 – 98)

Multiplication

Knowing multiplication tables up to 10 × 10 helps with multiplying single-digit numbers. You can use multiplication facts you already know to work out other multiplication calculations.

To multiply larger numbers you can write the calculation in columns or use the grid method. Both methods work by splitting the calculation into smaller ones.

Example

What is 20 × 12?

You know that 20 = 2 × 10

So, 20 × 12 = 2 × 10 × 12
= 2 × 12 × 10
= 24 × 10 = 240

Multiplying using columns

```
    25
×   36
──────
   150     6 × 25   ⎫
   750    30 × 25   ⎬ Add these to find 36 × 25
──────             ⎭
   900
```

Multiplying using the grid method

36 × 25 =

×	20	5
30	600	150
6	120	30

```
30 × 20 = 600
30 ×  5 = 150
 6 × 20 = 120
 6 ×  5 =  30
         ────
          900
```

Division

Division is the opposite of multiplication. Knowing the multiplication tables up to 10 × 10 also helps with division. Each multiplication fact gives two related division facts. For example:

4 × 6 = 24   24 ÷ 6 = 4   24 ÷ 4 = 6

Short division

When dividing by a single digit number, use short division.

161 √ 7 =

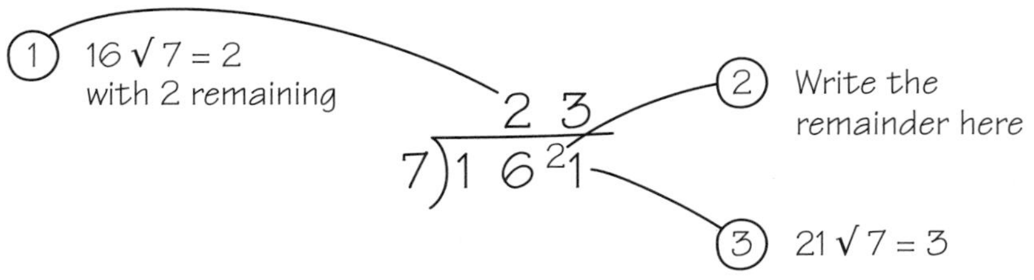

① 16 √ 7 = 2 with 2 remaining

② Write the remainder here

③ 21 √ 7 = 3

```
     2 3
7)1 6²1
```

Long division

When dividing by 10 or more, use long division.

$$\begin{array}{r} 246 \\ 12\overline{)2952} \end{array}$$

24	$2 \times 12 = 24$
55	$29 - 24 = 5$. Bring down the next 5
48	$12 \times 4 = 48$
72	$55 - 48 = 7$. Bring down the 2
72	$12 \times 6 = 72$
0	

Estimating

Sometimes an accurate answer to a calculation is not required. You can estimate an approximate answer by rounding all the values in the calculation to one **significant figure** (s.f.). For example:

Estimate the answer to the calculation 4.9×3.1

4.9 rounds to 5 to 1 s.f.
3.1 rounds to 3 to 1 s.f.
A sensible estimate is $5 \times 3 = 15$

Measures

In brickwork, quantities of material are presented in measurements. These measurements are used when ordering, and in plans and specifications. The mathematic skills described above will enable you to use these units of measurement.

Units of measurement

The metric units of measurement are shown in Table 2.5.

Length	millimetres (mm) centimetres (cm) metres (m) kilometres (km)
Mass (weight)	grams (g) kilograms (kg) tonnes (t)
Capacity (the amount a container holds)	millilitres (ml) centilitres (cl) litres (l)

milli means one thousandth	$1\ mm = \frac{1}{1000}\ m$	$1\ ml = \frac{1}{1000}$ litre
centi means one hundredth	$1\ cm = \frac{1}{100}\ m$	$1\ cl = \frac{1}{1000}$ litre
kilo means one thousand	1 kg = 1000 g	1 km = 1000 m

Table 2.5 Units of measurement

Table 2.6 shows some useful metric conversions.

Length	Mass	Capacity
1 cm = 10 mm	1 kg = 1000 g	1 l = 100 cl = 1000 ml
1 m = 100 cm = 1000 mm	1 tonne = 1000 kg	
1 km = 1000 m		

Table 2.6 Useful metric conversions

Remember

- To convert from a smaller unit to a larger one – divide
- To convert from a larger unit to a smaller one – multiply

To convert 2657 mm to metres:	2657 ÷ 1000 = 2.657 m
To convert 0.75 tonnes to kg:	0.75 × 1000 = 750 kg

For calculations involving measurements, you need to convert all the measurements into the same unit.

Example

A plasterer measures the lengths of cornice required for a room. He writes down the measurements as 175 cm, 2 m, 225 cm, 1.5 m. To work out the total length of cornice needed, we first need to write all the lengths in the same units:

175 cm
2 m = 2 × 100 = 200 cm
1.5 m = 1.5 × 100 = 150 cm
225 cm

So the total length is:

175 + 200 + 225 + 150 = 750 cm

Imperial units

In the UK we still use some imperial units of measurement (see Table 2.7).

Length	inches feet yards miles
Mass (weight)	ounces pounds stones
Capacity (the amount a container holds)	pints gallons

Table 2.7 Some imperial units of measurement

To convert from imperial to metric units, use the approximate conversions shown in Table 2.8.

Did you know?

A useful rhyme to help you remember the pints to litres conversion is: 'a litre of water is a pint and three quarters'

Length	Mass	Capacity
1 inch = 2.5 cm	2.2 pounds = 1 kg	1.75 pints = 1 litre
1 foot = 30 cm	1 ounce = 25 g	1 gallon = 4.5 litres
5 miles = 8 km		

Table 2.8 Converting imperial measurements to metric

Calculating perimeters and areas

Perimeter of shapes with straight sides

The perimeter of a shape is the distance all around the outside of the shape. To find the perimeter of a shape, measure all the sides and then add the lengths together.

Did you know?

You can use the perimeter to work out the length of picture rail to go all round a room

Example

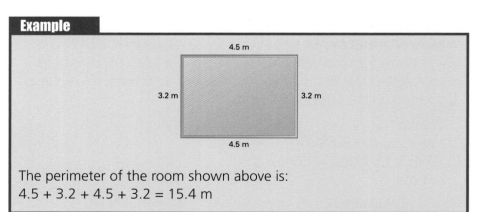

4.5 m
3.2 m
3.2 m
4.5 m

The perimeter of the room shown above is:
4.5 + 3.2 + 4.5 + 3.2 = 15.4 m

Units of area

The area of a two-dimensional (2-D; flat) shape is the amount of space it covers. Area is measured in square units, such as square centimetres (cm^2) and square metres (m^2).

The area of the square below is $10 \times 10 = 100 \text{ mm}^2$ or 1 cm^2.

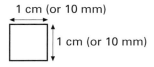

1 cm (or 10 mm)

1 cm (or 10 mm)

The area of the square below is $100 \times 100 = 10\ 000 \text{ cm}^2$ or 1 m^2.

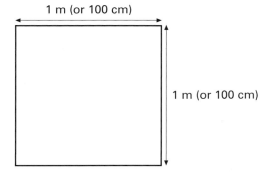

1 m (or 100 cm)

1 m (or 100 cm)

Area of shapes with straight sides

The rectangle below is drawn on squared paper. Each square has an area 1 cm^2.

You can find the area by counting the squares:

Area = 6 squares = 6 cm^2

You can also calculate the area by multiplying the number of squares in a row by the number of rows:

$3 \times 2 = 6$

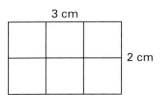

3 cm

2 cm

Example

If a wall is 32 feet long, what is its approximate length in metres?

1 foot = 30 cm
So, 32 feet = 32 × 30 cm
= 960 cm
= 9.6 m.

Remember

$1 \text{ cm}^2 = 100 \text{ mm}^2$
$1 \text{ m}^2 = 10\ 000 \text{ cm}^2$

Functional skills

FM 1.2.1c, d relates to using a formula to calculate perimeters and areas. This information is important in understandinga the amount of a material that is required to carry out a building task.

> **Example**
>
> If the length of a rectangular room is 3.6 m and the width is 2.7 m, the area is:
>
> $A = 3.6 \times 2.7 = 9.72$ m²

The area of a rectangle with length l and width w is:

$$A = l \times w$$

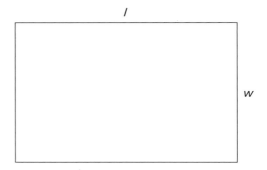

Area of a triangle

The area of a triangle is given by the formula:

$$A = \tfrac{1}{2} \times h \times b$$

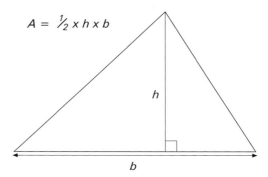

> **Key term**
>
> **Perpendicular** – at right angles to

$A = \frac{1}{2} \times h \times b$ where h is the **perpendicular** height and b is the length of the base. The perpendicular height is drawn to meet the base at right angles (90°).

> **Example**
>
> What is (a) the area and (b) the perimeter of the triangle opposite?
>
> 1. Perpendicular height = 4 m, base = 3 m
>
> $A = \frac{1}{2} \times h \times b = \frac{1}{2} \times 4 \times 3 = 6$m²
>
> 2. Perimeter = 5 + 4 + 3 = 12 m

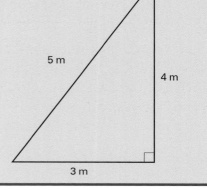

Pythagoras' theorem

You can use Pythagoras' theorem to find unknown lengths in right-angled triangles. In a right angled triangle:

- one angle is 90° (a right angle)
- the longest side is opposite the right angle and is called the **hypotenuse**.

Pythagoras' theorem says that for any right angled triangle with sides a and b and hypotenuse c:

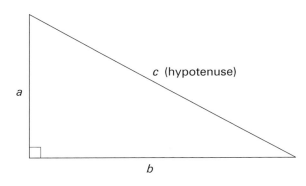

$c^2 = a^2 + b^2$

Example

What is the length of the hypotenuse of the triangle opposite?

We know $c^2 = a^2 + b^2$

where c is the hypotenuse.

$$c^2 = a^2 + b^2$$
$$= 9 + 16$$
$$= 25$$
$$c = \sqrt{25} = 5$$

Therefore the hypotenuse is 5 cm.

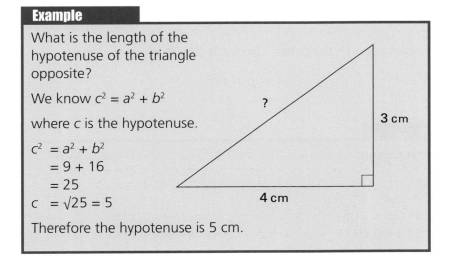

a^2 is 'a squared' and is equal to $a \times a$. a is '3 squared' and is equal to 3×3. The opposite or inverse of squaring is finding the square root. $\sqrt{25}$ means 'the square root of 25': $5 \times 5 = 25$, so $\sqrt{25} = 5$.

Learning these squares and square roots will help with Pythagoras' theorem calculations. Table 2.9 shows some squares and square roots you will often find useful to know.

$1^2 = 1 \times 1 = 1$	$\sqrt{1} = 1$
$2^2 = 2 \times 2 = 4$	$\sqrt{4} = 2$
$3^2 = 3 \times 3 = 9$	$\sqrt{9} = 3$
$4^2 = 4 \times 4 = 16$	$\sqrt{16} = 4$
$5^2 = 5 \times 5 = 25$	$\sqrt{25} = 5$
$6^2 = 6 \times 6 = 36$	$\sqrt{36} = 6$
$7^2 = 7 \times 7 = 49$	$\sqrt{49} = 7$
$8^2 = 8 \times 8 = 64$	$\sqrt{64} = 8$
$9^2 = 9 \times 9 = 81$	$\sqrt{81} = 9$
$10^2 = 10 \times 10 = 100$	$\sqrt{100} = 10$

Table 2.9 Useful squares and square roots

Using Pythagoras' theorem to find the shorter side of a triangle

You can rearrange Pythagoras' theorem like this:

$$c^2 = a^2 + b^2$$
$$a^2 = c^2 - b^2$$

Example

What is the length of side *a* in the right-angled triangle opposite?

$a^2 = c^2 - b^2$
$\quad = 12^2 - 6^2$
$\quad = 144 - 36 = 108$
$a \quad = \sqrt{108} = 10.3923…$ (using the $\sqrt{}$ key on a calculator)
$\quad = 10.4$ cm (to 1 decimal place (d.p.)).

12 cm

a

6 cm

Example

You can also use Pythagoras' theorem to find the perpendicular height of a triangle. For example, if we wanted to find the area of the triangle below, we would need to find the perpendicular height:

Using Pythagoras theorem:

$h^2 = 6^2 - 3^2$
$ = 36 - 9 = 27$
$h = \sqrt{27} = 5.196\ldots = 5.2$ cm (to 1 d.p.)

Area $= \frac{1}{2} \times b \times h$
$ = \frac{1}{2} \times 5 \times 5.2$ Base length $= 3 + 2$ cm
$ = 13$ cm^2

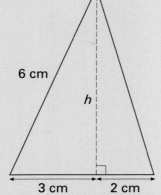

Areas of composite shapes

Composite shapes are made up of simple shapes such as rectangles and squares. To find the area, divide up the shape and find the area of each part separately. For example, to work out the area of the L-shaped room below:

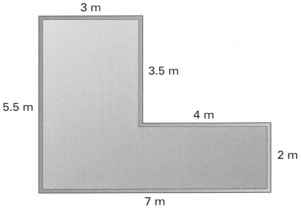

First divide it into two rectangles, A and B:

Area of rectangle A = $3 \times 5.5 = 16.5$ m^2
Area of rectangle B = $4 \times 2 = 8$ m^2
Total area of room = $16.5 + 8 = 24.5$ m^2

You could also divide the rectangle in the example above into two different rectangles, C and D, like this:

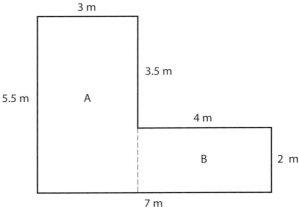

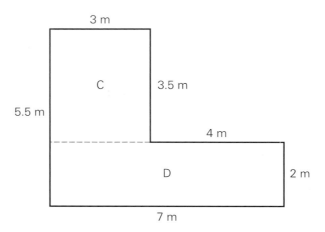

Check that you get the same total area.

Some shapes can be divided into rectangles and triangles. For example, to find the area of the wooden floor below:

divide the floor into a right-angled triangle A and a rectangle B.

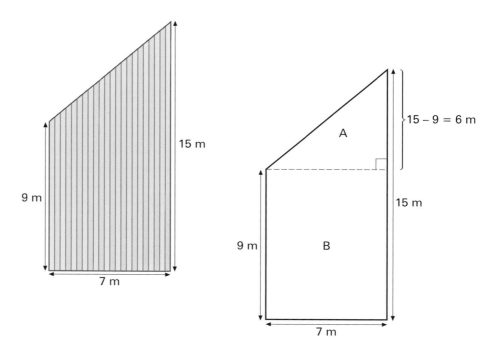

Triangle A has vertical height 6 m and base 7 m

Area of the triangle A = $\frac{1}{2}$ × b × h

$\qquad\qquad$ = $\frac{1}{2}$ × 7 × 6 = 21 m²

Area of the rectangle B = 9 × 7 = 63 m²
Total area = 21 + 63 = 84 m².

Circumference of a circle

The formula for the **circumference** of a circle of **radius** r is:

$$C = 2\pi r$$

The diameter is the distance across the circle through the centre (diameter = 2 × radius).

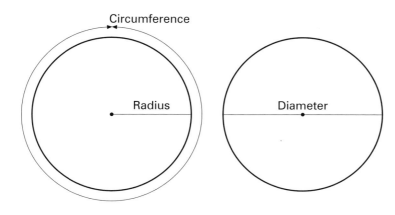

Circumference

Radius

Diameter

$$\pi = 3.141\ 592\ 654\dots$$

To estimate the circumference of a circle, use $\pi = 3$. For more accurate calculations use $\pi = 3.142$, or the π key on a calculator.

Example

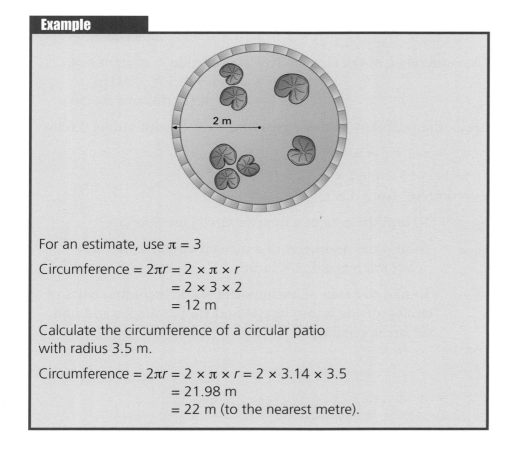

2 m

For an estimate, use $\pi = 3$

Circumference $= 2\pi r = 2 \times \pi \times r$
$= 2 \times 3 \times 2$
$= 12$ m

Calculate the circumference of a circular patio with radius 3.5 m.

Circumference $= 2\pi r = 2 \times \pi \times r = 2 \times 3.14 \times 3.5$
$= 21.98$ m
$= 22$ m (to the nearest metre).

Area of a circle

The formula for the area of a circle of radius r is

$$\text{Area} = \pi r^2$$

We can calculate the area of a circle with radius 3.25 m as:

$$\begin{aligned}\text{Area} &= \pi r^2 \\ &= \pi \times r^2 \\ &= 3.14 \times 3.25 \times 3.25 = 33.166\,25 \\ &= 33\ \text{m}^2\ \text{(to the nearest metre).}\end{aligned}$$

Area and circumference of part circles and composite shapes

You can use the formulae for circumference and area of a circle to calculate perimeters and areas of parts of circles, and shapes made from parts of circles. For example, we can work out the perimeter and area of the semicircular window below.

The diameter of the semicircle is 1.3 m, so the radius is $1.3 \div 2 = 0.65$ m.

The length of the curved side is half the circumference of the circle with radius 0.65 m.

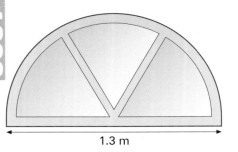

1.3 m

$$\text{Length of curved side} = \tfrac{1}{2} \times 2\pi r = \tfrac{1}{2} \times 2 \times \pi \times r$$

$$= \tfrac{1}{2} \times 2 \times 3.14 \times 0.65 = 2.041\ \text{m}$$

$$\begin{aligned}\text{Circumference of the semicircle} &= \text{curved side} + \text{straight side} \\ &= 2.041 + 1.3 = 3.341\text{m} \\ &= 3.34\ \text{m (to the nearest cm)}\end{aligned}$$

Area of semicircle = half the area of the circle with radius 0.65m

$$\begin{aligned}&= \tfrac{1}{2} \times \pi r2 = \tfrac{1}{2} \times \pi \times r^2 \\ &= \tfrac{1}{2} \times 3.14 \times 0.65 \times 0.65 = 0.663\,325\ \text{m}^2 \\ &= 0.66\ \text{m}^2\ \text{(to 2 d.p.)}\end{aligned}$$

To find the area of a quarter circle, use $\tfrac{1}{4} \pi r^2$.

To find the perimeter of a quarter circle, work out $\tfrac{1}{4}$ circumference + 2 × radius.

To find the area of a composite shape including parts of circles, divide it into circles and simple shapes and find the areas separately.

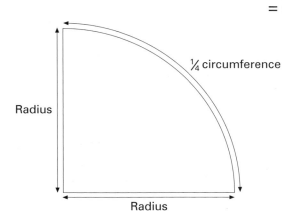

Radius

¼ circumference

Radius

K3. Communicating information in the workplace

Communication, in the simplest of terms, is a way or means of passing on information from one person to another. Communication is very important in all areas of life and we often do it without even thinking about it. You will need to communicate well when you are at work, no matter what job you do. What would happen if someone couldn't understand something you had written or said? If we don't communicate well, how will other people know what we want or need, and how will we know what other people want?

Companies that do not establish good methods of communicating with their workforce, or with other companies, will not function properly. They will also end up with bad working relationships. Co-operation and good communication are vital to achieve good working relationships.

Message taking

One of the most common reasons for communicating is to give a message to someone. You could often be the 'channel' passing a message from one person to another (the 'third party').

To ensure good and efficient communication there are certain things you can do when taking messages. When a phone call is made, many things may be discussed. Some of these things may need to be passed on to a third party. The main things that you need to record when receiving a phone call are:

- date
- time
- contact name and details.

The topic of conversation can also be recorded but, if it's complex or lengthy, this may not be possible. The most important thing to take is the person's contact details. This will allow the person the message is for to get in direct contact with the person sending the message, so that further conversations can take place.

Taking accurate information from a conversation is important because other people may use this as a source of information for making decisions. For example, a person receiving a message may decide when to call back, based on a message. If the message didn't indicate that the matter was urgent, the person may delay returning the call, which could have serious consequences.

Functional skills

Communicating effectively is an essential skill in every day work. FE 1.1.1 and FE 1.1.3 – 4 relate to speaking and listening. You might be expected to take part in discussions about your work and be asked for your opinions. You will also be required to write information, such as messages to supervisors and present information such as material orders or accident reports. The writing skills FE 1.3.1 – 1.3.5 will enable you to communicate information, ideas and opinions effectively.

Remember

Making sure that messages are as clear and complete as possible is an important rule to remember when you communicate with anyone – either through speaking (oral communication), writing or any other form of communication

Unit 1002 Information, quantities and communicating with others

Functional skills

While working through this unit, you will be practising the functional skills FE 1.2.1 – 1.2.3. These relate to reading and understanding information.

Did you know?

Some companies have their own forms to cover such things as scaffolding checks

Information relevant to communication

There are a number of different sources of information on site that are important for effective communication. By using these sources of information, you can improve the effectiveness of your communication.

General site paperwork

No building site could function properly without a certain amount of paperwork. Here is a brief description of some of the documents you may encounter, besides the ones already mentioned in the first part of this unit.

Timesheet

Timesheets record hours worked, and are completed by every employee individually. Some timesheets are basic, asking just for a brief description of the work done each hour, but some can be more detailed. In some cases timesheets may be used to work out how many hours the client will be charged for.

P. Gresford Building Contractors

Timesheet

Employee _____ **Project/site** _____

Date	Job no.	Start time	Finish time	Total time	Travel time	Expenses
M						
Tu						
W						
Th						
F						
Sa						
Su						
Totals						

Employee's signature _____

Supervisor's signature _____

Date _____

Figure 2.14 Timesheet

Day worksheets

Day worksheets are often confused with timesheets. However, they are different because day worksheets are used when there is no price or estimate for the work and so enable the contractor to charge for the work. Day worksheets record the work done, hours worked and, sometimes, the materials used.

Job sheet

A job sheet is similar to a day worksheet – it records work done – but is used when the work has already been priced. Job sheets enable the worker to see what needs to be done and the site agent or working foreman to see what has been completed.

P. Gresford Building Contractors

Day worksheet

Customer Chris MacFarlane   **Date** _____

Description of work being carried out _____

Hang internal door in kitchen

Labour	Craft	Hours	Gross rate	TOTALS
Materials	**Quantity**	**Rate**	**% addition**	
Plant	**Hours**	**Rate**	**% addition**	

Comments

Signed _____   **Date** _____

Site manager/foreman signature _____

Figure 2.15 Day worksheet

P. Gresford Building Contractors

Job sheet

Customer   Chris MacFarlane

Address   1 High Street
Any Town
Any County

Work to be carried out

Hang internal door in kitchen

Special conditions/Instructions

Fit with door closer

3 x 75 mm butt hinges

Figure 2.16 Job sheet

Variation order

This sheet is used by the architect to make any changes to the original plans, including omissions, alterations and extra work.

Confirmation notice

This is a sheet given to the contractor to confirm any changes that have been made in the variation order, so that the contractor can go ahead and carry out the work.

VARIATION TO PROPOSED WORKS AT 123 A STREET

REFERENCE NO:

DATE _____

FROM _____

TO _____

POSSIBLE VARIATIONS TO WORK AT 123 A STREET

ADDITIONS

OMISSIONS

SIGNED ....

Figure 2.17 Variation order

CONFIRMATION FOR VARIATION TO PROPOSED WORKS AT 123 A STREET

REFERENCE NO:

DATE _____

FROM _____

TO _____

I CONFIRM THAT I HAVE RECEIVED WRITTEN INSTRUCTIONS FROM _____
POSITION _____
TO CARRY OUT THE FOLLOWING POSSIBLE VARIATIONS TO THE ABOVE NAMED CONTRACT

ADDITIONS

OMISSIONS

SIGNED ....

Figure 2.18 Confirmation notice

Orders/requisitions

A requisition form, or order, is used to order materials or components from a supplier.

P. Gresford Building Contractors

Requisition form

Supplier _____	Order no. _____
_____	Serial no. _____
Tel no. _____	Contact _____
Fax no. _____	Our ref _____
Contract/Delivery address/Invoice address	Statements/applications
_____	For payments to be sent to
_____	_____
Tel no. _____	_____
Fax no. _____	_____

Item no.	Quantity	Unit	Description	Unit Price	Amount

Total £ _____

Payment terms _____ Date _____

Originated by
_____

Authorised by
_____

Figure 2.19 Requisition form

Remember

If there are any discrepancies or problems with a delivery, such as poor quality or damaged goods, you should write on the delivery note what is wrong *before* you sign it. You should also make sure that the site agent is informed so that they can rectify the problem

Delivery notes

Delivery notes are given to the contractor by the supplier, and list all the materials and components being delivered. Each delivery note should be checked for accuracy against the order (to ensure that what is being delivered is what was asked for) and against the delivery itself (to make sure that the delivery matches the delivery note).

Invoices

Invoices come from a variety of sources such as suppliers or subcontractors, and state what has been provided and how much the contractor will be charged for it.

Bailey & Sons Ltd
Building materials supplier

Tel: 01234 567890

Your ref: AB00671

Our ref: CT020   **Date:** 17 Jul 2010

Order no: 67440387

Invoice address: **Delivery address:**
Carillion Training Centre,   Same as invoice
Depford Terrace, Sunderland

Description of goods	Quantity	Catalogue no.
OPC 25kg	10	OPC1.1

Comments:

Date and time of receiving goods:
Name of recipient (caps):
Signature:

Figure 2.20 Delivery note

Remember

Invoices may need paying by a certain date – fines for late payment can sometimes be incurred, so it is important that they are passed on to the finance office or financial controller promptly

INVOICE   **JARVIS BUILDING SUPPLIES**
                                          3rd AVENUE
                                          THOMASTOWN
L. Weeks Builders
4th Grove
Thomastown

Quantity	Description	Unit price	Vat rate	Total
30	Galvanised joist hangers	£1.32	17.5%	£46.53
			TOTAL	£46.53

To be paid within 30 days from receipt of this invoice

Please direct any queries to 01234 56789

Figure 2.21 Invoice

Delivery records

Delivery records list all deliveries over a certain period (usually a month), and are sent to the contractor's head office so that payments can be made.

Daily report/site diary

This is used to pass general information (deliveries, attendance, etc.) to a company's head office.

JARVIS BUILDING SUPPLIES
3rd AVENUE
THOMASTOWN

Customer ref________________

Customer order date________________

Delivery date________________

Item no	Qty Supplied	Qty to follow	Description	Unit price
1	30	0	Galvanised joist hangers	£1.32

Delivered to: L. Weeks Builders
4th Grove
Thomastown
Customer signature -

Figure 2.22 Delivery record

DAILY REPORT/SITE DIARY

PROJECT____________________
DATE____________________

Identify any of the following factors, which are affecting or may affect the daily work activities and give a brief description in the box provided

WEATHER ( ) ACCESS ( ) ACCIDENTS ( ) SERVICES ( )
DELIVERIES ( ) SUPPLIES ( ) LABOUR ( ) OTHER ( )

SIGNED -
POSITION -

Figure 2.23 Daily report/site diary

Policies and procedures

Most companies will have their own policies and procedures in the workplace. All employees will be expected to follow these.

A policy states what the company expects to be done in a certain situation. Companies usually have policies for most things ranging from health and safety to materials orders. For example, in a health and safety policy the company will expect all employees to abide by rules and regulations and be safe.

To ensure that the policies are followed, the company will use certain procedures, for example, using a certain form to record data or use a certain method of working.

These policies and procedures are vital in a large organisation that may be doing work on several different sites in different locations. A senior manager should be able to walk onto any site at any location and see exactly the same set-up with the same forms and procedures being used everywhere.

Site rules

Site rules will cover most things ranging from safety to security. The company will have general policies covering rules that everyone on site must follow. These include important but basic things such as hours of work, behaviour etc.

However, a local site may have additional rules that apply only to that site. This is because each site will have some different situations. Site rules deal with those situations that could occur *only* on that site.

Remember

Your company's rules should be explained to you when you first start work. Any additional site rules should be made clear at your site induction (see Unit 1001, pages 12–13)

Positive and negative communication

You can communicate in a variety of ways, and the main methods of communication are explained below, with the advantages and disadvantages of each method.

The key point to remember is to make all your communication positive. Positive communication will basically have a positive outcome with the message being communicated successfully. This will lead to things getting done right first time. Negative communication will have the opposite effect and may lead to costly delays.

For positive communication, you need to ensure that no matter what method you use, the communication is clear, simple and – importantly – goes to the right people.

Methods of communication

There are many different ways of communicating with others and they all generally fit into one of these four categories:

- verbal communication (speaking), for example talking face-to-face or over telephone or radio
- written communication, for example sending a letter or a memo
- body language, for example the way we stand or our facial expressions
- electronic communication, for example e-mail, **fax** and text messages.

Each method of communicating has some good points (advantages) and some bad points (disadvantages).

Verbal communication	
Verbal communication is the most common method that we use to communicate with each other. If two people don't speak the same language or if someone speaks very quietly or not very clearly, verbal communication cannot be effective. Working in the construction industry you may communicate verbally with other people face-to-face, over the telephone or by radio/walkie-talkie.	
Advantages	**Disadvantages**
Verbal communication is instant, easy and can be repeated or rephrased until the message is understood.	Verbal communication can be easily forgotten as there is no physical evidence of the message. Because of this it can be easily changed if passed to other people. A different accent or use of slang language can sometimes make it difficult to understand what a person is saying.

Written communication	
Written communication can take the form of letters, messages, notes, instruction leaflets and drawings, among others.	
Advantages	**Disadvantages**
There is physical evidence of the communication and the message can be passed on to another person without it being changed. It can also be read again if it is not understood.	Written communication takes longer to arrive and understand than verbal communication and body language. It can also be misunderstood or lost. If it is handwritten, the reader may not be able to read the writing if it is messy.

Messages

To: Andy Rodgers

Date: Tues 10 Nov

Time: 11.10 am

Message: Mark from Stokes called with a query about the recent order. Please phone asap (tel 01234 567890)

Message taken by:
Lee Barber

Figure 2.24 A message is a form of written communication

Body language

It is said that, when we are talking to someone face-to-face, only 10 per cent of our communication is verbal. The rest of the communication is body language and facial expression. This form of communication can be as simple as the shaking of a head from left to right to mean 'no', or as complex as the way someone's face changes when they are happy or sad, or the signs given in body language when someone is lying.

We often use hand gestures as well as words to get across what we are saying, to emphasise a point or give a direction.

Some people communicate entirely through a form of body language called sign language.

Advantages	Disadvantages
If you are aware of your own body language and know how to use it effectively, you can add extra meaning to what you say. For example, when you are talking to a client or a work colleague, even if the words you are using are friendly and polite, if your body language is negative or unfriendly, the message that you are giving out could be misunderstood. By simply maintaining eye contact, smiling and not folding your arms, you have made sure that the person you are communicating with has not got a mixed or confusing message. Body language is quick and effective. A wave from a distance can pass on a greeting without being close, and using hand signals to direct a lorry or a load from a crane is instant and doesn't require any equipment such as radios.	Some gestures can be misunderstood, especially if they are given from very far away. Also, some gestures that have one meaning in one country or culture can have a completely different meaning in another.

Figure 2.25 Try to be aware of your body language

Electronic communication

Electronic communication is becoming more and more common and easy with the advances in technology. Electronic communication can take many forms, such as text messages, e-mail and fax. It is now even possible to send and receive e-mails via a mobile phone, which allows important information to be sent or received from almost anywhere in the world.

Advantages	Disadvantages
Electronic communication takes the best parts from verbal and written communication in that it is instant, easy and there is a record of the communication being sent. Electronic communication goes even further as it can tell the sender if the message has been received and even read. E-mails in particular can be used to send a vast amount of information and can even give links to websites or other information. Attachments to e-mails allow anything from instructions to drawings to be sent with the message.	There are few disadvantages to electronic communication, the obvious ones being no signal or a flat battery on a mobile phone and servers being down, which prevent e-mails etc. Not everyone is up to speed on the latest technology and some people are not comfortable using electronic communication. You need to make sure that the person receiving your message is able to understand how to access the information.

Computer viruses can also be a problem as can security, where hackers can tap into your computer and read your e-mails and other private information. A good security set-up and anti-virus software are essential. |

Functional skills

At the end of this unit you will have the opportunity to answer a series of questions on the material you have learnt. By answering these questions you will be practising the following functional skills:

FE 1.2.3 – Read different texts and take appropriate action.

FE 1.3.1 – 1.3.5 – Write clearly with a level of detail to suit the purpose.

FM 1.1.1 – Identify and select mathematical procedures.

FM 1.2.1c – Draw shapes.

FAQ

Why not just write the full words on a drawing?

This would take up too much space and clutter the drawing, making it difficult to read.

When working out the prices or materials for quotes is it important to be exact?

No. When estimating things it is easier to round up to the nearest whole number.

Which form of communication is the best?

No one way can be classed as best as it will depend on the circumstances, e.g. you wouldn't send a text regarding a job interview and you wouldn't send a formal letter to a friend asking them to meet. Always choose the method of communication that works best with the situation you are in.

Check it out

1. Describe four different methods of communication.
2. Describe the information that a schedule might give you.
3. Briefly explain why drawings are used in the construction industry.
4. What do the following abbreviations stand for: DPC; hwd; fnd; DPM?
5. Sketch the graphical symbols which represent the following: brickwork; metal; sawn wood; hardcore.
6. Explain the difference between day worksheets and timesheets.
7. What does a block plan show? Sketch an example of a block plan to show this.
8. Explain the importane of a Gantt chart.
9. What kind of information would you expect to find in a delivery note?
10. Describe and explain the type of information that can be found in specifications.
11. Describe the purpose of the Data Protection Act (1998).

Getting ready for assessment

The information contained in this unit, as well as continued practical assignments that you will carry out in your college or training centre, will help you with preparing for both your end of unit test and the diploma multiple-choice test. It will also aid you in preparing for the work that is required for the synoptic practical assignments.

Working with contract documents such as drawing, specifications and schedules is something that you will be required to do within your apprenticeship and even more so after you have qualified.

You will need to know about and be familiar with:

- interpreting building information
- determining quantities of material
- relaying information in the workplace.

To get all the information you need out of these documents you will need to build on the maths and arithmetic skills that you learnt at school. These skills will give you the understanding and knowledge you will need to complete many of the practical assignments, which will require you to carry out calculations and measurements.

You will also need to use your English and reading skills. These skills will be particularly important, as you will need to make sure that you are following all the details of any instructions you receive. This will be the same for the instructions that you receive for the synoptic test, as it will for any specifications you might use in your professional life.

Communication skills have been a particular focus of this unit and of learning outcome 3. This unit has explained the reasons behind recording a message and using relevant information to keep communication clear. You have also seen the benefits of positive communication over negative communication and the benefits of effective communication.

When working either professionally or for your practical assignments, you will need to communicate effectively with the people you are working with and alongside. While studying for your qualification, you will use a range of communication methods. These will include face-to-face, e-mail, phone and writing. You will also need to know about the message you give to people with your body language.

The communication skills that are explained within the unit are also vital in all tasks that you will undertake throughout your training and in life.

Good luck!

Knowledge check

1 A drawing that shows you a bird's eye view of a site and its surrounding area is known as a:

a) location drawing

b) component range drawing

c) assembly drawing

d) detail drawing.

2 What does the abbreviation 'ct' stand for?

a) Concrete

b) Cupboard

c) Column

d) Cement

3 A scale of 1 to 50 means that 1 mm represents:

a) 5 mm

b) 50 mm

c) 500 mm

d) 5000 mm

4 Add together the following dimensions: 3 m + 60 cm + 9 mm.

a) 36 090 mm

b) 3690 mm

c) 3609 mm

d) 30 609 mm

5 Calculate the following: 6 m – 60 cm.

a) 54 cm

b) 5400 mm

c) 5.54 m

d) 544 cm

6 What is 250 × 8?

a) 1750

b) 2000

c) 2250

d) 2500

7 What is 12^2?

a) 144

b) 156

c) 160

d) 172

8 What is the area of a room that is 4 m long and 3.4 m wide?

a) 13 m²

b) 1.36 m²

c) 13.6 m²

d) 136 m²

9 Which of these is an advantage of spoken communication?

a) It is quick.

b) It can be forgotten.

c) There is no record of it.

d) All of the above.

10 The written form of communication that tells us the layout of a building is known as a:

a) specification

b) timesheet

c) drawing

d) schedule.

Building methods and construction technology

Whatever type of building is being constructed there are certain principles that must be followed and certain elements that must be included. For example, both a block of flats and a warehouse have a roof, walls and a floor.

These basic principles are applied across all the work carried out in construction and will apply to nearly all the possible projects you could work on. This unit contains material that supports TAP Unit 2: Set Out for Masonry Structures. It also contains material that supports the delivery of the five generic units.

This unit will cover the following learning outcomes:

- Foundations, walls and floor construction
- Construction of internal and external masonry
- Roof construction.

K1. Foundations, walls and floor construction

The majority of buildings need to be constructed so that they have a level internal surface and walls. To do this, we need to have a standard level across the whole site, to ensure that all construction is being carried out to this same height. This information is given by datum points on the construction site.

Datum points

The need to apply levels is required at the beginning of the construction process and continues right up to the completion of the building.

Datum points are used to transfer levels for a range of construction jobs, including for the following:

- roads
- brick courses
- paths
- excavations
- finished floor levels.

The same basic principles are applied throughout all these jobs.

Ordnance bench mark (OBM)

Ordnance bench marks (OBMs) are found cut into locations such as walls of churches or public buildings. The height of the OBM can be found on the relevant Ordnance Survey map or by contacting the local authority planning office. Figure 3.1 shows the normal symbol used, though it can appear as shown in Figure 3.2.

Site datum

It is necessary to have a reference point on site to which all levels can be related. This is known as the site datum. The site datum is usually positioned at a convenient height, such as the finished floor level (FFL).

The site datum itself must be set in relation to some known point, preferably an OBM and must be positioned where it cannot be moved.

Figure 3.2 shows a site datum and OBM, illustrating the height relationship between them.

If no suitable position can be found a datum peg may be used.

Did you know?

The whole of the UK is mapped in detail and the Ordnance Survey places datum points (bench marks) at suitable locations from which all other levels can be taken

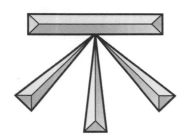

Figure 3.1 Ordnance bench mark

Functional skills

While working through this unit, you will be practising the functional skills FE 1.2.1 – 1.2.3. These relate to reading and understanding information.

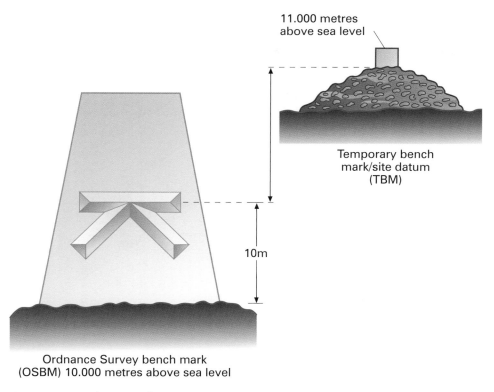

11.000 metres above sea level

Temporary bench mark/site datum (TBM)

10m

Ordnance Survey bench mark (OSBM) 10.000 metres above sea level

Figure 3.2 Site datum and OBM

Its accurate height is transferred by surveyors from an OBM, as with the site datum. The datum peg is usually a piece of timber or steel rod positioned accurately to the required level and then set in concrete. However, it must be adequately protected and is generally surrounded by a small fence for protection (Figure 3.3).

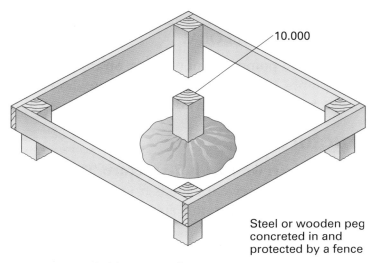

10.000

Steel or wooden peg concreted in and protected by a fence

Figure 3.3 Datum peg suitably protected

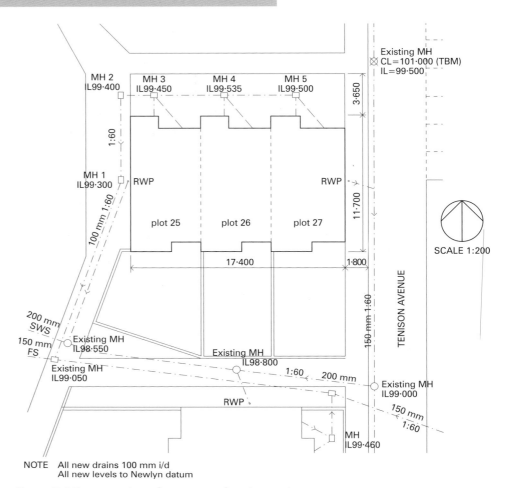

Figure 3.4 Datum points shown on a drawing

NOTE   All new drains 100 mm i/d
All new levels to Newlyn datum

Figure 3.5 All buildings have a substructure

Key terms

Substructure – all of the structure below ground and up to and including the damp proof course (DPC)

Superstructure – the main building above the ground

Load-bearing – something that carries a load such as a wall that supports the structure above

Temporary bench mark (TBM)

When an OBM cannot be conveniently found near a site, a temporary bench mark (TBM) is usually set up at a height suitable for the site. Its accurate height is transferred by surveyors from the nearest convenient OBM.

All other site datum points can now be set up from this TBM using datum points, which are shown on the site drawings. Figure 3.4 shows datum points on drawings.

Substructure

All buildings will start with the **substructure**. The purpose of the substructure is to receive the loads from the **superstructure** and transfer them safely down to a suitable **load-bearing** layer of ground.

The main material used in foundations and floors is concrete. Concrete is made up of sand, cement, stones and water.

The main part of the substructure is the foundations. When a building is at the planning stage, the entire area – including the soil – will be surveyed to check what depth, width and size of foundation will be required. This is vital: the wrong foundation could lead to the building subsiding or even collapsing.

The main type of foundation is a strip foundation. Depending on the survey reports and the type of building, one of four types of foundation will usually be used.

- **Narrow strip foundation** – the most common foundation used for most domestic dwellings and low-rise structures.
- **Wide strip foundation** – used for heavier structures or where weak soil is found.
- **Raft foundation** – used where very poor soil is found. This is basically a slab of concrete that is thicker around the edges.

Did you know?

During the surveying of the soil, the density and strength of the soil are tested and laboratory tests check for harmful chemicals contained within the soil

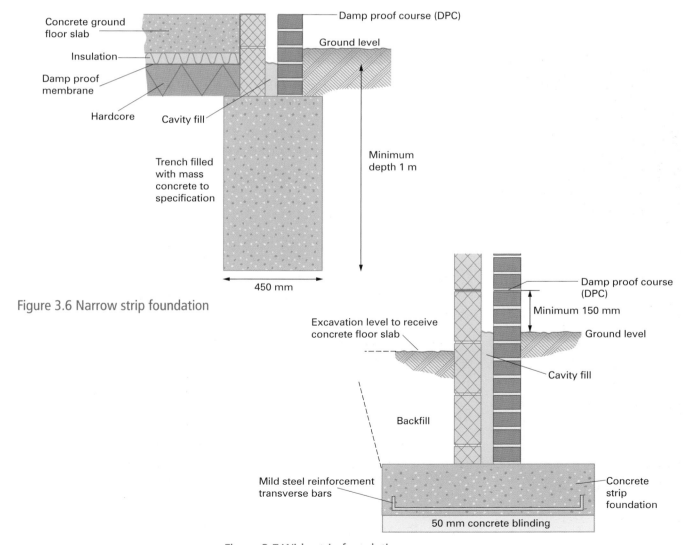

Figure 3.6 Narrow strip foundation

Figure 3.7 Wide strip foundation

Building methods and construction technology **Unit 1003**

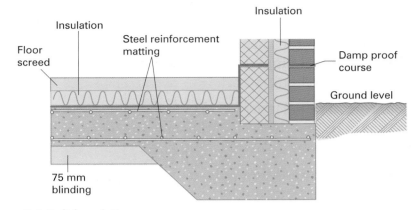

Figure 3.8 Raft foundation

Damp proof course

A damp proof course (DPC) and damp proof membranes are used to prevent damp from penetrating into a building. Flexible DPC may be made from polythene, **bitumen** or lead and is supplied in rolls of various widths for different uses.

Slate can also be used as a DPC. Older houses often have slate, but modern houses normally have polypropylene.

Damp proof membrane is used as a waterproof barrier over larger areas, such as under the concrete on floors etc.

For more information on DPCs, see Unit 1006, page 189–190.

Floors

There are two main types of floor: ground and upper.

Ground floors

There are several types of ground floor. The ones you will most often come across are:

- **Suspended timber floor** – this is a type of floor where timber joists are used to span the floor. The size of floor span determines the depth and thickness of the timbers used. The joists are either built into the inner skin of brickwork, set upon small walls (dwarf/sleeper wall), or some form of joist hanger is used. The joists should span the shortest distance; sometimes dwarf/sleeper walls are built in the middle of the span to give extra support or to go underneath load-bearing walls. The top of the floor is decked with a suitable material (usually chipboard or solid pine tongue and groove boards). As the floor is suspended, usually with crawl spaces underneath, it is vital to

Key terms

Bitumen – also known as pitch or tar, bitumen is a black sticky substance that turns into a liquid when it is heated. It is used on flat roofs to provide a waterproof seal

Slate – is a natural stone composed of clay or volcanic ash that can be machined into sheets and used to cover a roof

Figure 3.9 Damp proof course (DPC)

Did you know?

DPC is usually made of 1000-gauge polypropylene and comes in large rolls, usually black or blue in colour

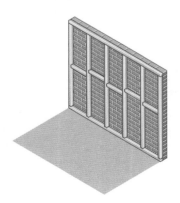

Figure 3.10 Ground lats

have air bricks fitted, allowing air to flow under the floor, preventing high moisture content and timber rot.

- **Solid concrete floor** – concrete floors are more durable and are constructed on a sub-base incorporating hardcore, damp proof membranes and insulation (Figure 3.12). The depth of the hardcore and concrete will depend on the building and are set by the Building Regulations and the local authority. Underfloor heating can be incorporated into a solid concrete floor. You must take great care when finishing the floor to ensure that it is even and level. See page 190 for more information on solid concrete floors.

- **Floating floor** – these are the basic timber floor constructions that are laid on a solid concrete floor. The timbers are laid in a similar way to joists, though they are usually 50 mm thick maximum as there is no need for support. The timbers are laid on the floor at predetermined centres and are not fixed to the concrete base (hence floating floor). The decking is then fixed on the timbers. Insulation or underfloor heating can be placed between the timbers to enhance the thermal and sound properties.

Upper floors

Again, solid concrete slabs can be used in larger buildings, but the most common type of upper floor is the suspended timber floor. As before, the joists are either built into the inner skin of brickwork or supported on some form of joist hanger. Spanning the shortest distance, with load-bearing walls acting as supports, it is vital that **regularised joists** are used because a level floor and ceiling are required. The tops of the joists are again decked out, with the underside being clad in plasterboard and having insulation placed between the joists to help with thermal and sound properties.

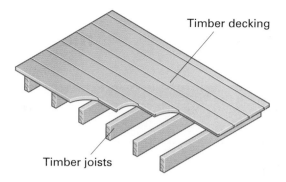

Figure 3.11 Suspended timber floor

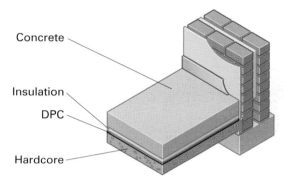

Figure 3.12 Section through a concrete floor

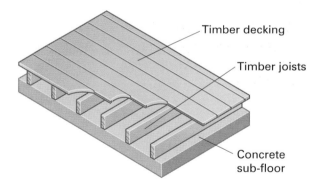

Figure 3.13 Floating floor

Key term

Regularised joists – joists that are all the same depth

K2. Construction of internal and external masonry

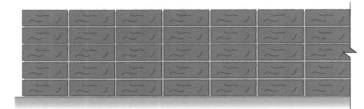

Figure 3.14 Unbonded wall

Figure 3.15 Stretcher bond wall

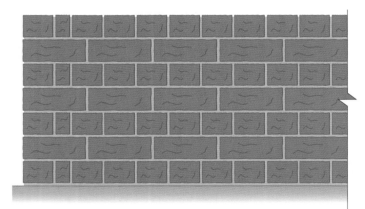

Figure 3.16 English bond wall

Bonding

Bonding is the term given to the different patterns produced when lapping the bricks to gain the most strength from the finished item. The most common type of lapping is half brick lap – better known as half bond.

If bricks were just put one on top of the other in a column, there would be no strength to the wall, and with sideways and downward pressure this type of wall would collapse. The main reasons for bonding brickwork are:

- strength
- distribution of heavy loads
- help resist sideways and downward pressure to the wall.

Other types of brick bonding are:

- stretcher bond walling
- English bond walling
- Flemish bond walling.

Figure 3.17 Flemish bond wall

Walls

External walls come in a variety of styles but the most common is cavity walling. Cavity walling is simply two brick walls built parallel to each other, with a gap between acting as the cavity. The cavity wall acts as a barrier to weather, with the outer leaf preventing rain and wind penetrating the inner leaf. The cavity is usually filled with insulation to reduce heat loss.

External walling is often load-bearing.

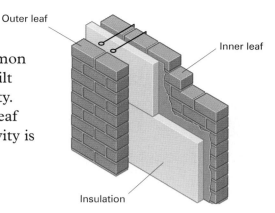

Figure 3.18 A cavity wall

Internal walls

There are several different designs of internal walls. Each has advantages and disadvantages. These methods include:

- **Blockwork** – simple blockwork, covered with plasterboard or plastered over for a smooth finish. Its disadvantage is low thermal and sound insulation.
- **Timber stud partition** – this is preferred when dividing an existing room, as it is quicker to erect. It is clad in plasterboard and plastered to a smooth finish. Insulation can make the partition more fire and sound resistant. It can also be made load-bearing by using thicker timbers.
- **Metal stud partition** – this is similar to timber, but metal studs are used.

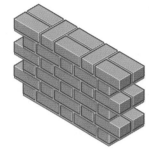

Figure 3.19 A solid brick wall

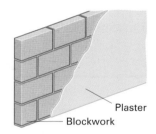

Figure 3.20 Cross section of blockwork

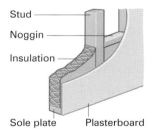

Figure 3.21 Cross section of timber stud partition

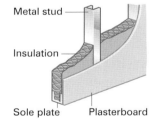

Figure 3.22 Cross section of metal stud partition

Wall ties

Wall ties are a very important part of a cavity wall. They tie the internal and external walls together, resulting in a stronger job. If we built cavity walls to any great height without connecting them together, the walls would be very unstable and could possibly collapse.

Figure 3.23 General purpose wall tie

Figure 3.24 Stacked lintels

Pre-cast concrete lintels

Lintels are components placed above openings in brick and block walls to bridge the opening and support the brick or blockwork above. Lintels made from concrete have a steel reinforcement placed near the bottom for strength, which is why pre-cast concrete lintels will have a 'T' or 'Top' etched into the top surface.

Mixing mortar

Mortar is used in bricklaying for bedding and jointing the bricks when building a wall. Mortar is made of sand, cement, water and plasticiser. The mortar must be 'workable' so that it can roll and spread easily. The mortar should hold on to the trowel without sticking.

Mortar can be mixed to the appropriate strength through two methods.

Gauging materials

Accurate measuring of materials to the required proportion before mixing is important to ensure consistent colour, strength and durability of the mortar. The most accurate method of **gauging** the mortar materials is by weight. However, this method is usually only used on very large sites. The next best way to gauge the materials is by volume using a gauge box.

A gauge box is a bottomless box made to the volume of sand required (to a proportion of a bag of cement). The box is placed on a clean, level, flat surface and filled with the sand. The sand is levelled off and any spillages cleaned away. The box is then removed, leaving the amount of sand to be mixed with the bag of cement. If a gauge box is not available, a bucket could be used. A bucket is filled with sand and emptied on a clean, flat surface for the number of times specified in the proportion. A separate bucket should be used to measure the cement.

Mixing by hand

If mixing by hand, the materials should be gauged first into a pile with the cement added. The cement and sand should then be 'turned' to mix the materials together. The pile should be turned a minimum of three times to ensure that the materials are mixed properly. The centre of the pile should be 'opened out' to create a centre hole.

Gradually add the water, mixing it into the sand and cement, making sure not to 'flood' the mix. Turn the mix another three times, adding water gradually to gain the required consistency.

Mixing by machine

Mixing by machine can be carried out by using either an electric mixer or a petrol or diesel mixer. Always set the mixer up on level ground.

- If using an electric mixer – the voltage should be 110 V and all cables and connections should be checked before use for splits or a loose connection (see page 36). Cables should not be in contact with water and the operation should not be carried out if it is raining.
- If using a petrol or diesel mixer – make sure that the fuel and oil levels are checked and topped up before starting. If using the mixer for long periods, the levels should be checked regularly so as not to run out.

Gauge the materials to be used, fill the mixer with approximately half of the water required (add plasticiser if being used). Add half the amount of cement to the water and add half of the sand. Allow to mix, and then add the remaining cement, then sand. Add more water if required, allowing at least two minutes for the mix to become workable and to ensure all the materials are thoroughly mixed together.

Once the mix has been taken out of the mixer, part fill the mixer with water and allow the water to run for a couple of minutes to remove any mortar sticking to the sides. If the mixer will not be used again that day, it should be cleaned thoroughly, either using water (and adding some broken bricks to help remove any mortar stuck to the sides) or ballast and gravel (which should then be cleaned out and the mixer washed with clean water). This will keep the mixer drum clean, and any future materials used will not stick to the drum sides so easily.

On most large sites, mortar is brought in already mixed.

K3. Roof construction

Although there are several different types of roofing, all roofs will either technically be a flat roof or a pitched roof.

Flat roofs

A flat roof is a roof with a **pitch** of 10° or less. The pitch is usually achieved through laying the joists at a pitch, or by using **firring pieces**.

The main construction method for a flat roof is similar to that for a suspended timber floor, with the edges of the joists being supported either via a hanger or built into the brickwork, or even a

Did you know?

On cold mornings, brickwork should not be started unless the temperature is 3°C and rising

Remember

Never hit the drum with a hammer etc. to clean it out – this could result in needing costly repairs to the drum

Key terms

Pitch – the angle or slope of the roof

Firring pieces – tapered strips of timber

Key term

Felt – is a bitumen-based waterproof membrane

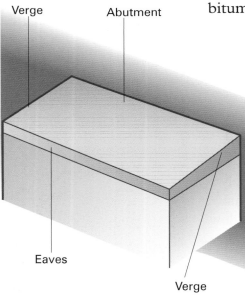

Figure 3.25 Flat roof terminology

Figure 3.26 Duo pitch roof with gable ends

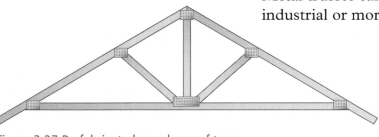

Figure 3.27 Prefabricated wooden roof truss

combination of both. Once the joists are laid and firring pieces are fitted (if required), insulation and a vapour barrier are put in place. The roof is then decked on top and usually plasterboarded on the underside. The decking on a flat roof must be waterproof, and can be made from a wide variety of materials, including fibreglass or bitumen-covered boarding with **felt** layered on it.

Drainage of flat roofs is vital. The edge where the fall leads to must have suitable guttering to allow rainwater to run away without draining down the face of the wall.

Pitched roofs

There are several types of pitched roof, from the basic gable roof to more complex roofs such as mansard roofs. Whichever type of roof is being fitted to a building, it will most likely be constructed in one of the following ways.

Prefabricated truss roof

As the name implies, this is a roof that has prefabricated members called trusses. Trusses are used to spread the load of the roof and to give it the required shape. Trusses are factory-made, delivered to site and lifted into place, usually by a crane. They are also easy and quick to fit: they are either nailed to a wall plate or held in place by truss clips. Once fitted, bracing is attached to keep the trusses level and secure from wind. Felt is then fixed to the trusses and tiles or slate are used to keep the roof and dwelling waterproof.

Traditional/cut roof

This is an alternative to trusses and uses loose timbers that are cut in situ to give the roof its shape and to spread the relevant load. More time-consuming and difficult to fit than trusses, the cut roof uses rafters that are individually cut and fixed in place, with two rafters forming a sort of truss. Once the rafters are all fixed, the roof is finished with felt and tiles or slates.

Metal trusses can also be used for industrial or more complex buildings.

Figure 3.28 Individually cut rafters

Finishing roofs

To finish a roof where it meets the exterior wall (eaves), you must fix a vertical timber board (fascia) and a horizontal board (soffit) to the foot of the rafters or trusses. The fascia and soffit are used to close off the roof space from insects and birds.

Ventilators are attached to the soffits to allow air into the roof space. This prevents rot. Guttering is attached to the fascia board to channel the rainwater into a drain.

Roof components

Ridge

A ridge is a timber board that runs the length of the roof and acts as a type of spine. It is placed at the apex of the roof structure. The uppermost ends of the rafters are then fixed to this. This gives the roof central support and holds the rafters in place.

Purlin

Purlins are horizontal beams that support the roof at the midway point. They are placed mid way between the ridge and the wall plate. They are used when the rafters are longer than 2.5 m. The purlin is supported at each end by gables.

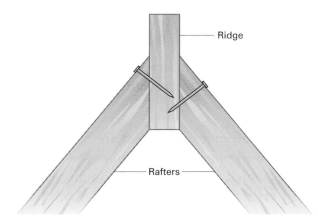

Figure 3.30 A ridge

Firrings

A firring is an angled piece of wood, laid on top of the joints on a flat roof. They provide a fall. This supplies a pitch of around 10° or less to a roof. This pitch will allow the draining of flat roofs of water. This drainage is vital. The edge where the fall leads to must have suitable guttering to allow rainwater to run away and not down the face of the wall.

> **Did you know?**
>
> Because hot air rises, the majority of heat loss that occurs is through a building's roof. Insulation such as mineral wool or polystyrene must be fitted to roof spaces and ideally any intermediate floors

Figure 3.29 Fascia and soffit in roof construction

Figure 3.31 A purlin

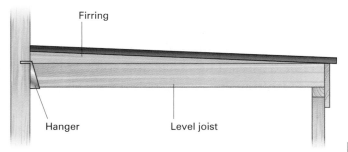

Figure 3.32 Firrings

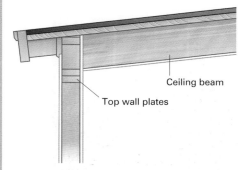

Figure 3.33 Battens on a roof

Figure 3.34 Wall plate and roof

Batten

Battens are wooden strips that are used to provide a fixing point for roof sheet or roof tiles. The spacing between the battens depends on the type of roof and they can be placed at right angles to the trusses or rafters. This makes them similar to purlins.

Some roofs use a grid pattern in both directions. This is known as a counter-batten system.

Wall plate

Wall plates are timber plates laid flat and bedded on mortar. These plates run along the wall to carry the feet of all trusses, rafters and ceiling joists. They can serve a similar role as lintels, but their main purpose is to bear and distribute the load of the roof across the wall. Because of this vital role that wall plates play in supporting the roof and spreading the pressure of its weight across the whole wall, it is important that they stay in place.

Wall plates are held in place by restraint straps along the wall. These anchor the wall plates in place to prevent movement.

Hangers and clips

Hangers, or clips, are galvanised metal clips that are used to fix trusses or joists in place on wall plates. This anchors the trusses and joists to the wall plate, which is in turn firmly anchored to the wall. This gives the roof a stable and firm construction and helps it to avoid the pressures of wind and weather.

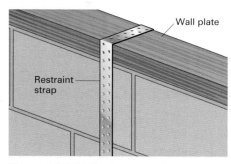

Figure 3.35 Wall plate restraint straps

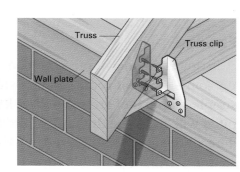

Figure 3.36 Truss clips

Bracing

Bracing consists of lengths of timber laid diagonally across the trusses. This holds them in place and help to prevent any movement in high winds. Combined with the wall plates and truss clips, bracing is a major part of ensuring the stability of the roof in all conditions.

Felt

Felt is rolled over the top of the joists to provide a waterproof barrier. It is then fastened down to provide a permanent barrier. Overlapping the felt strips when placing them will help make this barrier even more effective, as will avoiding air bubbles in the felt.

Slate and tile

Slate is flat and easy to stack. The supplier will recommend the spacing between the battens on the roof. The slate is then laid onto the battens, with the bottom of each slate tile overlapping the top of the one below. The top and bottom rows are made up of shorter slates to provide this lapping for the slate below/above. This provides waterproofing to the roof. Slate is often nailed into place.

Roofing tiles are made from concrete or clay. They are moulded or formed into a shape that allows them to overlap each other. This provides weatherproofing to the roofs, similar to the technique used for slate.

Figure 3.37 Bracing

Figure 3.38 Roofing felt

Did you know?

Some roofing tiles are made from slate

Figure 3.39 Roofing slate

Figure 3.40 Roofing tiles

Flashings

Flashings are made from aluminium or lead. They are used to provide water resistance around openings in a roof, such as chimneys or roof windows or when a roof butts up to an existing wall.

Metal flashing can be purchased in rolls or in sections specifically designed for certain jobs – such as around a chimney.

Figure 3.41 Roof flashing

FAQ

How do I know what type of foundation is needed?

A site survey, including taking soil samples and checking the area for tree roots etc., will help determine which type of foundation is used. A site survey will need to be carried out before you begin any construction work. Without it you may overlook a potential problem with the area you are planning to build on.

How do I know which height things should be on site?

The site datum will give you a baseline to which all measurements can be taken and the drawing will give you a measurement such as 1000 mm above site datum. You can use this information to set the height that things will need to be on site in relation to each other.

Check it out

1. Explain the main purpose of substructure.
2. List the three different types of foundation. Sketch each type and explain the differences between them.
3. Give a brief description of external walling.
4. Explain the difference between a truss roof and a cut roof.
5. Sketch English and Flemish brick bonds.
6. Describe the purpose of a gauge box.
7. Describe the purpose of a site datum.
8. List four materials which can be used as DPC.
9. Sketch diagrams showing the cross section of two types of internal wall.
10. Describe what mortar is used for and explain what it is made from.

Getting ready for assessment

The information contained in this unit, as well as continued practical assignments that you will carry out in your college or training centre, will help you with preparing for both your end of unit test and the diploma multiple-choice test. It will also aid you in preparing for the work that is required for the synoptic practical assignments.

The information in this unit will help you to understand the basics of your own trade as well as the basic information on several other trade areas.

You will need to be familiar with:

- foundations, walls and floor construction
- construction in internal and external masonry
- roof construction.

It is important to understand what other trades do in relation to you and how the work they do affects you and your work. It is also good to know how the different components of a building are constructed and how these tie in with the tasks that you carry out. You must always remember that there are a number of tasks being carried out on a building site at all times and many of these will not be connected to the work you are carrying out. It is useful to remember the communication skills you learnt in Unit 1002, as these will be important for working with other trades on site. You will also need to be familiar with specifications and contract documents and to know the type of construction work that other trade workers will be doing around you on site.

For learning outcome 1 you saw how datum points work on-site and the purpose that they serve in construction. You have seen that these are vital when building a range of constructions, such as roads, brick courses, paths and excavations for floor levels. You have also seen the materials used in concrete foundations and floors and the reasons for DPM and DPC.

You will need to use this knowledge to demonstrate your understanding of construction on-site. Part of this is being able to sketch basic cross sections of strip foundations and concrete floors. You will also need to be able to sketch the different types of foundation found in domestic buildings, including strip and raft concrete floor slab.

Remember, that a sound knowledge of construction methods and materials will be very useful during your training as well as in later life in your professional career.

Good luck!

Knowledge check

1 What is a datum point?

a) A point from which you take all your levels.

b) A point from which you take the time and date.

c) A point that tells you which way is north.

d) A point from which you draw.

2 The most common type of foundation is:

a) raft foundation

b) wide strip foundation

c) narrow strip foundation

d) none of the above.

3 The type of foundation used when the soil is very poor is called:

a) raft foundation

b) wide strip foundation

c) narrow strip foundation

d) none of the above.

4 What can damp proof course (DPC) be made from?

a) Slate

b) Lead

c) Polypropylene

d) Any of the above

5 What are wall ties used in?

a) Brick walls

b) Timber stud walls

c) Block walls

d) Cavity walls

6 What is the component placed above openings in brick and block walls called?

a) Lintel

b) Cavity tray

c) DPC

d) Wall tie

7 What is a roof with a pitch of 10° or less called?

a) Lean to roof

b) Pitched roof

c) Flat roof

d) Domed roof

8 What is the horizontal timber board called that is fixed to the foot of a rafter and finishes the roof?

a) Soffit

b) Fascia

c) Eaves

d) Gable

9 Which of these statements about fixing slates to a roof is *not* correct?

a) The bottom of each tile should overlap the top of the one below.

b) The architect will specify the spacing between the battens on the roof.

c) The top and bottom rows are made up of shorter slates.

d) Slate is often aniled into place.

10 A roof made with loose timbers and cut in-situ is a:

a) cut roof

b) truss roof

c) gable roof

d) flat roof.

UNIT 1014

How to carry out basic blocklaying skills

Walls can be constructed from concrete blocks or bricks. This unit will look at the use of concrete blocks in the construction of walls.

The unit also contains information about complying with working drawings. This information will be applicable to all constructions that you will study. This unit also supports NVQ Unit VR 36 Prepare and Mix Concrete and Mortars and Unit VR 37 Lay Bricks and Blocks to Line.

This unit contains material that supports TAP Unit 3: Erect Masonry Structures and Unit 5: Carry Out Masonry Cladding to Timber Framed Structures. It also contains material that supports the delivery of the five generic units.

This unit will cover the following learning outcomes:

- Setting out blockwork to comply with workshop drawings
- Setting out and building block walling using dense and lightweight insulation blocks.

K1. Setting out blockwork to comply with workshop drawings

Interpreting working drawings

With any wall that you build you will need a drawing in the workshop. The drawing should have a plan and an elevation so you can see what you will be building. It will also have any measurements or block lengths marked. From this you can work out what materials you will need. For example, if the wall was six blocks long and four blocks high you would need 24 blocks.

The preferred scales used for drawings are described in Unit 1002 (page 75). In a blocklaying workshop, the scales commonly used are 1:5, 1:10, 1:20, 1:50, 1:100 and 1:500.

On more complicated tasks you may have an opening, such as a window or door. You will need to know the size of the opening.

If the drawing is based just on measurements you will need to measure a block and remember its size in order to calculate the amount required.

Information sources

You will be using a number of information sources when complying with workshop drawings. Many of these you will already be familiar with from earlier units. The main sources of information you will use when planning are:

- location drawings, specifications and schedules (pages 80–81)
- scales (page 75)
- symbols and abbreviations (page 78–79)
- job sheets (page 103)
- safety data sheets
- workshop safety rules
- COSHH hazard warning data sheets.

Safety data sheets

These can come in different forms, but the main two types are:

- method statements
- risk assessments.

Method statements

A method statement is a written document. It explains exactly how a task should be carried out, stage-by-stage, from beginning to end. This is based on **best practice** and should take into account all aspects of health and safety.

The method statement is normally written by the site management, including a safety manager on a larger site and given to the person carrying out a task by their supervisor. It should be read and agreed so that the person understands exactly what to do. It should then be signed, with the supervisor giving a copy to the person to keep as reference, in case the person forgets something. A copy is kept on file. The same method statement could be used again if the same task has to be done again. On a smaller site, the builder will have his own method of doing this but would base it on previous work done and tried and tested safety methods employed previously.

Key term

Best practice – a method of carrying out work that has been proved to get the best results

Remember

Method statements are tried and tested methods based on previous work. Don't think you can do it differently to cut time or costs – you will find yourself spending more time and money repairing the work later

	Contract No	Ref. No
	Sheet No	Date

Safety Method Statement

1. Contractors Name:	2. Contract Name:

3. Location of works on site:

4. Description of the works to be carried out:

5. Start Date:	6. End Date:	7. Duration of works:

8. Supervisor Name:	9. Contact Telephone Numbers:

10. Description of the works including sequence and technical detail as appropriate:

THIS DOCUMENT MUST BE READ IN CONJUNCTION WITH THE ATTACHED RISK AND COSHH ASSESSMENTS

SEMS-FO-084 Rev: 0

Figure 4.1 A company method statement

Working life

Ahmed is writing a method statement on how a task should be completed stage by stage.

Think about:

- Who he should work with when completing this statement?
- What information should he collect?
- Who should he talk to?
- What information should he be including?

Ahmed will have to be sure he consults everyone who is or will be involved in the task on site – not only the site manager but also the workers carrying out the task.

When the statement is written, Ahmed will have to make sure that it contains all the information needed.

- Who could he check this with?
- What could he do to test the statement?
- Who will need to approve the statement?
- What should Ahmed do about risks in the area?

Ahmed must make sure that the statement helps everyone on site to work safely.

- How should he make sure that the statement meets with health and safety requirements?

Find out

On your next practical task, carry out a risk assessment on the task you are performing. Discuss the results with your trainer, e.g. the issues you identified and the best way to deal with them

Safety tip

As you will be new to the industry you are the most vulnerable person in the working environment. Therefore, you need to make sure that you follow all the rules and regulations you are learning. Failure to do so usually ends in accidents and injury not just to yourself but also to others

Risk assessments

A risk assessment is a written document based on a task to be carried out. It looks at all possible areas that could cause a risk or hazard (see pages 22–23) to a person in carrying out that task – from the materials, tools and equipment to be used, to cutting and laying blocks and bricks.

To read more about risk assessments, see page 24.

Workshop safety rules

Workshop safety rules are rules to be followed within the workshop to safeguard everyone working there. They will state clear dos and don'ts in the workshop and should be explained at the start of your training during your induction (see pages 12–13).

Workshop safety rules should also be on show at all times as they are there to ensure your and others' safety while in that area.

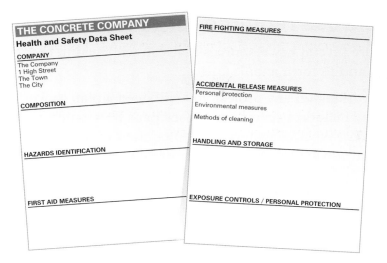

Figure 4.2 A COSHH hazard warning data sheet

COSHH hazard warning data sheets

COSHH stands for Control of Substances Hazardous to Health (see page 7 for more details). A COSHH data sheet states all the information on a particular material:

- what it is made of
- how to use it
- any hazards associated with it.

You should read these so as to understand about that material, especially if there are any hazards involved with its use.

Reporting inaccuracies in information

Sometimes information given to you may be wrong or have mistakes in it. This might be an inaccuracy in measurements, or the inclusion of material requirements that not actually suitable for the job. If you notice any inaccuracies, you should report them immediately to your line manager. You will need to explain what the problem is.

Your manager may be able to give you the correct information straight away, but often he or she will probably need to speak to their line manager. This could be the site foreman or they in turn may need to speak to the clerk of works or the architect, if the problem is related to drawings etc. These people may, in turn, need to speak to the client to resolve the problem. However, no work should be carried out until this is resolved.

From the point of view of your training in the workshop and the drawings you will be using there, your supervisor will probably be best placed to resolve your problem.

Resources required for erecting walling

There are several key resources that you will need in order to erect walling and to form a joint finish.

When working on any project you will need a plan to work to. This may include a specification (see page 81), which explains briefly what types of material are to be used in the task you are to carry out. It will also state the type of joint finish required.

In some instances if you were on site you may follow an existing joint finish, for example, if working on an extension to an existing building. Using the plan measurements you can then calculate the amount of materials you will need to carry out the task.

Make a list of the different materials you will be using, as this should make things easier so as not to forget anything. Having identified the types of materials you require, now think about the tools you will need to carry out the task as well as the personal protective equipment (PPE; see pages 63–66) you will need to wear. Add this to your list and ask your supervisor to check the list.

Basic working calculations

Block sizes can vary slightly, but when working out amounts required you can base it on a block being 440 mm long and 215 mm high.

When calculating amounts, remember that you must include 10 mm for the bed joint and **perp joint**. Therefore if the wall is two blocks long it would be:

440 mm + 10 mm + 440 mm = 890 mm

For basic calculations this is normally taken as two blocks plus two joints equals 900 mm.

For height, one block equals 215 mm plus a 10 mm joint which, when added, equals 225 mm. When working out for larger areas, the formula is based on 10 blocks to a square metre (m^2).

Key term

Perp joint – this is the vertical joint between two bricks or blocks

---

Example

If a wall is 3 m long and 2 m high the following formula would be used to complete building calculations:

Length × height or $l \times h$

3 × 2 = 6 m^2
1 m^2 = 10 blocks

Therefore 6 × 10 = 60 blocks

The total number of blocks required is 60.

Example

A wall is 1.5 m by 4.5 m. How many blocks do we need?

The same principle is used as in the previous example:

1.5 × 4.5 = 6.75 m^2
6.75 × 10 = 67.5 blocks

In this case, as you need 0.5 of a block, you would round up the figure to 68 blocks.

Try doing some calculations yourself based on the above formula, and ask your supervisor to check them.

Checks on materials

There are several checks that you need to make to ensure that the materials are correct and meet the specification. Some of these checks are:

- Are they the right materials asked for?
- Do you have enough?
- Are they free from defects or are they chipped or cracked or damaged in any way?
- Have I got the right tools to carry out the task?
- Have the tools been maintained appropriately?
- Is the correct PPE available and appropriately maintained?

K2., K3. Setting out and building block walling using dense and lightweight insulation blocks

Laying blocks

The area of blockwork that can be built during a working day is greater than with brickwork, but be very careful about the height that you build. The type of block used will govern this, as well as the weather conditions.

There are two main types of blocks used in the building industry:

- concrete blocks
- lightweight insulation blocks.

Concrete blocks

These blocks are made from concrete. This means they are quite heavy, but they do produce strong finished work. They are used mainly where a lot of weight will be put on top of, or against, the wall.

Concrete blocks are also used for forming **footings** below ground, on walls that support steel, internal walls for car parks and shopping centres, and retaining walls for embankments. These blocks can be solid, hollow or cellular (Aircrete blocks, see page 141) depending on what they are required for. They can also have a finished texture for paint finishes.

> **Remember**
> If a wall blows down, it will cost time and money to replace it

> **Did you know?**
> Trench blocks are often used to replace building two separate skins below ground level. They are solid lightweight blocks and range from 255 mm up to 355 mm wide, 440 mm long and 125 mm in depth

> **Key term**
> **Footings** – the supporting base of a building, which supports the weight of the floors and walls

Unit 1014 How to carry out basic blocklaying skills

Find out

Most manufacturers show their range of blocks on their website or in their catalogue. Use the Internet to discover more about the different types of block available on the market and their uses

Figure 4.3 Solid block

Key term

Beam and pot floors – this type of flooring consists of shaped concrete beams that span the floor area. These are then in-filled with concrete blocks to form the oversite area

Figure 4.5 Hollow blocks

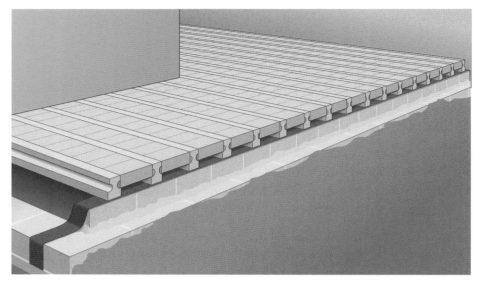

Figure 4.4 Beam and pot floor

Solid blocks

These are mainly used for making walls above ground for commercial, industrial and leisure buildings. They are used for both internal and external walls. They can also be used for **beam and pot floors**. They are hard-wearing and provide good fire and sound insulation.

Hollow blocks

These are used on areas where reinforcement is required. These blocks have the same finish as solid blocks, but have hollow sections in them. They can have reinforcement rods running vertically through them. They are then filled with concrete. This creates a very strong wall and is used in areas where a lot of weight is to be placed on top. It might also be used for other purposes, such as retaining walls for embankments.

Hollow block sizes vary from 100 mm up to 215 mm in thickness, depending on requirements. The specification for the job would state the type and size of block needed.

Lightweight blocks

Concrete manufacturers are now producing lightweight concrete block products. This is because health and safety regulations have placed restrictions on lifting and handling units heavier than 20 kg. The Concrete Block Association, which represents the majority of manufacturers, aims to offer products that would be acceptable to use in order to comply with these regulations. Some manufacturers have reduced the thickness size requirements, while others have substituted hollow blocks in place of thicker solid blocks.

Aircrete blocks

Aircrete blocks are another kind of block. They are produced under different trade names by several manufacturers. These blocks are made of a microcellular composition called Aircrete. This makes the blocks lightweight but durable. They can be used for most work associated with concrete products. The blocks can be used for foundations, beam and block floors as well as internal and external cavity walling, dependent on the external finishes required.

Aircrete blocks have a higher insulation rating than concrete blocks. Their sizes range from 75 mm up to 215 mm for standard blocks.

Using blocks

Lightweight block walls can usually be built higher. This is because the water content in the mortar is absorbed into the blocks, drying the joints faster and so giving stability more quickly. Concrete blocks are a lot heavier and do not absorb mortar water as quickly. Because of this, they are more likely to compress (swim), with the water inclined to run down the face of the work. Also, because of the weight, the blockwork can start to bow out of plumb.

Hazards in laying blocks

On site, blocks should be unloaded and transported by forklift. If they are being used on scaffolding, they should again be lifted by forklift, and not carried up ladders by hand or on a shoulder.

Blocks should not be laid too high if working in windy conditions as walls can be blown down, causing damage to property or injury to people.

Another reason to avoid laying too high is that you will not be able to see the setting out line correctly. This could mean the block touching the line. This will move it and cause the wall to bow. (See Unit 1017 for more information on setting out.)

When performing joint finishes, you should be aware of the hazard of your skin coming into contact with the mortar. When brushing down the joints there is also the risk of particles being blown into your eyes. These can be avoided by wearing the correct personal protective equipment (PPE).

Figure 4.6 Lightweight concrete blocks

Did you know?

Because of their design and composition, Aircrete blocks can be cut, sawn and drilled using basic hand tools

Figure 4.7 Aircrete blocks

Safety tip

For guidance on the dangers of working at height, see pages 48–54

Safety tip

When lifting blocks, because of the weight, you must carry only one block at a time. If a new stack of blocks is to be opened use a Stanley knife to cut plastic bands and metal cutters for metal straps

Remember

Always ask yourself some key questions:

- Have I got enough mortar boards?
- Are the materials in the right place?
- Are they not too close but also not too far away?
- Have I mixed enough mortar?

Did you know?

It takes 1.65 tonnes of raw material to make 1 tonne of cement. Almost half the weight of the limestone is lost because of carbon dioxide emissions during the manufacturing process

Location of blocks, mortar and components

Once you have a drawing to work to, you will need to look at preparing your working materials in the workshop ready for building your wall, as shown in Figure 4.8.

After working out the amount or volume of material required, you will have to stack them in your area. Each site will have different rules for arranging materials. On some smaller sites, you might need to position materials close ready for use. Other sites may hold all materials in a compound until needed and then transport to position them via forklift as required.

Your supervisor will explain the correct method of setting out the job to you. Setting out is covered in more depth on pages 139–141. You will need to use the drawings and measurements given to you by your supervisor.

Mortar

Mortar is used in brick and block laying for bedding and jointing bricks and blocks together when building a wall. Mortar was introduced on pages 124–125, which looked at the methods used to mix mortar.

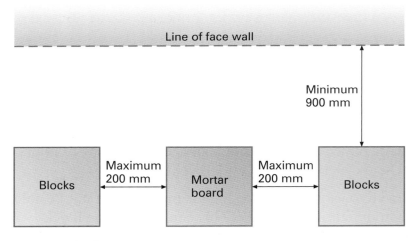

Figure 4.8 Setting out your area

Sand

Sand for bricklaying mortar should be 'well graded', having large, medium and small grains (see Figure 4.9). If all the grains were of an even size, this would be 'poorly graded' and require more cement to fill in the voids between each grain.

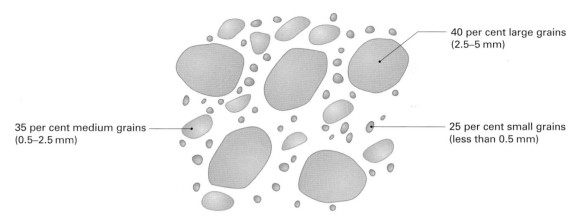

40 per cent large grains
(2.5–5 mm)

35 per cent medium grains
(0.5–2.5 mm)

25 per cent small grains
(less than 0.5 mm)

Figure 4.9 Graded samples of sand

Cement

Cement is made from limestone or chalk and a chemical combination of calcium, aluminium, silicon and iron.

Cement is used to bind the grains of sand together. A layer of cement slurry coats the particles of sand, which chemically sets after the addition of water. This results in a hardened layer holding the bricks in place. The most common form of cement used is Ordinary Portland Cement (OPC). This is suitable for general work and will produce high quality, strong mortar.

Water

Water is used to make cement paste and to cause the cement to set. This reaction is called **hydration**. The water used for mixing must be clean enough to drink.

Cutting and preparing components

When preparing to build walls, you may need to cut and prepare blocks. There are three different methods that can be used:

- by hand using a bolster chisel and hammer
- by hand using a saw
- by machine using a portable disc cutter or fixed table saw.

The method used sometimes depends on the type of block being used. For example, a hand saw would be no good to cut concrete blocks but is fine for lightweight blocks.

A hammer and bolster is adequate for concrete blocks but can chip the edges of the cut. If the cut blocks are to be covered by another material this would be acceptable, but if the blocks have a face finish then machine cutting would be the better option, especially if a large number of cuts are required.

Did you know?

Masonry cement is often used for bricklaying mortar. It is similar to OPC but has a plasticiser added to the cement powder. As this contains 25 per cent plasticiser, a higher proportion of cement must be used

Key term

Hydration – the addition of water to cement paste to produce a chemical reaction to set mortar

Safety tip

As well as your normal PPE always wear goggles, gloves and a facemask when cutting blocks

Safety tip

Cutting by machine should only be carried out by a trained, competent person

Mark out the cutting position on the block

This should be marked on all sides

The bolster should be tapped along the cut line

The face edge of the block is the most important

Rough ends can be trimmed with a brick or scutch hammer

Figure 4.10 Cutting a block by hand

Cutting by hand

If blocks are cut by hammer and bolster, the cutting position should be marked on all sides. The bolster should then be positioned face side first and tapped sharply along the cut line. Then the same method should be followed on the back side, top and bottom of the block, repeating the process until the block cuts.

The face edge is most important, as a neat straight line is required with little or no chipping. If excessive chipping has happened, then a new block should be cut or another method used. If the block cut is good but slightly rough on the cut end, it can be trimmed down using a brick or scutch hammer.

Tools for cutting blocks

Angle grinders

Angle grinders are cutting tools that run by electricity using 110 V and 230 V supplies or are battery powered. They cut using an abrasive or diamond-type disc. They range from 100 mm to 230 mm diameter disc size.

Angle grinders are used by bricklayers mainly for cutting bricks, blocks, concrete and stone to size or for cutting existing material for alteration. Great care should be taken when using them as the disc travels at very high speed and takes time to slow down after release of the trigger, and therefore can still cut.

Owing to the cutting speed, large amounts of dust and particles are released from the material, so goggles and mask should always be worn in addition to the usual PPE. Ear defenders (see page 65) should also be worn. All leads should be checked before and after use for cuts or splits. With a 110 V supply, a transformer must be used.

Petrol cutters

This type of cutter is the same as the angle grinder but is motorised, running on petrol. The disc size is 300 mm and it runs at a slower speed than the angle grinder. It uses abrasive or diamond cutting discs and is used for heavier duty cutting.

> **Safety tip**
>
> Always wear goggles and facemask to prevent chippings going into your eyes and inhaling the dust. Also, carry out cutting in a separate place away from other people to prevent them from being affected by your actions

> **Did you know?**
>
> In the construction industry only 110 V type or battery-type angle grinders are allowed to be used on site according to health and safety law

> **Safety tip**
>
> No person is allowed to change a cutting disc unless they hold an Abrasive Wheels Certificate

Figure 4.11 100 mm / 4 inch electric grinder   Figure 4.12 225 mm / 9 inch electric grinder

Figure 4.13 A 300 mm / 12 inch petrol cutter

Great care must be taken when using these cutters, and fuel and oil levels should be checked regularly. Discs should also be regularly checked for wear or damage.

To ensure that no movement occurs when the disc is spinning, the locking nut must be securely tightened and a shim (a flat metal plate) fitted over the main spindle either side of the disc.

Working life

Josh is asked by his supervisor to cut 30 bricks to a set size using a petrol cutter. He has had training and is competent using it, but he isn't sure what blade is on the cutter as it's covered up by the shim that holds it tight.

- What should he do?
- What hazards must Josh be aware of if he is checking the blade?

Josh should be certain that the cutter is switched off and unplugged before inspecting it.

- What else will Josh need to do?
- What type of PPE should Josh be wearing?

Did you know?

You have to be 18 or over to use a disc cutter on site

Figure 4.14 Block cutter

Block cutters

These are used for cutting bricks, blocks, paviers and concrete slabs and have a sharp cutting edge and use high compression to break the material to the correct size.

They can be moved around fairly easily, but are more time-consuming to use than cutting bricks and blocks by hammer and bolster. However, they are better for slabs and paviers, than cutting with disc cutters or grinders.

Establishing bonds for block walling

Bonding is the lapping of bricks or blocks to give a wall maximum strength. Lapping the blocks spreads the weight of the wall.

Blocks should be laid so they are bonded for maximum strength to the wall, so they should be laid to half bond or, as in brickwork, stretcher bond (see page 122). The minimum lap that should be used is quarter bond.

With half bond, the perp joints of the second course blocks should be in the centre of the block below as shown in Figure 4.15.

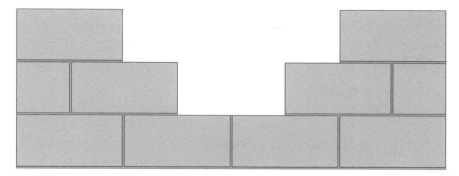

Figure 4.15 Independent wall showing half bond

If the wall is an **independent wall**, the second course should start with a half block at each end, minus the thickness of a joint of 10 mm.

If the wall has a return, the corner blocks should overlap **flush** and a cut block placed next to it to attain half bond. The cut will vary in size depending on the thickness of the blocks being used (see Figure 4.16).

Key terms

Independent wall – a wall not connected to another wall at either end

Flush – when one surface is exactly even with another one

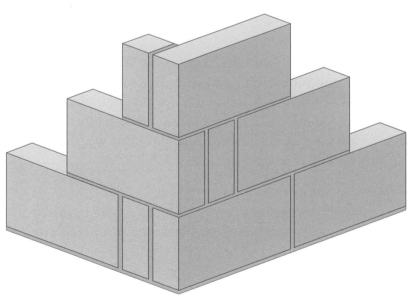

Figure 4.16 Return corner

Safety tip

You should also understand how to use the tools correctly. If you are not sure how to use a tool, ask your supervisor to demonstrate to you the correct use

Figure 4.17 Brick trowel

Figure 4.18 Pointing trowel

Figure 4.19 Club or lump hammer

Correct use of hand tools and equipment

Whilst carrying out blockwork, or any other task, you must ensure that you use the correct tool for the right job. A lot of accidents happen purely because the person tries to 'make do' with unsuitable tools for a job. Make a list of tools needed before you start a task to ensure that this doesn't happen to you.

Tools required for blockwork

Brick trowel

The brick trowel is used by the bricklayer to take the mortar off the mortar board, lay it on to the wall and spread it to form a uniform bed joint ready for the bricks or blocks to be laid on it.

Brick trowels can be purchased in different sizes and for left- or right-handed people. They are made from solid, rolled, forged carbon steel, with a hickory handle. Always clean your trowel with water after use, dry it thoroughly and lightly oil it to prevent rust from forming.

Pointing trowel

Pointing trowels can be purchased in different sizes depending on requirement and preference. They are used for filling in joints and pointing certain types of joint finishes. They are made from solid, rolled, forged carbon steel, with a hickory handle. They should be cleaned in the same way as brick trowels.

Club or lump hammer

This is a heavy hammer that is used together with a bolster chisel for cutting bricks and blocks by hand. It is also used with other chisels for cutting out bricks, knocking holes through walls and removing joints using a plugging chisel. It is made from forged steel, with a hickory handle, and comes in different weights, usually ranging from 2.5 lb to 4 lb (1.2 to 1.8 kg).

Bolster chisel

This is used mainly for cutting bricks or blocks to the required size and angled shape. It is made from hardened tempered steel,

Figure 4.20 Bolster chisels

usually in cutting blade sizes from 64 mm to 100 mm. Some come with safety handle grips.

Lines and pins

Lines and pins are used for laying bricks and blocks once the corners have been erected to ensure that work is in a straight line. The pins are placed into the perp joints at each end of the run so that the line runs from the top of the laid brick at each end. This ensures that the bricks that are to be laid run in a straight line. Also, by putting the top of the brick to the line, this keeps the bricks level between the two points, assuming that the corners are correct.

Figure 4.21 Brick line and line pins

The pins are normally made from forged steel for light duty work. Some are made from thicker steel for heavier duty work.

The line can be made of nylon or cotton. Nylon is more durable but less flexible, whereas cotton is the opposite. While using either, care should be taken when laying the bricks as they cut very easily.

Tape measure

Tape measures come in many sizes, from 3 m up to 10 m for the pocket type, and from 10 m up to 30 m for larger setting out tapes – some can go up to 100 m. They are used for measuring or checking sizes.

Figure 4.22 Steel tape measure

Tape measures are usually made with plastic or steel cases, with a steel measure. Some come with both metric (centimetres and metres) and imperial (inches and feet) measurements, although most only have metric measures. Larger tapes are made of steel or fibreglass.

Spirit levels

Made from aluminium, spirit levels come in various sizes from 225 mm to 2000 mm. The main size used in bricklaying is 1200 mm. They are used for levelling things and for plumbing vertically.

Remember

In Scotland, a large spirit level is also known as a large bead

Spirit levels contain bubbles that give a reading between set lines to determine the accuracy of the work. Some levels have an adjustable bubble at the bottom for levelling angled work.

Great care must be taken when using levels as they can easily go out of **true**. This means that work that could seem to be level or plumb but the reading is actually wrong. This could result in work having to be taken down and redone.

Figure 4.23 Spirit level

The main cause of a spirit level going out of true is that the level has been hit with a trowel or hammer, dropped or misused in other ways.

Always wash the spirit level with water to keep it clean.

Key term

True – giving an accurate reading

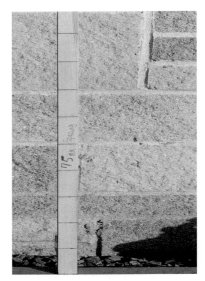

Figure 4.24 Gauge rod in use

Key terms

Gauge – the blockwork course height. For a block size of 215 mm this would be the size plus the 10 mm joint – 225 mm

Reverse bond – when the two ends of a wall start with opposite ends, i.e. one end with full block, the other with half block

Methods used to maintain industrial standards

Industrial standards are the standards and tolerances allowed on site or in the workshop covering:

- the plumbness, level and finish of a wall
- if the wall is to **gauge**
- if the joints on courses run true and plumb
- the cleanliness of the wall once built.

Gauge can be maintained by using a gauge rod, a storey rod or a tape measure.

Sequences of work and recommended heights

When in the workshop, the first course of blocks should be set out to the drawing and measurements given. The difference on site is that you will only have the measurements. This means that you will need to set out the first course before you will know if the measurements used work to the block sizes, or whether you will need to cut the blocks.

If a cut block is required, this should be placed in the middle of the wall. However, this may change depending on the circumstances. For example, if there is to be an opening in the wall or if **reverse bond** will be used at one end.

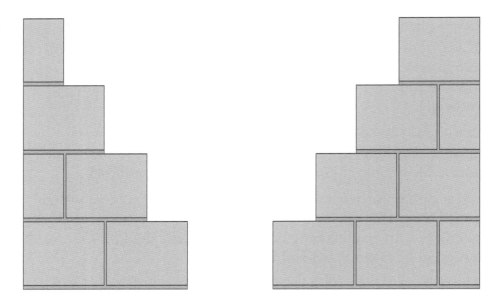

Figure 4.25 Reverse bond

Once the bond has been established, blocklaying can commence. The requirements will change from wall to wall. First lay a half block in the correct position at one end, ensuring that it is gauge, plumb and level. Then repeat this sequence at the other end. When both end blocks are built, use a line and pin to place and lay the central blocks.

Once the first course is in place, corners can be built at each end as in Figure 4.25 and the centre filled in. If the wall has return corners, the same sequence occurs at each end before **in-filling** and then as above.

Reasons for carrying out checks

The work should be checked periodically as it progresses to ensure that the wall is straight, plumb and level. This is because a slight knock or accidental touch could cause blocks in the wall to move or a corner to move slightly out of plumb.

Blocks could also move if they are wet, especially in the case of concrete blocks as the moisture does not soak into the blocks. Therefore the water from the mortar mix can run out of the joint and down the wall, causing voids in the joints. This is usually called **swimming**.

As well as the weight of the blocks pushing downwards, it is important not to build the wall too high at any point. The British Standards (BS 5628) recommends that a single wall should not be raised by more than six courses of blocks. The only exception to this is with a cavity wall, where the two leaves are raised together and incorporate wall ties – although the number of block courses may have to be less if the blocks are wet.

> **Key term**
>
> **In-filling** – positioning the blocks to complete the course

> **Key term**
>
> **Swimming** – the movement of the block because of too much water either in the mortar or saturation of the block. It's also caused by the weight of the block not allowing enough time for initial setting into position

> **Functional skills**
>
> At the end of this unit you will have the opportunity to answer a series of questions on the material you have learnt. By answering these questions you will be practising the following functional skills:
>
> FE 1.2.3 – Read different texts and take appropriate action.
>
> FE 1.3.1 – 1.3.5 – Write clearly with a level of detail to suit the purpose.
>
> FM 1.1.1 – Identify and select mathematical procedures.
>
> FM 1.2.1c – Draw shapes.

Unit 1014

How to carry out basic blocklaying skills

FAQ

Why are blocks used?

Blocks are often used for load-bearing walls, such as in cavity walls. They are then supported by concrete columns and wall ties.

Why aren't bricks used on corners to gain bond, to save having to cut blocks?

If bricks are used at corners, they will leave what are called 'cold spots' in the wall. This is because bricks do not have the same thermal value as blocks. These cold spots can attract condensation and increase the risk of damp and mould.

What type of mortar should I use for blockwork?

You will need to carefully select the correct type of mortar. Guidance on this is given in BS 5628 of the masonry design standards. You will need to think about the final planned location of the blockwork. For example, in places where the blockwork is going to be exposed, you will need a stronger mortar than you would for an internal wall.

Check it out

1. Describe six of the key tools used in the building of blockwork, explaining what they are used for and why.
2. Explain the purpose of a risk assessment when building blockwork. Complete a sample risk assessment, detailing some of the hazards you may encounter.
3. Describe the purpose of a beam and pot floor, using sketches and diagrams.
4. Explain what 'swimming' is and why it happens. What can be done to prevent it?
5. Name three types of information on a COSHH data sheet and explain what each piece of information means. What effect does the COSHH data sheet have on the work you will be doing?
6. Describe what a hollow block is used for and where. Draw a diagram of a hollow block, labelling its key features.
7. Explain what a method statement is and complete an example method statement for a task you have carried out.
8. Describe the process used to create mortar. Explain what hydration is and how it can be prevented.

Getting ready for assessment

At the end of studying this unit you will need to carry out a synoptic test on blockwork. To prepare for this you will need to use both the information contained in this unit and your practical experience.

You will need to be familiar with:

- identifying and calculating the materials and equipment required
- setting up your area
- how to set out, level, gauge and plumb blocks
- cutting blocks to given size.

This unit has introduced the facts that help you to make decisions in your practical work. In your synoptic test you will need to use the knowledge you have gained from this unit to carry out the practical task.

For example, for learning outcome 2 you will need to position all the materials you will use, such as blocks, mortar and tools, in a safe way. Remember that there are serious health and safety issues when moving blocks. We looked at manual handling earlier in the book on pages 31–33. Using this knowledge in your practical activity is very important for making your work safe.

This unit has looked at cutting blocks and preparing straight block walls. This gives you the information that you need in order to carry out the work yourself. Remember that following the methods you have learnt about in this unit will help to make your work accurate and complete.

A big part of all practical work is checking that your completed work is accurate and correct. Use the knowledge you have gained from this unit to make sure that what you have constructed is secure, safe and fit for purpose.

Before you start work, think of a plan of action, which will tell you the order you need to do things in. You will need to refer back to this at each stage to check that you are not making any mistakes as you work. Your tolerances must be correct on plumbing, gauge and level as you progress with the work. Without checking this, you could make serious mistakes in your construction that will have a big impact on the final build.

Your speed in carrying out these tasks in a practice setting will also help to prepare you for the time set for the test. However, you must never rush the test! Always make sure that you are working safely. Make sure throughout the test that you are wearing appropriate and correct PPE and using tools correctly.

Good luck!

Knowledge check

1 What is the British Standard that recommends the maximum height a block wall should be raised in a single stage, without being backed up?

a) BS 5286

b) BS 5628

c) BS 6582

d) BS 4628

2 How many blocks are there in 1 m²

a) 7

b) 8

c) 10

d) 12

3 What document explains all about the materials on site?

a) Method statement

b) Risk assessment

c) COSHH data sheet

d) Specification

4 A wall is planned to be 12 m long and 3.5 m high. How many blocks will be required to complete its construction?

a) 310

b) 320

c) 410

d) 420

5 What document explains fully how a task should be carried out, often in a stage-by-stage way?

a) Method statement

b) Risk assessment

c) COSHH data sheet

d) Specification

6 What tool should be used to cut plastic bands around new sets of blocks?

a) Hammer

b) Metal cutters

c) Stanley knife

d) Chisel

7 A wall is planned to be 2.02 m high. How many courses will it have?

a) 6 courses

b) 7 courses

c) 8 courses

d) 9 courses

8 What is the minimum lap that should be used in blockwork?

a) Three-quarter bond

b) Half bond

c) Quarter bond

d) Stretcher bond

9 What is an independent wall?

a) A wall with a return.

b) A wall that is not connected to another.

c) A wall connected to another at one end.

d) A wall connected to another at both ends.

10 What bond is used when a wall is started with a full block at one end and a half block at the other?

a) Half bond

b) Header bond

c) Reverse bond

d) Stretcher bond

UNIT 1015

How to carry out basic bricklaying skills

Bricklaying requires time and practice, as well as a willingness to follow the correct procedures, which have been tried and tested over a number of years.

This unit will also give you information about preparing and cutting components and about many of the tools that you will need to use to complete walling. This unit also supports NVQ Unit VR 36 Prepare and Mix Concrete and Mortars and Unit VR 37 Lay Bricks and Blocks to Line. This unit contains material that supports TAP Unit 3: Erect Masonry Structures, Unit 5: Carry Out Masonry Cladding to Timber Framed Structures and Unit 6: Co-ordinate Self and Others to Erect Complex Masonry Structures. It also contains material that supports the delivery of the five generic units.

This unit will cover the following learning outcomes:

- Setting out brickwork to comply with workshop drawings
- Building straight walls in half-brick stretcher bond
- Building return corners in half-brick stretcher bond
- Building straight walls in one-brick walling
- Building return corners in one-brick walling
- Forming junctions in brick and block walling.

Example

To build a wall 2.5 m long and 1.6 m high, how many bricks would we need?

We first need to work out the area.

   2.5 × 1.6 = 4 m²

If 60 bricks = = 1 m²

   4 × 60 = 240

We need 240 bricks to build the wall.

Find out

Check out the size of some of the walls around you – how many bricks would be needed to build these walls? Do some calculations and then get them checked. How much would one of these walls cost to build – check some supplier websites to find out the average cost of bricks

K1. Setting out brickwork to comply with workshop drawings

The skills and knowledge needed to set out brickwork using workshop drawings are largely the same as those you used when working with blocks. Refer back to pages 139–141, to refresh your memory about the use of these materials.

The information sources, methods of reporting inaccuracies, and the resources required are the same as those discussed on pages 139–141.

Using bricks

Bricks are obviously smaller than blocks, therefore more are required per square metre. A brick is 215 mm long or half the length of a standard block. Allowing for a joint, two bricks make up the length of a block. A brick is 65 mm high. This means that three courses of bricks with bed joints make up a full block with a joint (225 mm). Therefore to build a wall the same size as a block you would need six bricks: 3 × 2 = 6.

Basic calculations for using bricks

As with working with blocks, there are a few basic calculations that you will need to make for most of your brickwork. These calculations will be essentially the same for each job you carry out.

Example

To build a wall 4.8 m long and 2.4 m high, how many bricks would we need?

Again, first we calculate the area.

   4.8 × 2.4 = 11.52 m²

We know 60 bricks = 1 m²

   11.52 × 60 = 691.2 bricks

Of course you cannot have 0.2 of a brick, so you need to round up to a full brick (692).

Health and safety in bricklaying

Bricks can vary in weight depending on the type. For instance, engineering and concrete bricks are heavier than clay bricks. Water absorption by the bricks also increases their weight. The same applies for blocks.

You must always remember that bricks and blocks are a source of danger when handling them in your daily work. When lifting bricks and blocks always use the correct method – this is called kinetic lifting (see pages 31–33). Heavy dense concrete blocks can cause back and hand injuries when lifting and, if dropped on your foot or hand, can cause serious damage.

K2. Building straight walls in half-brick stretcher bond

Preparing components

The main component you will need to prepare is, of course, the bricks you will be using.

Before carrying out any work, you must understand the basic sizes and names of the different parts of a brick, and the cuts used to enable you to set out a wall correctly.

As you can see in Figure 5.1, the length of a brick is called the stretcher and the end of a brick is called the header. The length of the stretcher is 215 mm and the header length is 102.5 mm. Two headers plus a 10 mm joint equal the length of the stretcher. These measurements can vary slightly as all bricks are not exactly the same and depend on the mould sizes used when produced at the factory. This means the joint size may have to be adjusted.

Mortar

Mixing mortar components was covered on pages 124–125. However, there are some different elements of mortar creation for brickwork that need to be taken into account when carrying out bricklaying.

Plasticisers

Sand, cement and water will make a mortar difficult for a bricklayer to use. To make a bricklaying mortar 'workable', a plasticiser must be added to the mix. Most plasticisers come in a powder or a liquid form. This should be added to the water as per the product instructions. The plasticiser works by coating the grains of the sand with tiny bubbles of air. This allows the sand to flow easily when being spread.

Hydrated lime may be used as a plasticiser, but washing-up liquid must never be used as you can't control the amount of air bubbles, and you would create a weak mortar mix because the chemicals and detergents react to the cement, breaking down the hydrant.

Colouring agents

Colouring agents are available in powder or liquid form, but are only really suitable for pointing brickwork as it is difficult to keep a consistent colour in a large amount of mortar by this method. Therefore a ready mix mortar should be used when a large amount is needed.

This is available from mortar suppliers.

Safety tip

Be mindful when stacking:

- Never stack too high as overreaching can cause injury. Also, collapse of the stack could cause crush injuries which could be fatal
- When laying bricks and blocks, mortar can splash onto skin, causing irritation, or into eyes, and when cutting, hand and eye injury is possible

Remember

There can be quite a big difference in the sizes of bricks

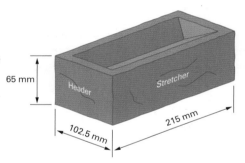

Figure 5.1 Sizes of brick, header and stretcher

Remember

Never use plasticiser below ground level. Natural minerals and acids in the ground will react with the plasticiser, breaking down the structure and weakening the mortar joint

Remember

When using colouring pigments, always follow the instructions on the packaging

Mark out the cutting position on the block

This should be marked on all sides

The bolster should be tapped along the cut line

The face edge of the brick is the most important

Rough ends can be trimmed with a brick or scutch hammer

Figure 5.2 Cutting a brick by hand

Cutting bricks

If bricks need to be cut, there are two different methods that can be used:

- by hand using a hammer and bolster chisel
- by machine using a portable disc cutter or fixed table cutter.

The method used can depend on the type of brick to be cut. Some bricks, if cut by hand, can break or shatter. This can cause a lot of wastage and cost. For situations such as this, machine cutting is a better option.

For bricks that are cut by hammer and bolster, the cutting position should be clearly marked on all sides. The bolster should be positioned face side first and tapped sharply. Then repeat at the opposite position on the back of the brick. If you need to, return to the face position and repeat the cut. The face edge is the most important as a neat straight cut is required with no chipping of the face.

If the face is chipped, the cut brick should not be used, as bricks that are chipped look unsightly and spoil the look of the wall. In this situation, a new brick should be cut. If the cut is slightly rough on the rest of the cut edges, the brick can be trimmed down using a brick or scutch hammer.

Setting out and laying bricks

A bricklayer has to lay bricks level and straight with equally sized joints in order to achieve a sound wall and a good overall appearance. In the next few pages we will look at how this is achieved.

Once you understand the basic sizes, you can start to set out your wall. Remember that in most cases the wall to be built is governed by measurements given on a drawing. These do not always work to brickwork sizes, therefore always set out the wall **dry**, puting in the required bond using a stretcher course to establish if cut bricks will need to be used.

If a cut is required it should be placed in the centre of the wall, with the smallest cut being a half brick (102.5 mm). Sometimes the cut can be put under a door or window, or a reverse bond may be another option.

Establishing bonds for straight brick walling

Bond is the name given to the pattern of the bricks in a wall. The purpose of bonding brickwork is to distribute the weight of the wall evenly along its length and onto the foundation below.

Functional skills

FM 1.2.1c, d relates to using a formula to calculate perimeters and areas. This information is important in understanding the amount of a material that is required to carry out a building task.

Remember

Cutting by machine should only be carried out by a trained and competent person

Find out

There are many different types of brick available on the market. Carry out some research on the Internet into the different types of brick available. What sort of builds are each type used for? Write a summary of the information you find

Safety tip

As well as your normal personal protective equipment (PPE) requirements, always wear goggles, gloves and a facemask when cutting

Key term

Dry – a course set out without the use of mortar. This it to help make decisions about how to lay the bricks, such as the most suitable bond and the need for any cuts to the bricks

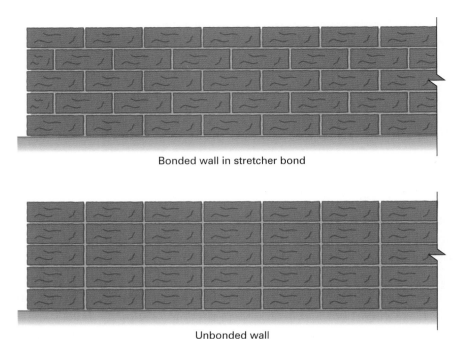

Bonded wall in stretcher bond

Unbonded wall

Figure 5.3 Bonded and unbonded walls

The length of the wall should be set out dry first to see if full size bricks can be used along the length or whether cut bricks will be needed. In some instances reverse bond (see page 150) may be required to keep the wall to full bricks. For example, one end could be started with a header and the other with a stretcher.

If cut bricks are required this is called broken bond. In most instances architects and designers will try to keep to measurements that will work to brick sizes, but this is not always the case. Sometimes differences in the sizes of the bricks may require the perp joints to be opened or closed slightly to achieve the overall length required. If this is still not correct, setting the wall out to incorporate windows or doorway may give enough scope to achieve full bond.

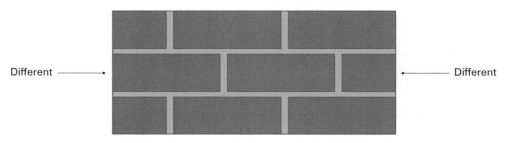

Different — • • — Different

Figure 5.4 Wall formed with reverse bond

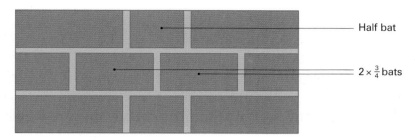

Figure 5.5 Broken bond

As windows in most cases do not start at damp proof course (DPC; see pages 120, and pages 189–191) level you may need to set out with a broken bond underneath. This means that once the window is set in place, correct bond will work from this level onwards. Broken bond should consist of a minimum of a **half bat** on one course with two three-quarter bricks on the alternate course.

Types of bond

There are many different types of bond that can be used. The choice of bond is usually determined by the purpose of the wall and the strength required, incorporating the thickness.

Stretcher bond

As mentioned previously, stretcher bond is the most common bond and is used mainly in the construction of the outer **leaf** in cavity wall brickwork (Figure 5.6) and the inner leaf in block walling.

Sometimes you may come across a project where the outer leaf of brickwork may be built using a bond other than stretcher bond. In most cases this is when an extension is carried out to an older property and the brickwork needs to blend with the existing bond.

Figure 5.6 Stretcher bond brickwork (cavity wall)

Key term

Half bat – a brick cut to 102.5 mm, which is half the full size of a brick (less a joint)

Key term

Leaf – the two walls that form cavity walls are referred to as leaves, with the inner leaf being the one on the 'inside' and the outer leaf being on the 'outside'

Remember

If a quarter of a brick is to be gained, use half-brick and three-quarter brick to fill

Remember

In Scotland, a half bat is also known as a half brick

Quarter bond

Quarter bond is used in the construction of solid walling used for garden walls, load-bearing walls, retaining walls and inspection chambers are 215 mm thick or above. It is used for its strength and, on some work, for its appearance. There are many different types of quarter bond, but the four main bonds that are regularly used are:

- English bond
- English garden wall bond
- Flemish bond
- Flemish garden wall bond.

English bond

English bond is the strongest of all the bonds and uses alternate courses of stretchers and headers (see Figure 5.7). It is used for inspection chambers, garden walls, etc. It can have a monotonous appearance but strength is the priority here.

English garden wall bond

English garden wall bond may consist of either three, five or seven courses of stretchers to one course of headers. Figure 5.8 shows the use of three stretchers to one course of headers. This bond is not as strong as English bond as there is a straight joint in the centre of the wall on the three stretcher courses. As the name suggests, English garden wall bond is mainly used for garden wall construction as downward pressure is not a problem.

Figure 5.7 English bond

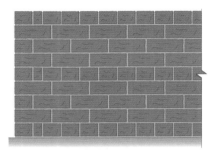

Figure 5.8 English garden wall bond

Functional skills

When working on site with different levels of wall, it is important that you read any instructions or specifications carefully, and use the correct calculations for your work. When you do this you will be practising the following functional skills:

FE 1.2.1 – 1.2.3 – Reading and understanding information including different texts and taking appropriate action.

FM 1.1.1 – Identifying and selecting mathematical procedures.

FM 1.2.1a – Using appropriate mathematical procedures.

Working life

Peter needs to build a wall in the garden of a property to retain the earth to a raised area. The difference in the levels is 680 mm.

- What size wall and which bond might be best suited for the job?
- What factors would affect Peter's decision?
- What could Peter do about any water that collects from the raised area?

Peter will need to think about the strength that the wall will need, and the impact that the water will have. He will need to think about ways to stop the water from collecting above the wall.

- Should he talk to the client about any of these decisions?
- Which ones would the client like to be consulted on?

A client is unlikely to want to be consulted on minor details, but may want to know about brick choice or larger issues that could affect other areas of the project. Peter will have to be sure that he is working safely.

- What are the possible risks Peter might face when working on this wall?

Remember there is a lot of on-site information and paperwork that Peter could check when deciding on the safest way to work.

Flemish bond

Flemish bond uses alternate stretchers and headers in each course (Figure 5.9). The header should be positioned in the centre of the stretcher of the course below and above, making it the most attractive bond used, especially if the headers are carried out in an alternative coloured brick.

Figure 5.9 Flemish bond wall

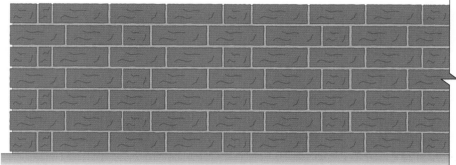

Figure 5.10 Flemish garden wall bond

Flemish garden wall bond

Flemish garden wall bond consists of three stretchers and then one header alternating in each course (Figure 5.10). The header is positioned in the centre of the middle stretcher each time.

In all cases where quarter bond is used, the corner header should have a queen closer next to it to form the quarter bond (Figure 5.11).

Did you know?

Flemish garden wall bond is stronger than English garden wall bond as the headers tie across more regularly

Remember

For bonding purposes never use a closer in the wall other than at the corner

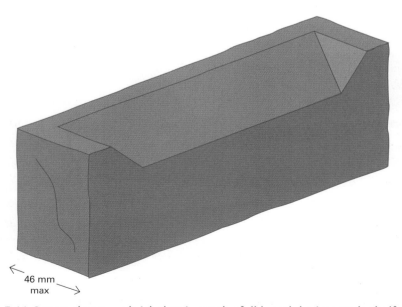

Figure 5.11 Queen closer – a brick that is cut the full length by just under half the width (46 mm maximum) to allow for a joint

46 mm max

Working life

Alfie is setting out a wall for a new extension. The existing brickwork is in Flemish bond. He starts setting out in stretcher bond as the bricks add up to the same measurements, that is two half bricks equal one stretcher.

- Is this correct?
- If not what should Alfie be doing?

Alfie's bond choice may be incorrect. Take a look again at the types of bond and their uses and discuss which bond Alfie should consider using and why.

Laying bricks below ground level

Bricks laid below ground level are laid in much the same way as those laid above – the bonding and laying principles remain the same. However, the practice of laying bricks and blocks in trenches can be affected by certain factors such as limited space within the trench, making it difficult to move around and meaning that materials have to be stacked above the ground level, on the sides of the trenches.

Modern foundation designs have alleviated this problem to some degree. Using deep-fill concrete in trenches, for instance, means that less brickwork or blockwork is required below ground level, with as few as four or five courses actually required within the trench itself.

Where there is a requirement to construct walling deeper than four or five courses, foundation blocks can be used. These blocks are a much larger unit than the individual brick, so this is a less costly method of providing walling requirements. It also means

Brickwork under DPC level

Ground area blocks

Figure 5.12 Bricks laid below ground level

that the bricklayer spends less time within the confines of the trench. Foundation blocks can be obtained in sizes to suit the width of cavity walling, removing the need to construct an inner leaf and an outer leaf for much of the depth of the trench.

Other difficulties to overcome when building below ground level are:

- making provision for services such as gas, electric or water pipes, which may have to pass through the brickwork or blockwork
- maintaining the gauge of the brick and/or block courses to ensure that appropriate levels are achieved, such as ground level, DPC level or, more importantly, ground floor level.

Provision for services

Where any service passes through brickwork or blockwork below ground level, you must ensure that the weight of the brick or block does not sit directly on the service pipe. This could cause severe damage to the service pipe, resulting in loss of service and creating potential health and safety hazards for workers and the public.

Any opening provided within the masonry to accommodate the passage of services needs to be bridged by means of a suitable **lintel**, normally made from concrete.

Building masonry walling up to DPC level

It is essential that the correct height is achieved when constructing walling from the base of the trench up to the required DPC level. You can achieve this easily by using a gauge rod and spirit level as shown in the illustration below.

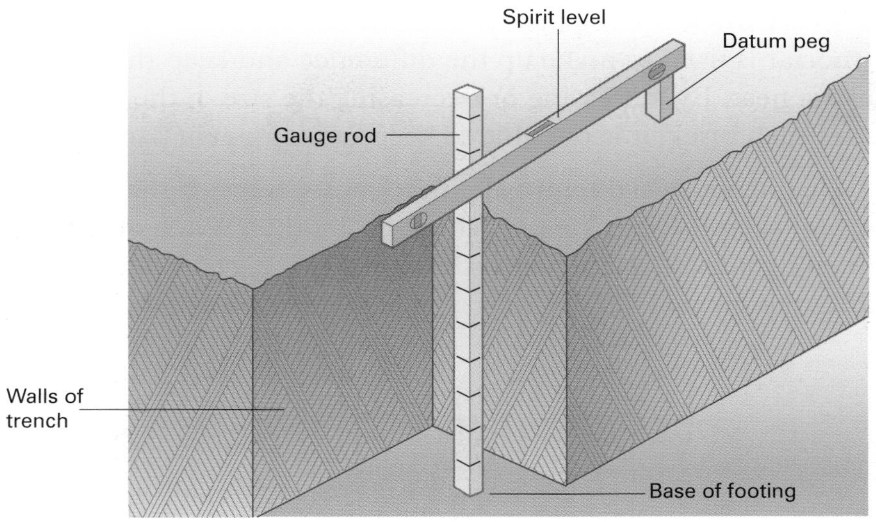

> **Key term**
>
> **Lintel** – component placed above an opening in brickwork or blockwork to bridge the opening and support the bricks or blocks above it

> **Did you know?**
>
> Where the distance from the datum peg to the point above the wall is greater than the spirit level, a straight edge can be used to span the distance

Figure 5.13 Using a gauge rod and spirit level to ensure the correct height

Remember

Transferring must be carried out with care and accuracy to ensure that the building elevations remain truly vertical

Where the depth from DPC level to the concrete below does not work to the normal 75 mm course heights, you may need to lay a thicker bed joint underneath the first course.

Where there is a difference of half a course, you will need to lay a split brick course. If this method is used, the split course must always be laid as the first course and not anywhere else within the height of the wall. This is because it can cause significant weakness within the construction.

Before construction of the walling below ground level can commence, you will need to transfer the line of the face of the brickwork, down from the ranging or setting-out lines onto the concrete in the base of the trench.

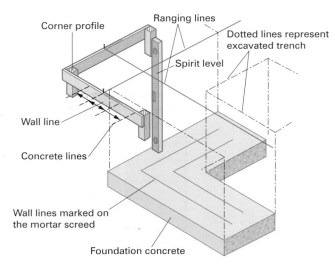

Figure 5.14 Transferring the ranging lines

The ranging or setting-out lines will be attached to wooden profiles (see pages 216–217). A spirit level is used to transfer this line down onto the concrete. A mortar bed is spread over the area directly below the setting out line, which identifies the face of the wall to be built.

When using the spirit level to transfer the face line down onto the concrete, you should use a straight edge to steady the spirit level. This helps maintain the level's upright position and obtain accurate positioning of the markings in the mortar bed.

The purpose of joints

Bricks are often not regular in shape or size (see Figure 5.15), so mortar is used to make up the difference and keep the wall looking neat. By increasing or decreasing the size of the bed joint under each brick, it is possible to keep the top **arris** flat.

By opening up or tightening the perp joints between the bricks, you can keep the joints neatly above each other. When opening or tightening joint sizes, the joint size should not vary more than 3 mm either way, giving a final joint size of between 7 mm and 13 mm.

Key term

Arris – the edge of a brick

Top arris kept flat despite different size and shape bricks

Figure 5.15 Irregular shaped bricks

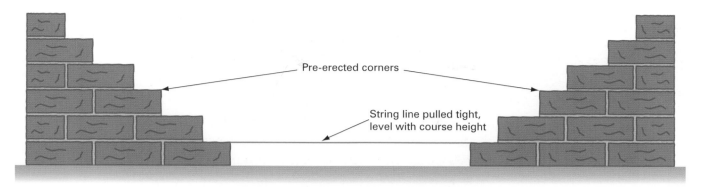

Figure 5.16 Corners with line attached

The building process

Fixing lines to the corners

To build any wall, corners have to be built in the correct positions first (unless you are using corner profiles – see pages 172–173). To lay the bricks between corners and to maintain accuracy, the bricklayer will use a line. The string line is attached, level, to the course height and to a pre-erected corner using pins or corner blocks. The line is then pulled tight to take out any 'sag' in the line, and attached to the other corner.

Laying the bricks

The bricks can now be laid to the line, which will ensure that they are the correct height and are laid in a straight line. The bricks should be tapped down until the top arris is level with the top of the string line.

To ensure that the bricks are laid in a straight line upwards (face), the bricklayer should look from above the line downwards (see Figure 5.18). There should be a slight gap between the line and the face of the brick. This gap should be about the thickness of a trowel and should be even along the length of the brick.

1   Correct
2   Too high – tap down to line
3   Too low – take off and re-bed
4   Tilting one end high – tap down highest end
5   Tilting one end low – take off and re-bed
6   Tilting one end high and one end low – take off and re-bed

Figure 5.17 Bricks laid to a string line

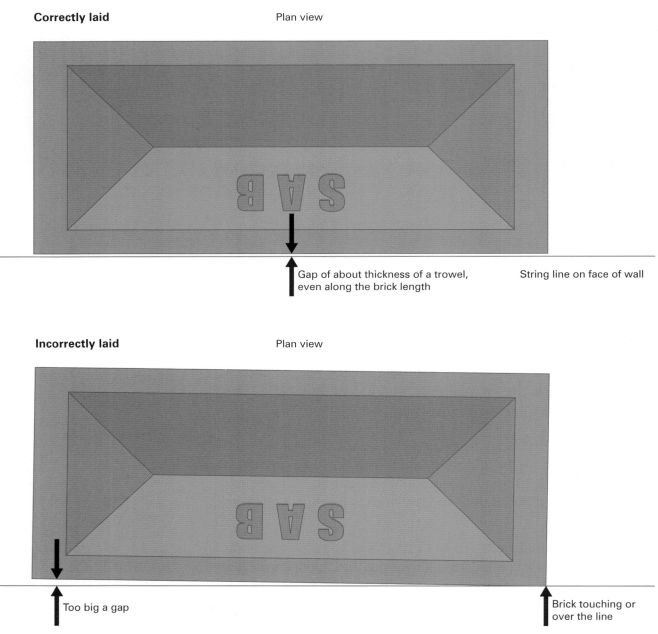

Correctly laid   Plan view

Gap of about thickness of a trowel, even along the brick length

String line on face of wall

Incorrectly laid   Plan view

Too big a gap

Brick touching or over the line

Figure 5.18 Plan view of line

It is important that the brick should not touch the line at any time as this can cause the line to be pushed outwards, resulting in the wall becoming 'curved'. It will also be a nuisance to any other bricklayer who is using the same line.

Unit 1015 How to carry out basic bricklaying skills

Correct use of hand tools and equipment

Many of the hand tools and equipment you will use for bricklaying are identical to those you used for blocklaying. The following tools will be familiar from blockwork.

Trowels, hammers and chisels

Brick trowel

This is used to take the mortar off the mortar board and lay it on the wall, spreading it to form a uniform bed joint ready for bricks. It is made from solid carbon steel and available for left- and right-handed people.

Figure 5.19 Brick trowel

Pointing trowel

This is used for filling in joints and pointing certain types of joint. They are available in different sizes and need cleaning like the brick trowel.

Figure 5.20 Pointing trowel

Club or lump hammer

A club or lump hammer is a heavy hammer used with a bolster chisel to cut bricks by hand. It is also used for knocking holes in walls and removing joints using a plugging chisel. Made in forged steel it comes in a number of different weights.

Figure 5.21 Club or lump hammer

Bolster chisel

This is used mainly for cutting bricks or blocks to the correct size and shape. It is made from hardened tempered steel in blade sizes from 64 mm to 100 mm.

Figure 5.22 Bolster chisels

Tape measure

Tape measures come in many sizes, usually up to 10–30 m. They are made with plastic or steel cases with a steel measure.

Figure 5.23 Steel tape measure

Spirit levels

Spirit levels are made from aluminium and available in various sizes from 225 mm to 1200 mm. They are used for levelling things horizontally and for plumbing vertically. Some levels have an adjustable bubble at the bottom for levelling angled work.

Other tools used in brickwork

Brick hammer

Brick hammers are used for rough cutting and shaping of bricks and are made from forged steel with a hickory handle. The brick should be held stable, with the hammer held in the appropriate hand. With the square edge of the hammer you tap the brick at the position where you require the cut.

Lines and pins

Lines and pins are used for laying bricks and blocks, once the corners have been erected to ensure that work is in a straight line. This ensures that the bricks that are to be laid run in a straight line.

Using line pins

The line should be wound onto the blade of the pin so that the line is on top of the pin, pointing towards the wall.

Figure 5.24 Spirit level

Figure 5.25 Brick hammer

Figure 5.26 Brick line and line pins

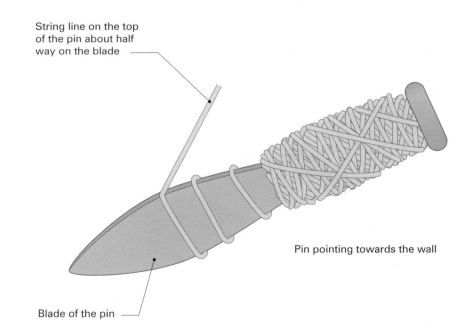

String line on the top of the pin about half way on the blade

Pin pointing towards the wall

Blade of the pin

Figure 5.27 Pin

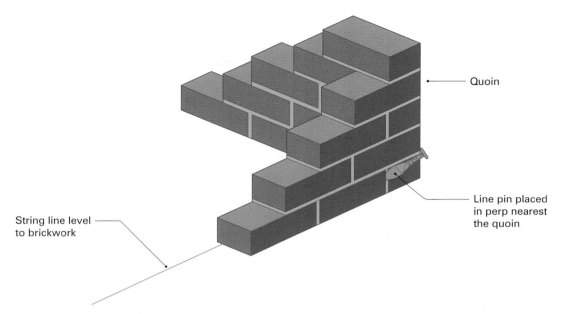

Quoin

Line pin placed in perp nearest the quoin

String line level to brickwork

Figure 5.28 Perp joint nearest the internal corner

The blade is then placed into the perp joint nearest the **quoin**. The pin should be angled slightly downward with the line level to the top of the pre-laid brick.

Corner blocks

Corner blocks are used to attach the line to keep the brickwork straight. They are made from wood, plastic or steel and fit onto the corners of the brickwork with the lines pulled tight to hold them in place. They are then raised to complete each course as it progresses.

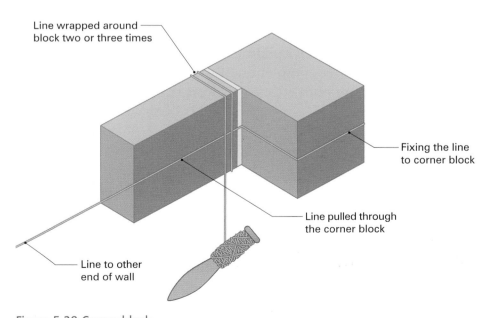

Line wrapped around block two or three times

Fixing the line to corner block

Line pulled through the corner block

Line to other end of wall

Figure 5.29 Corner block

> **Key term**
>
> **Quoin** – the corner of a wall

> **Remember**
>
> Be careful not to over-tighten as the line can break or the corner blocks could be pulled out of plumb

> **Remember**
>
> Corner blocks can only be used on external corners

> **Remember**
>
> In Scotland, a right angled quoin is also known as a right angled corner

To avoid the 'pin-holes' left in the quoin, the line could be fixed in place using corner blocks. The blocks can be made of wood, plastic or metal (see Figure 5.29). The line is pulled through the corner block and attached to screws or tied.

The corner block is placed onto one quoin with the line pulled tight at all times. The other corner block is then fixed to the line about a quarter brick short of the quoin, depending on the length of the wall to be built – sometimes it may require more. The block is then pulled and fixed to the second quoin. Both blocks are adjusted so that the line is level with the course of bricks to be laid.

Tingle plate

When building very long courses of brickwork, the line may sag even when pulled tight. If this was not corrected the courses of bricks would dip in the middle. To hold the line up in the middle of the wall a tingle plate is used. A tingle plate is a flat piece of steel with three prongs, and the line is fed under the ends and over the middle prong so that the line stays at the bottom.

The tingle plate is placed on top of a previously lined, levelled and gauged brick at the centre of the wall. A brick is then placed on top of the plate to hold it secure, and the course is then laid to the line in the normal way.

Corner profiles

Corner profiles are used to save time, as there is no need to build corners. They are secured to existing brickwork at the bottom and are adjustable so as to allow for making plumb. They are made of right-angled steel and the bricks sit hard against the internal corner of the profile when building. If set up correctly, once they are removed after completion of the brickwork, the corner should be plumb on both edges, which should be more accurate

Remember

A tingle plate is worth having in your kit. It could stop work from having to be rebuilt due to the wall sagging in the middle

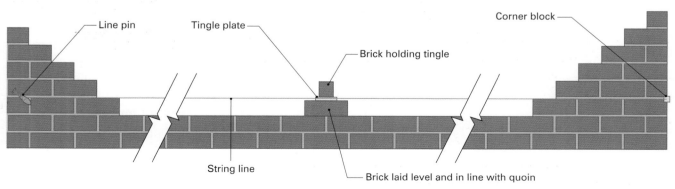

Figure 5.30 Tingle plate on the line

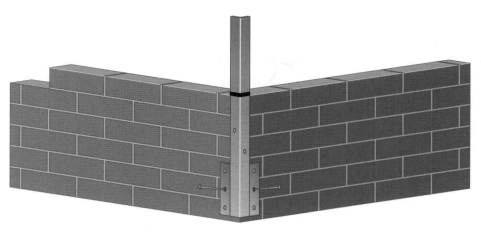

Figure 5.31 A corner profile

than hand-built corners using the conventional method. Profiles can be set on each corner. They can then be marked for correct gauge and lines pulled from corner to corner. This speeds up the building process.

Working life

Ray is building a brick wall 10 m long. He is using his line and the wall looks nice and straight. When he steps back and looks, there is a sag in the middle.

- Why has this happened?
  Ray will need to check that he has used all the possible equipment for building a level wall.
- How can Ray correct this?
  Ray will need to make sure that this line is straight before he continues constructing the wall.
- What would be the effect on the finished wall if Ray did not check the line?
  If Ray did not check his work at regular intervals, he could find that he has a time-consuming job putting everything right at the end.

Functional skills

If you have made mistakes in your work, you will be practising the skill of problem solving while you work out what went wrong. To correct a mistake in building a wall you will need to check any instructions. Here you will be practising the following functional skill:

FE 1.2.1 – 1.2.3 – Reading and understanding information including different texts and taking appropriate action, e.g. responding to advice/instructions.

Maintaining industrial standards

As with blockwork, industrial standards cover the standards and tolerances allowed on site for the plumbness, level and finish of a wall. They also cover if the wall is to gauge, if the joints run true and plumb as well as the cleanliness of the wall.

The standards that the project has to meet are usually set out in the specification or the bill of quantities on site. As well as checking all the measurement requirements throughout the building stages, experience and a good eye will also help you to tell whether a job looks right or not.

> **Remember**
>
> Bricks are lighter than blocks so you will need to be aware of this difference in weight. However, the danger of movement remains the same

If there are no specifications for the work, an experienced bricklayer should know that whatever he or she builds needs to be level and plumb with a good appearance. If nothing else, these serve as a good advert for bricklaying skills and help get future work.

Reasons for carrying out checks

As with blockwork, you should periodically carry out checks to ensure that the wall is straight, plumb and level. Slight knocks or the movement of a corner can move the wall out of plumb. Make sure that bricks are kept dry to avoid moisture not soaking in.

Brick and one-brick walling

The skills and techniques covered are the key resources that you will use for all parts of wall construction. However, there are several different types of wall and construction that you will need to work on, which have different construction requirements.

K3. Building return corners in half-brick stretcher bond

A return corner is formed when the two walls that make up the corner are joined using only full bricks. This makes the walls tightly bonded together.

On return corners, rather than having a half bat to start the second course, a full brick is used in its place to continue the half bond. This is shown in Figure 5.32.

You will need to use corner profiles in order to correctly set out corners.

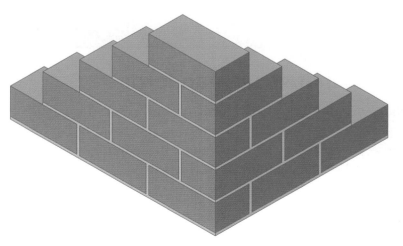

Figure 5.32 Return corner

K4. Building straight walls in one-brick walling

One-brick walls are 215 mm thick and enable bricklayers to place headers across the wall. This makes it possible to create several different types of bond. This type of wall is used where more strength is required, for example, fire walls, garden walls, inspection chambers, areas where steelwork has to sit and for sound proofing. The four main bonds used here are:

- English bond
- Flemish bond
- English garden wall bond
- Flemish garden wall bond.

With these bonds, the bricks lap the course below by a quarter brick. A queen closer should always be used at the corner (quoin) next to the header.

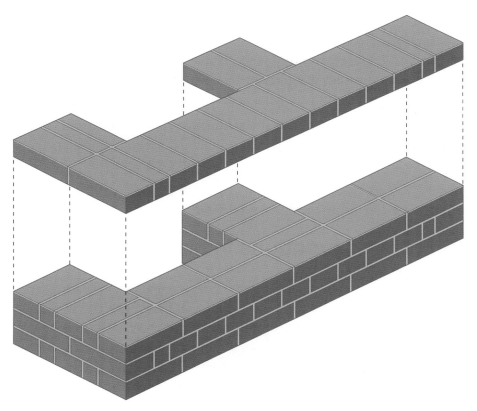

Figure 5.33 One-brick wall

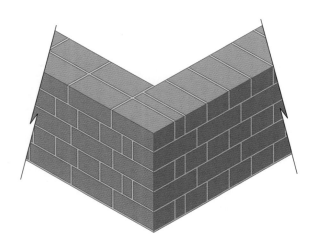

Figure 5.34 Return in English bond

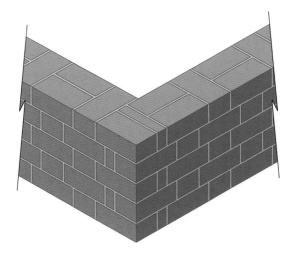

Figure 5.35 Return in Flemish bond

K5. Building return corners in one-brick walling

The different types of bonds used in one-brick wall construction may determine the return bond on a course. For example, if English bond is used the opposite course will be on the returned wall. So, for example, if the main face wall is started with stretcher bricks the return would be headers and vice versa.

In the case of Flemish bond, the main face should start with a full brick and on the return side will be header, queen closure and then stretcher. Again this will alternate for each course.

Information on using English and Flemish garden wall bonds can be found earlier in this unit on pages 162–163.

K6. Forming junctions in brick and block walling

A junction is a position where another wall joins into the main wall at a given point. This could be as a boundary wall, joining two properties at the end of a garden or the separation of two gardens. It could also be an internal wall that divides the rooms in a house. In all these examples, the point where the walls meet is called the junction.

The junction can be built at the same time as the main wall. However, in some instances this may be built at later date for ease of work. This is so that only one wall is being worked on at any given any time.

Figure 5.36 The end of a wall with bricks left out on alternate course for a new wall to be built in

Figure 5.37 A wall with a hole left for a junction

Figure 5.38 Reinforcing mesh

It may also be because the wall is quite high and scaffolding is being used that is in the way of the place where the junction wall will be built. In these circumstances, **indents** will be left in alternate courses to tie the two walls together.

The indents left must be the size of the return wall, plus a joint each side.

For a one-brick wall they must be at least a quarter of the thickness of the main wall to allow for bonding. For a half-brick wall or block wall they must be full width.

If indents are used all joints must be well filled when joining. This is because this point of the wall will be weaker than in walls where the junction section was constructed at the same time as the rest of the wall. In most instances reinforcing mesh should be used to stop any movement that might otherwise take place.

Key term

Indents – holes left in a wall to join another wall to it

Remember

- The indents must be kept plumb, because when building the return wall, this could lean as the join area is not upright
- Always check when using indents that you are working within the acceptable practice for the site

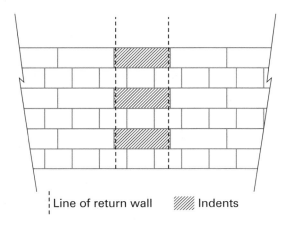

⋮ Line of return wall   ▨ Indents

Figure 5.39 Indents in a brick wall

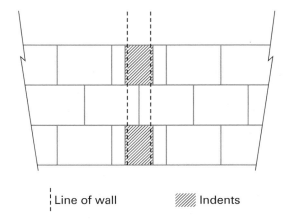

⋮ Line of wall   ▨ Indents

Figure 5.40 Indents in a block wall

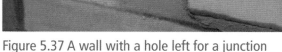

FAQ

What is the most commonly used bond for one-brick walls?

English bond is used most often when constructing a one-brick wall, as this type of bond is the strongest.

Why are bricks laid frog up? Why can't I lay them frog down?

A frogged brick is one that has an indent or 'depression'. Laying frogged bricks downwards means that the frog is then filled with mortar. If laid frog down, the frog cannot be fully filled. Therefore the strength of the wall will be reduced.

Why should you not stretch the line from the corner block too tight? Surely it should be as tight as possible so that the wall is straight?

If you over-tighten the line it could break, or the corner blocks could be pulled out of plumb. Either way you will end up damaging the wall rather than improving it.

Check it out

1. Describe what a tingle plate is used for and the best way of using it. Use diagrams to help explain.
2. Draw a sketch of English bond. Where might you use this type of bond? What benefits does it have over other bonds?
3. A drainage pipe is to run through the wall that you are building. Explain what is needed to let this happen and why. Use diagrams to help explain your answer.
4. Explain why mortar is used when building walls. What would happen if you didn't use mortar?
5. Draw a sketch of a corner block and explain where it is used and why.
6. Name the bond used mainly on half-brick walls and draw a sketch of a typical corner in this type of walling.
7. Explain why it is important to dry bond a wall.
8. Explain why plasticiser is used in mortar.
9. State three scales used on workshop drawings. Complete a sketch of a floor plan using one of these three scales.

Getting ready for assessment

At the end of studying this unit you will need to carry out a synoptic test on brickwork. To prepare for this you will need to use both the information contained in this unit and your practical experience. You should be given the opportunity to gain this and practise these skills by your college or training centre. These should provide you with the opportunity to practise and prepare for this test.

You will need to be familiar with:

- identifying and calculating the materials and equipment required
- setting up your area
- how to set out half- and one-brick walls and the different bonds used for these walls
- how to set out, level, gauge and plumb bricks for straight walls, junctions and return corners
- cutting bricks to given size.

This unit has introduced the facts that help you to make decisions in your practical work. In your synoptic test you will need to use the knowledge you have gained from this unit to carry out the practical task.

For learning outcome 6 you have learnt why it is important to position bricks, mortar and components in a safe manner. This knowledge will be very important for you to prepare for any practical task, whether on the test or in the working environment. Remember that there are serious health and safety considerations when moving bricks. We looked at manual handling earlier in the book on pages 31–33, and you will need to follow this to make sure that you are working safely.

This unit has looked at cutting blocks and preparing straight block walls. This gives you the information that you need in order to carry out the work yourself. Remember that following the methods you have learnt about in this unit will help to make your work accurate and complete.

A big part of all practical work is checking that your completed work is accurate and correct. Use the knowledge you have gained from this unit to make sure that what you have constructed is secure, safe and fit for purpose.

You will know that junctions are formed where two walls meet and that indents are left in the wall to allow another wall to be built in. When working on these walls you will need to remember that these indents are weaker points in the wall and need to be well filled. Again, this will affect the work you are doing in any practical.

Before you start work, think of a plan of action, which will tell you the order you need to do things in. You will need to refer back to this at each stage to check that you are not making any mistakes as you work. Your tolerances must be correct on plumbing, gauge and level as you progress with the work. Without checking this, you could make serious mistakes in your construction that will have a big impact on the final build.

Your speed in carrying out these tasks in a practice setting will also help to prepare you for the time set for the test. However, you must never rush the test! Always make sure that you are working safely. Make sure throughout the test that you are wearing appropriate and correct PPE and using tools correctly.

Good luck!

Unit 1015 How to carry out basic bricklaying skills

Knowledge check

1 What is the length of a standard brick?

a) 200 mm

b) 215 mm

c) 225 mm

d) 230 mm

2 What is the end of a brick called?

a) Stretcher

b) Header

c) Bat

d) Closer

3 What is the strongest bond used in one-brick thick walling?

a) Flemish garden wall bond

b) Flemish bond

c) English garden wall bond

d) English bond

4 A brick wall is planned to be 2.4 m long and 1.2 m high and half a brick thick. How many bricks will be needed to construct the wall?

a) 172

b) 173

c) 182

d) 184

5 What is a perp?

a) A tool to finish joints.

b) A vertical joint between two bricks.

c) A noise made by bricks scraping together.

d) A horizontal joint between two bricks.

6 What is the width of a standard brick?

a) 100 mm

b) 102.5 mm

c) 105 mm

d) 110 mm

7 What is a quoin?

a) The edge of a brick.

b) The side of a brick.

c) The width of a brick.

d) The external corner of a wall.

8 What is the length of a brick called?

a) Header

b) Closer

c) Bat

d) Stretcher

9 If a wall is 1 m high, 3 m long and 1 brick thick, how many bricks will be needed to build it?

a) 360

b) 260

c) 250

d) 350

10 What is the name of the document that explains the types of material you will use on a particular job?

a) Method statement

b) Risk assessment

c) COSHH data sheet

d) Specification

UNIT 1016

How to carry out basic cavity walling

Cavity walls are mainly used for house building and extension work to existing homes and flats. They consist of two separate walls built with a cavity between, joined together by metal ties. In most cases the outer wall is made of brick with the inner skin made of block.

The main reason for this type of construction is to protect the inside from water penetration, caused by rain and other weather elements. This unit also supports NVQ Unit VR 39 Joint Brick and Block Structures.

This unit contains material that supports TAP Unit 2: Set Out for Masonry Structures and Unit 3: Erect Masonry Structures. It also contains material that supports the delivery of the five generic units.

This unit will cover the following learning outcomes:

- Selecting the required quantity and quality of resources to construct cavity walling and form joint finishes

- Constructing cavity walling straight lengths and forming joint finishes

- Constructing cavity walling return corners and forming joint finishes.

Functional skills

While working through this unit, you will be practising the functional skills FE 1.2.1 – 1.2.3. These relate to reading and understanding information.

Safety tip

Always make sure that you understand the potential hazards of a task before you begin it. With this knowledge you can ensure that you have all the PPE you need to carry out the task safely and without putting yourself at risk

Remember

You will need to make sure that the PPE you are using is up to date and correctly maintained. See page 63 for advice on how to complete checks on PPE and maintain it in a good condition

Remember

You will need several tools for erecting cavity walling. These are similar to the tools for bricklaying, which are covered on pages 169–173

K1. Selecting the required quantity and quality of resources to construct cavity walling and form joint finishes

What is cavity walling?

Cavity walls are used for house building and extension work to existing homes and flats. They are made from two separate walls built with a cavity – or space – between them. These walls are then joined together by metal ties (for more about wall ties, see pages 185–186). Usually the outer wall is brick and the inner is made from block.

The main reason for this type of construction is to protect the inside from water penetration. The cavity forms a barrier: as the outer wall becomes wet, due to the weather and elements, water does not pass through because the two walls do not touch. Air circulating around the cavity dries the dampness caused, and also keeps the inner wall dry. In positions that the walls do meet, for example at door and window openings, a damp proof course is used to stop water penetration. The cavity can be insulated either partially or fully to make the building warmer and energy-efficient.

Resources for erecting cavity walling

PPE for cavity walling

Protective personal equipment (PPE) is covered on pages 63–66. However, there is never a complete list of all the PPE you could use for walling, as each job is different. Some jobs involve tasks that will need you to be safe for working at height. Others will need you to be safe when working in excavations. The basic PPE you will always need is:

- hard hat
- boots
- high visibility jacket
- gloves
- goggles.

Bricks and blocks

The mains resources needed for walling are of course bricks and blocks. Bricks and blocks are available in several different types. The type you will need to use depends on the job that will be carried out.

There are several factors that you need to take into account when working on bricks. These are known as working characteristics. The main working characteristics that are likely to be important on most constructions are:

- insulation
- **solar gain**
- resistance to moisture
- resistance to fire.

Most bricks and blocks have good fire resistance and provide thermal insulation, which is particularly important for cavity walling. Some bricks are also designed to provide good resistance of moisture. Particular qualities of certain bricks are described below.

Bricks are often identified by the manufacturer's name, which could be taken from:

- their place of origin: Swanage, Ashdown, Tonbridge
- colour: red, buff, blue, multi-coloured
- method of manufacture: **pressed**, **wire-cut**, **handmade**
- surface texture: rustic, smooth, dragface.

Brick types

Clay bricks

The most common type of brick is the clay brick. These are usually pressed, cut or moulded and then fired in a kiln at a very high temperature. Their density, strength, colour and surface texture depends on the variety of clay used and the temperature of the kiln during firing. There are three main types of clay brick.

- **Engineering bricks** – these have a high **compressive strength** and low water absorption rate. They are rated either as class A or B, with A being the stronger. Class B bricks are sometimes known as semi-engineering bricks. Engineering bricks are ideal for use below ground level and for damp proof courses (DPCs). They are ideal for structures that will carry heavy loads, bridge abutments and lining chimney shafts. As well as clay, they can also be made from calcium silicate and concrete.
- **Facing bricks** – these are literally the bricks that 'face' the person looking at the building. They are designed to be used externally to provide an attractive appearance. They come in a huge range of colours and sizes and have a finished surface that is either sanded, smoothed or textured.
- **Common bricks** – these have lower compressive strength and are lower quality than engineering or facing bricks. They are not decorative as no attempt is made to control their colour or appearance. They should only be used for internal brickwork.

Key term

Solar gain –the increase in temperature of an object or structure from being exposed to the sun. The amount of solar gain increases with the strength of the sun

Find out

Here are some example names that describe bricks: Nottingham red rustic, Stratford sandfaced brindle, Tonbridge handmade grey. Use the Internet to find out some names of other types of brick

Key terms

Pressed – regular in shape, arrises with a frog in the top

Wire-cut – no frog, sharp arrises, wire cut marks on top and bottom

Handmade – irregular in shape with shallow frog

Remember

For information about storage of bricks, see pages 37–38

Key term

Compressive strength – the ability to withstand heavy pressure or weight load without movement or crush problems

Find out

There are several different types of design and quality of clay bricks available – use the Internet to research this by looking at the websites of leading manufacturers

Other types of brick

Some other types of brick that you will encounter are listed below:

- **Concrete bricks** – these are similar to blocks and are available in several colours and patterns. These bricks deaden exterior noise and provide good fire protection and thermal insulation. They are made from a mixture of Portland cement and aggregate of sand or crushed rock, with a colouring agent if required. They are made by thumping, vibrating or pressing, and will develop their strength naturally, or by steam curing.
- **Sand lime bricks** – these are decorative bricks sometimes used in place of facing bricks. They are made from sand and lime or crushed flint and lime, pressed into shape and steamed at a high temperature in an autoclave. Pigments may be added during the manufacturing process to achieve a range of colours.

Types of block

There are two main types of block that you will use:

- **Lightweight insulation blocks** – these should be used above DPC, and provide good insulation qualities. This is particularly important for cavity walls.
- **Dense concrete blocks** – these should be used up to DPC.

Other resources needed for cavity walling

The main resources you will need for cavity walling are given below – many of these resources have been covered earlier in the book.

Damp proof course

This is used to prevent the penetration of damp. For more information about this, see page 120.

Lintels

These are placed above openings in brick and block walls to bridge the opening and support the brickwork and blockwork above. Lintels made from concrete have a steel reinforcement placed near the bottom for strength. For more information about lintels, see page 124.

Cavity frames linings

Frames and linings are fitted around openings and are used to allow components such as windows and doors to be fitted. The frame or lining is fitted to the wall and usually finished flush with

> **Safety tip**
>
> Blocks have the same storage and potential hazards as bricks – make sure you are storing them safely and correctly (see page 38), as well as using them correctly

the wall; the joint between the frame or lining and the wall is covered by an **architrave**.

Cavity tray

This is a moisture barrier placed above a window or a door opening. It is designed to force any moisture to flow away from the inner wall to the outer facing brick. This keeps the moisture out rather than allowing it into the building.

A cavity tray is two bricks long and has interlocking edges for the next section. A flapped back edge adjusts to the internal wall. The bricks are bedded into the wall, and the curve downwards of the tray pushes any moisture out and away from the interior of the house.

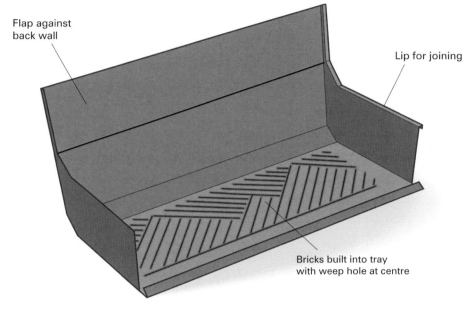

Flap against back wall

Lip for joining

Bricks built into tray with weep hole at centre

Figure 6.1 A cavity tray

Wall ties

Wall ties are a very important part of a cavity wall as they link the internal and external walls together, resulting in a stronger job. If we built cavity walls to any great height without connecting them together, the walls would be very unstable and could possibly collapse.

A wall tie should be:

- rust-proof
- rot-proof
- of sufficient strength
- able to resist moisture.

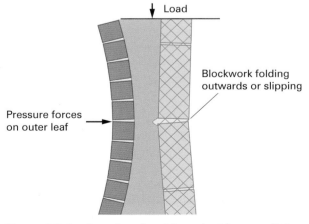

Load

Blockwork folding outwards or slipping

Pressure forces on outer leaf

Figure 6.2 Section of walls with and without wall ties

Figure 6.3 General purpose wall tie

There are many designs of wall tie currently on the market, with a wide selection suitable for different types of construction methods. One of the most common types used when tying together brick and block leaves is the general purpose masonry tie (Figure 6.3). These ties are made from very strong stainless steel, and incorporate a twist in the steel at the mid point of the length. This twist forms a drip system, which prevents the passage of water from the outer to the inner leaf of the structure.

Checks on materials

There are several key checks that you need to carry out on materials to make sure that they are ready to use. The key facts to remember when using materials are:

- The specification – this will tell you exactly what is needed for the job and to what quality. This document should always be your first reference point when ordering materials.
- Any defects to the materials – do not use materials that have been damaged; for example, do not use bricks that have been cracked or chipped, as these will not be of a reliable strength for the wall.
- Are the materials correctly maintained – materials need to be protected to make sure that they remain free of defects and of a high quality.

Remember

Correct storage of materials is a vital part of good housekeeping

How to construct cavity walls

Cavity walls mainly consist of a brick outer skin and a blockwork inner skin. There are instances where the outer skin may be made of block and then rendered or covered by tile hanging. The minimum cavity size now allowed is 100 mm, but the cavity size is usually governed by:

- the type and thickness of insulation to be used
- whether the cavity is to be fully filled or partially filled with insulation.

The thickness of blocks used will also govern the overall size of the cavity wall.

In all cases, the cavity size will be set out to the drawing with overall measurements specified by the architect and to local authority requirements.

Did you know?

On older properties, the internal blocks were always of 100 mm thickness. Nowadays, due to the emphasis on energy conservation and efficiency, blocks are more likely to be 125 mm or more

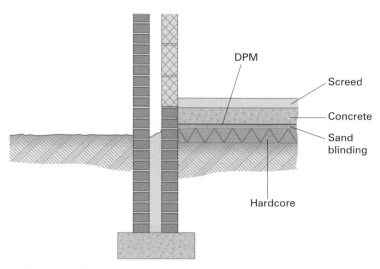

Figure 6.4 Section of footings

DPM

Screed

Concrete

Sand
blinding

Hardcore

Once the **foundations** have been concreted, the **footings** can be constructed. This is done usually by using bricks for both walls (see Figure 6.4).

In some situations trench blocks may be used below ground level and then traditional cavity work constructed up to the DPC. A horizontal DPC must be inserted at a minimum height of 150 mm above ground level to both walls. This is to prevent damp rising, from below ground, up through the blockwork and brickwork to penetrate to the inside.

The cavity must also be filled with weak concrete to ground level to help the footing resist the pressure of the soil against the external wall and oversite fill material.

K2. Constructing cavity walling straight lengths and forming joint finishes

Setting out, and tools and equipment

Setting out

Setting out refers to the marking out and positioning of a building. Setting out indicates exactly where the building will be constructed and mistakes made at this stage can be very costly.

Your supervisor will explain the correct method of setting out the job with you. Setting out is covered in more depth in pages 139–141. You will need to use the drawings and measurements given to you by your supervisor.

Key terms

Foundations – concrete bases supporting walls

Footings – brickwork between the foundation concrete and the horizontal DPC

Remember

The correct size of block must be used for the internal wall, with the cavity size to suit

Positioning materials

To begin construction work you should first position the components you will need to work with on the construction site. After working out the materials you require, you will have to stack them in the area where you are working.

Each site will have different rules for arranging materials, either placing them nearby or keeping them in a holding compound until needed. There may be written instructions for storing and placing materials or you may be given verbal instructions by a site manager.

In either case it is important to check any information you find confusing, and to confirm that you have understood how materials are to be placed. This is because:

- decisions on material placement will affect everyone on site, as everyone will need to know how to access them
- placing materials in the wrong place could lead to health and safety issues.

Preparing components

Bricks and blocks will both need to be cut and prepared for individual walls. The main methods for carrying out this cutting is covered on pages 143–146 for blocks and pages 158–159 for bricks. Refer back to these sections to remind yourself of the different ways of cutting by both hand and machine.

Datum heights

Site datum points are reference points on site to which all levels can be related. One is usually positioned at a convenient height, such as finished floor level (FFL). For more information on datum points, see pages 116–118.

Erecting basic cavity walling

The older, traditional way to build a cavity wall is to build the brickwork first and then the blockwork. Nowadays, due to the introduction of insulation into the cavity, the blockwork is generally built first, especially when the cavity is partially filled with insulation. This is because the insulation requires holding in place against the internal block wall, by means of special clips that are attached to the wall ties.

In most cases the clips are made of plastic as they do not rust or rot. The reason for clipping the insulation is to stop it from moving away from the blocks, which would cause a loss of warmth

Safety tip

Remember to always wear the correct PPE for cutting components, in addition to the normal PPE you wear on site. Machine cutting can only be carried out by a qualified person to the interior of the building, as well as causing a possible **bridge** of the cavity, which could cause a damp problem.

The brick courses should be gauged at 75 mm per course but sometimes course sizes may change slightly to accommodate window or door heights. In most instances these positions and measurements are designed to work to the standard gauge size. This will also allow the blockwork to run level at every third course of brick, although the main reason is to accommodate wall tie positioning as shown in diagram on page 199.

Bonds and cavity walling

Most cavity walling will require cut bricks, or broken bond even though architects try to design as much as possible within known brick sizes. Setting the wall out to incorporate windows or doorways may also give enough scope to achieve full bond. However, this is often not possible so many cavity walls used broken bond. For more information on broken bond, see pages 160–161.

Cavity walling uses a range of face bonds. These types of bond, and the reason for using them, are covered on pages 159–163.

Damp proof barriers

Damp proof course

DPC is a layer of non-absorbent material bedded on to a wall to prevent moisture penetrating into a building. There are three main ways that moisture can penetrate into a building:

- rising up from the ground
- through the walls
- moisture running downwards from the top of walls around openings or chimneys.

There are three types of DPC:

- flexible
- semi-rigid
- rigid.

Flexible DPC

Flexible DPC comes in rolls of various widths to suit various requirements. Metal can be used as a DPC (copper and lead) but because of the cost it is mainly used in specialised areas. The most widely used and economic DPC material is polythene. Flexible DPC should always be laid on a thin bed of mortar and lapped by a minimum of 100 mm on a corner or if joining a new roll.

Key term

Bridge – where moisture can be transferred from the outer wall to the inner leaf by material touching both walls

Safety tip

One safety hazard that is often forgotten when working with cavity walling is exposed wall ties. If walls are built too high and wall ties left exposed, it is very easy to catch your head on the wall tie, cutting or injuring yourself in the process

Remember

Broken bond should consist of a minimum of a half bat on one course with two three-quarter bricks on the alternate course

Key term

Tanking – system of continuous damp proofing e.g. floor and walls to stop moisture or water penetration; this is normally carried out using bitumen

Semi-rigid DPC

This type of DPC is normally made from blocks of asphalt melted and spread in coats to form a continuous membrane for **tanking** basements or underground work.

Rigid DPC

Rigid DPC uses solid material such as engineering bricks or slate, which were the traditional materials used. Slate is more expensive to use than other DPC materials and has no flexibility. If movement occurs, the slate could crack, allowing damp to penetrate. Engineering bricks could be used for a garden wall if a DPC was required.

Floors

There are two main types of floor used for most modern-day houses – solid floor construction and suspended concrete flooring.

Solid floor

A solid floor consists of a hardcore base of a porous material with a minimum depth of 150 mm on which a solid concrete slab is laid. The concrete should have a minimum thickness of 100 mm. A thin layer of sand should be laid on top of the hardcore to fill any voids – this is usually called sand 'blinding' – onto which a polythene membrane is laid to stop any dampness rising up through the ground and making the concrete slab (floor) wet.

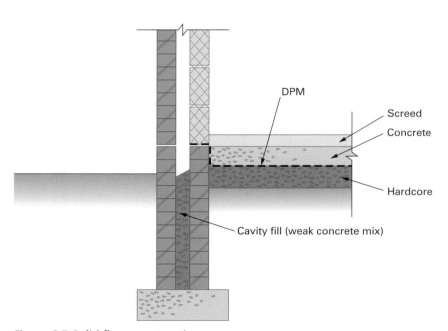

Figure 6.5 Solid floor construction

The membrane should be returned up the wall so as to under the DPC on top of the wall. The slab should finish at the same height as the DPC level, so existing ground should be dug out to provide the correct levels to accommodate the hardcore etc. The floor is normally finished with a 50 mm cement and grit screed.

Suspended concrete floor

A suspended concrete floor consists of reinforced concrete beams that lie on the inner leaf of the blockwork with standard dense concrete blocks laid between to form the floor. There should be a minimum depth of 150 mm between the bottom of the floor and the ground to allow air circulation and to stop damp from rising.

Airbricks must be situated in the outer leaf below DPC level, to allow a free flow of fresh air, and **cavity liners** inserted into the inner leaf connected to the airbricks. A DPC tray must be situated above the liner to prevent damp penetration to the inner leaf, usually caused by dropped mortar being left on top of the liner (see Figure 6.7).

The floor can be finished with a 75 mm reinforced screed, or timber flooring laid on a polythene membrane.

Key terms
Airbricks – bricks with holes to allow air to pass through a wall
Cavity liner – placed behind an airbrick to form an air duct

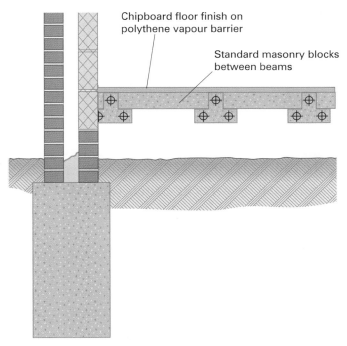

Figure 6.6 Suspended floor construction

Chipboard floor finish on polythene vapour barrier

Standard masonry blocks between beams

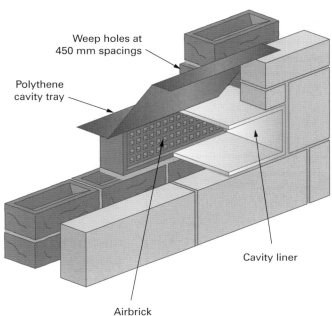

Weep holes at 450 mm spacings

Polythene cavity tray

Cavity liner

Airbrick

Figure 6.7 Airbricks with cavity liner and tray

Functional skills

Choosing the correct method when building will mean you need to understand the specification and the qualities of the materials you are building with. By doing this you will be practising the following functional skills:

FE 1.2.1 – 1.2.3 – Reading and understanding information including different texts and taking appropriate action, e.g. responding to advice/instructions.

FM 1.1.1 – Identifying and selecting mathematical procedures.

FM 1.2.1a – Using appropriate mathematical procedures.

Remember

Simple checks at regular intervals will help to ensure that the work you are doing is correct and to a high standard

Key term

Cavity batten – a timber piece laid in a cavity to prevent mortar droppings falling down the cavity

Remember

Clean up at the end of each day, as the mortar will go hard. Good practice is to lay hessian across the wall ties and remove it at the end of each day to clear any mortar that has dropped down the cavity

Working life

Kevin works for a medium-size construction company on the sheltered housing building section. The work has been completed up to DPC level by groundwork contractors, using a beam and block system. The external brickwork is continuous up to DPC in 105 mm bricks.

- Is this method correct?

Look back at the section on suspended concrete floors and check the diagram.

- Would this method create a stable floor?

Maintaining industrial standards and cleanliness

Each site and company will have slightly different standards, with the specification outlining principles for the materials used on the construction but not the specific standards that the work has to be carried out to. However, all clients will demand that work is of a high quality and fit for purpose. There are also several building regulations and pieces of legislation (see Unit 1001) that you will need to be aware of when you are working on site.

Checking that work is plumb and level at regular intervals, and double checking measurements are very simple jobs that can save you a great deal of time and expense later in the process.

Keeping a cavity wall clean

It is important to keep the cavity clean to prevent dampness. If mortar is allowed to fall to the bottom of the cavity it can build up and allow the damp to cross and enter the building. Mortar can also become lodged on the wall ties and create a bridge for moisture to cross. We can prevent this by the use of **cavity battens**. These are pieces of timber the thickness of the cavity laid onto the wall ties and attached by wires or string (to prevent them dropping down the cavity) to the wall and lifted alternately as the wall progresses.

The bottom of the wall can be kept clean by either leaving bricks out or bedding bricks with sand so they can be taken out to clean the cavity. These are called core holes and are situated every fourth brick along the wall to make it easy to clean out each day. Once the wall is completed the bricks are bedded into place.

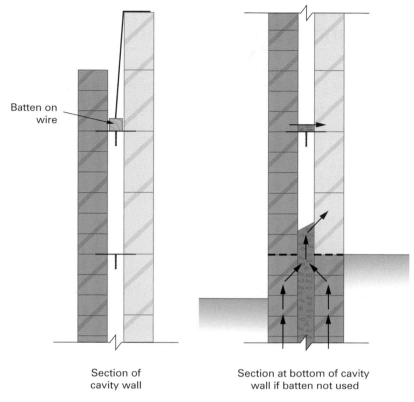

Batten on wire

Section of cavity wall

Section at bottom of cavity wall if batten not used

Figure 6.8 Cavity batten in use

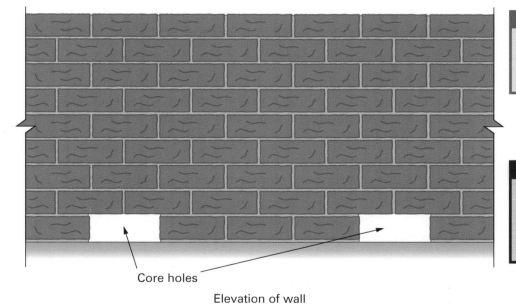

Core holes

Elevation of wall

Figure 6.9 Core holes

Did you know?

Any batten can be used as long as the width is the same as the cavity space

Remember

Bricks bedded on sand and removed for cleaning purposes are referred to as core holes

K3. Constructing cavity walling return corners and forming joint finishes

On most large sites, corner profiles are used rather than building traditional corners (see pages 172–173). These allow the brickwork to be built faster and, if set up correctly, more accurately. But they must be marked accurately for the gauge. It also makes sense to mark window sill heights or **window heads** and door heights so that they do not get missed, which would result in brickwork having to be taken down.

Joint finishes to brickwork

Jointing is carried out to make sure that the mortar joint is completely filled and in contact with each brick. This will prevent rainwater penetration and possible damage by frost, which would crumble the joint. Another reason for jointing is to give the overall appearance of the wall a pleasing look to the eye. Once the jointing is completed, rainwater should run down the surface of the wall and not into any gaps left in joints.

Jointing

On larger sites, before commencement of any brickwork, sample brick panels may be constructed and pointed to show how the finished product will look, giving architectural staff a chance to change the type or colour of pointing required. This is because sometimes coloured mortar may be used for the joints.

One of the most important things to consider is at what time jointing should be carried out. As the brickwork is carried out over the course of the day, lower courses will dry out, but other factors need to be taken into consideration:

- The type of brick used – stock or engineering bricks do not absorb moisture as fast as some softer bricks. Therefore the joints will take longer to dry to the required texture for jointing.
- The moisture content – the bricks may be damp before use. Therefore moisture absorption will be slow.
- The weather – when working in summer the heat will dry out joints faster, due to the warmth of the bricks, than in damper conditions, when moisture stays in the air.

Joints need to be checked by touching to see if they are ready for jointing. If they are too dry it will be difficult to carry out jointing. If they are too wet the joint mortar is inclined to 'drag', giving poor adhesion to the bricks and a poor quality appearance.

This operation has no given time span, so understanding and experience are key to knowing when is the right time.

Pointing

Pointing is the process of joint filling to brickwork when the mortar joints have been previously raked out to approximately 12 mm on work that is fresh and 12–18 mm on older work that has had existing mortar ground out and is to be re-pointed at a later date. This type of work requires more skill and patience than jointing as it is very time-consuming and great care must be taken not to smear the new mortar onto the face of the brick.

There are different types of joint finishes, which we will cover in this unit. Some take longer to carry out than others, hence the cost of pointing varies considerably as some types can take twice as long to complete.

Remember when pointing:

- Always start from the top and work downwards – dropped mortar, or mortar brushed off, can fall onto already completed work.
- Make sure the joints are clean of any loose old mortar.
- Brush the area to be pointed to remove dust.
- Wet the wall so that the bricks absorb the water to give good adhesion for the new mortar. Some bricks will require more water than others.
- Apply the mortar filling to the preps first so as to keep a continuous bed joint when applied.
- When sufficiently dry, brush off with a fine brush to remove any excess particles of mortar.

Raking out

Joints need to be raked to a depth of 12–18 mm. This can be carried out in several ways:

- By using a raking out tool (or chariot) set to the required depth to rake out the joints evenly. This is perfect for very soft joints, but may not be so good for harder or variable joints.
- By using an angle grinder, but great care and expertise are required not to touch and mark the brick faces or damage the arrises of the brick as joint depths can be varied. Dust from the cutting can cause problems if working in a built-up area (dust gets on to people's property).
- Sometimes a combination of the above may be the best solution. Once raking out is complete, pointing can be carried out.

Figure 6.10 Tooled joint

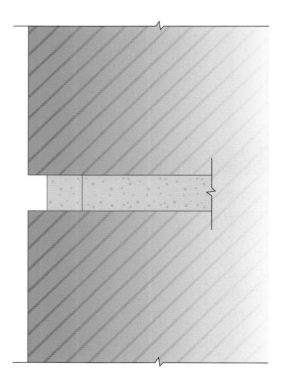

Figure 6.11 Recessed joint

Types of joint finish

Ironed or tooled joint

This type of joint is the most commonly used as it covers up slight impurities in the brick arrises and is the quickest to carry out (Figure 6.10).

There are different sizes, so care should be taken to use the same size each time. Smaller sizes give a deeper profile whereas the larger diameters give a shallower, rounded look. The jointing is carried out as work progresses.

Recessed joint

With this type of joint the mortar is dragged out to a maximum depth of 4 mm and then ironed to compress the joint's surface (Figure 6.11). Great care should be taken to ensure that all of the joint is removed.

A recessed joint is better used when the bricks are of a harder, more frost-resistant type because water can lie on the edge of the recessed arris on the brick. Care must be taken to ensure that all the joints are full before commencing the raking out process. Again, jointing is carried out as the work progresses.

Flush joint

This type of joint gives a simple look but it is quite difficult to keep a flush surface finish (Figure 6.12).

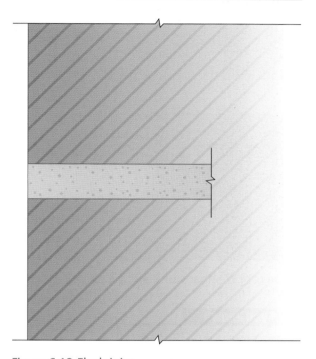

If modern type finishes are not required, it gives a **rustic** look, which may be more in keeping with the surroundings. This type of joint is carried out by using a hardwood timber or plastic block to smooth and compact the surface of the mortar into place.

A flush joint is not ideal if the bricks used are not regular in shape as the joints will show any deviation and could look wider than they are. Jointing is always carried out as work progresses.

> **Key term**
>
> **Rustic** – old and natural looking; traditional

Figure 6.12 Flush joint

Weather struck joint

This type of joint is slightly sloping to allow rainwater to run down the face of the brick rather than lying at the joint (Figure 6.13).

The mortar is smoothed with a trowel, with the mortar the thickness of the trowel below the top brick and flush with the brick below. The same process is carried out with the perps and the left side of the joint is below the surface.

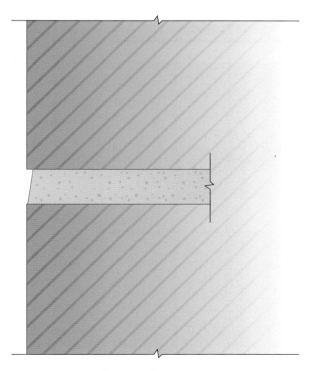

Figure 6.13 Weather struck joint

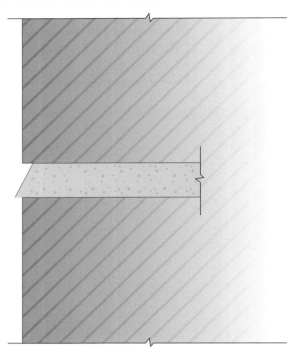

Figure 6.14 Weather struck and cut joint

Did you know?

Sometimes a glue (PVA) can be added to the mortar to give a better adhesion to the brick and help bond to the existing mortar

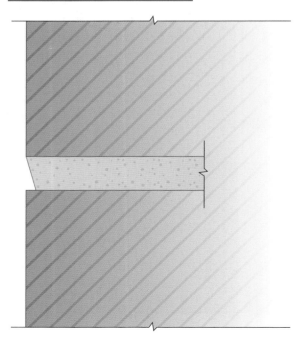

Figure 6.15 Reverse struck joint

Weather struck and cut pointing

This is the most common type of jointing carried out on previously raked joints. It can cover any irregularities in the bricks, creating a straight appearance (Figure 6.14). This type of pointing is the hardest and most time-consuming to do. The mortar is smoothed flush to the brick at the top of the joint and about a trowel thickness proud of the brick at the bottom. The mortar is then allowed to dry slightly and is then 'cut' in a straight line using a tool called a Frenchman.

The straight edge should be kept off the wall using cork pads, nails or screws, so that the cut excess can drop and not be squashed against the face of the wall. Perps are again angled to the left and finished in the same way as the bed joints, but cut with a pointing trowel. All perps should be completed before the bed joint so as not to mark the beds with the trowel and to keep a continuous joint to the bed. This should then be lightly brushed sideways so as not to drag the edges of the bed joints.

Reverse struck joint

This type of finish is normally used for internal walls, giving a smooth finish to work that is not plastered that no shadows appear at the joint area (Figure 6.15). Care must be taken to ensure that the bottom edge is flush to the brick to stop the joint becoming a dust trap when work is completed. The wall would then be given a paint finish.

With all types of pointing, it is essential that the new mortar bonds well to the existing material, otherwise moisture will be trapped between and, with frost, will break the newer material down, resulting in more costly repairs.

Positioning of wall ties

In cavity walling where both the outer and inner leaves are 90 mm or thicker, you should use ties at not less than 2.5 per square metre, with 900 mm maximum horizontal distance by a maximum 450 mm vertical distance.

At positions such as vertical edges of an opening, unreturned or unbonded edges and vertical expansion joints, you need to use additional ties at a maximum of 300 mm in height (usually 225 mm to suit block course height) and located not more than 225 mm from the edge.

You must take care to keep the wall ties clean when they are placed in the wall: if bridging occurs, it may result in moisture penetrating the internal wall.

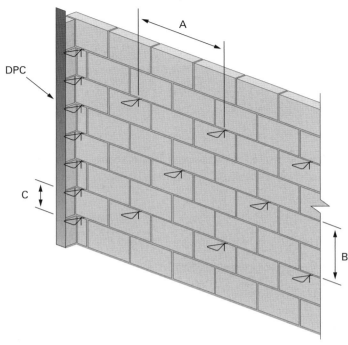

Figure 6.16 Spacing of wall ties

FAQ

How will I know if the materials I have chosen are strong enough to carry the load?

On the specification you will find all the details you need about the sizes and types of material to be used. This will help you to build a wall that will be strong enough to support the weight it is designed to take.

Why do the block courses have to be level to meet the brick courses? Surely it would be stronger if the levels were different?

Wall ties are used to strengthen the wall, not the courses. However, if the courses were at different levels then it would not be possible to insert the wall ties. Without them the wall would be much weaker. So if the levels were different, then the wall would actually be weaker!

Why is insulation placed in cavity walls?

Cavity wall insulation will help to keep warmth inside the building. This will be an effective way to save energy (and therefore money) as it makes it easier to both heat a building and then keep it warm. Cavity wall insulation can also help reduce carbon dioxide emissions, as less energy is being used. This means that it is also good for the environment.

Check it out

1. Explain the process used to make clay bricks.
2. What is the purpose of a wall tie? State three of the design features of a wall tie and explain what they are for.
3. Sketch a section showing foundation work up to DPC. Label this sketch with the key features, explaining what they are for.
4. Describe the key features of common bricks. Where would these bricks be used when constructing walls?
5. Name three types of DPC and give one example of each. What are these different types of DPC used for and when?
6. Sketch a typical section of a suspended floor, and explain how the floor must be constructed and why.
7. State the reason why lintels are used in wall construction. Use a diagram to demonstrate what a lintel does and why it is important.
8. Why are cavity trays used above airbricks? With a written answer, and sketches, show how cavity trays are placed above airbricks and what they help to avoid.
9. Sketch the four different types of joint finish and explain why they are used at different times.
10. Explain the difference between pointing and jointing.

Getting ready for assessment

At the end of studying this unit you will need to carry out a synoptic test on cavity work. To prepare for this you will need to use both the information contained in this unit and your practical experience. You should be given the opportunity to gain this and practise these skills by your college or training centre. These should provide you with the opportunity to practicse and prepare for this test.

You will need to be familiar with:

- identifying and calculating the materials and equipment required
- setting up your area
- how to set out, level, gauge and plumb bricks and blocks
- cutting bricks and blocks to given size.

This unit has introduced the facts that help you to make decisions in your practical work. In your synoptic test you will need to use the knowledge that you have gained from this unit to carry out the practical task.

For learning outcome 2 you have learnt why it is necessary to confirm verbal and written instructions. This skill will be vital not just in the test, but in any work that you may be hired to carry out professionally. You will also need to be able to identify all hazards in your area, including positioning bricks, mortar and components in a safe manner. This knowledge will be crucial for you in any practical task, whether on the test or in the working environment.

The knowledge you have gained on brick and block types, the advantages and disadvantages of each as well as their features will be vital to decide which of these to use on any particular task. For the test, you will need to know the conditions in which the wall will be constructed and the purpose it will be used for, in order to make the correct decision on brick or block type. The same skills will also be used for any wall that you may build later in your career.

You will also need to apply the correct joint finish to the wall, again using your knowledge of the types of joint finish to select the correct one for the purpose of the wall. Information about the purpose of the wall will be found in its specification.

Before you start work, think of a plan of action, which will tell you the order you need to do things in. Your tolerances must be correct on plumbing, gauge and level as you work. Without checking this, you could make serious mistakes in your construction that will have a big impact on the final build. Your speed in carrying out these tasks in a practice setting will also help to prepare you for the time set for the test. However, you must never rush the test! Always make sure that you are working safely. Make sure throughout the test that you are wearing appropriate and correct PPE and using tools correctly.

Good luck!

Unit 1016 How to carry out basic cavity walling

Knowledge check

1 What material could be used as rigid damp proof course?

a) Concrete block
b) Lightweight block
c) Face brick
d) Engineering brick

2 What is left in order to clean out a cavity?

a) Core holes
b) Airbricks
c) Cavity tray
d) Weep holes

3 What is the correct gauge for brickwork course heights?

a) 60 mm
b) 65 mm
c) 75 mm
d) 100 mm

4 How many blocks are there in a square metre of blockwork?

a) 15
b) 12
c) 10
d) 8

5 What are used to stabilise the inner and outer leaves of a cavity wall?

a) Insulation
b) Frames
c) Damp proof course
d) Wall ties

6 How many bricks are there to a square metre in a half-brick wall?

a) 50
b) 60
c) 70
d) 80

7 What material could be used as flexible damp proof coursing?

a) Engineering brick
b) Pitch-polymer
c) Slate
d) Asphalt

8 What is the minimum height that a horizontal damp proof course should be inserted above ground level?

a) 200 mm
b) 150 mm
c) 100 mm
d) 75 mm

9 What is the smallest cut brick that can be used in a broken bond?

a) Closer
b) Half bat
c) Queen closer
d) Three-quarter cut

10 What is meant by the term 'footings'?

a) Brick/block between concrete foundation and damp proof course.
b) Brickwork above a lintel.
c) Blockwork above damp proof course.
d) Blockwork next to a frame.

UNIT 1017

How to contribute to setting out and building masonry structures up to damp course level

Setting out refers to the marking out and positioning of a building. It is a very important operation as the setting out of a building must be as accurate as possible as mistakes can prove very costly later.

This unit will explain the basic rules and methods used when setting out. This unit also supports NVQ Unit VR 38 Contribute to Setting Out Basic Masonry Structures. This unit contains material that supports TAP Unit 2: Set Out for Masonry Structures. It also contains material that supports the delivery of the five generic units.

This unit will cover the following learning outcomes:

■ Interpreting given instructions to establish setting out work to be carried out

■ Selecting required quantity and quality of resources when setting out and building masonry structures

■ Assisting in the setting out and building of masonry structures to working drawings.

K1. Interpreting given instructions to establish setting out work to be carried out

In order to carry out setting out correctly, you need to refresh your knowledge of how to use diagrams, working drawings and project start-up documents. This material has been covered earlier in the book. Please look back at the pages below to refresh your memory:

- For the types of drawings and documents used, and their purpose, see pages 80–85.
- For information on the scales commonly applied to drawings, see pages 75–77.
- Also refer to Unit 1002 for information on the methods of reading and taking measurements from drawings, the range of information sources for interpreting drawings and the methods of reporting inaccuracies in sources.

K2. Selecting required quantity and quality of resources when setting out and building masonry structures

The materials you will need to set out a building

The exact materials you will need to set out a building will depend on the size of the job. The following list would be adequate for, say, a small detached house:

- plans and specifications
- two measuring tapes (30 m), preferably steel
- optical level
- site square (optional)
- 50 mm × 50 mm timber pegs
- 25 mm × 100 mm timber for profiles
- lump hammer
- claw hammer
- hand saw
- a line
- concrete (ballast and cement) to secure pegs (although sometimes unnecessary)
- sand (for marking out trenches)
- 50 mm round head nails
- 75 mm round head nails.

The list is not exhaustive, but should give you some idea of what is required.

Functional skills

While working through this unit, you will be practising the functional skills FE 1.2.1 – 1.2.3. These relate to reading and understanding information.

Resources for transferring levels

Generally speaking most buildings are built level (horizontal) so it makes sense to do the setting out on a level plane. A building is kept level by various methods. See pages 116–118 on the use of datum points and Ordnance Survey bench marks (OBM) in transferring levels.

Figure 7.1 shows the position of the average sea level of the UK (which is the average level of the sea in Newlyn, Cornwall) and this is called 0.000 metres. As explained in Unit 1003, bench marks are positioned countrywide (shown dotted) in relation to this sea level and are often carved in stone walls, churches, government buildings, or sometimes cast in a concrete pedestal as shown in Figure 7.2.

When the Ordnance Survey system is used for reference, the nearest OBM is used and a relative temporary bench mark (TBM), or site datum (see page 116), is positioned on site as shown in Figure 7.3. It can be in the form of a steel or wooden peg set in concrete and is very often protected by a fence.

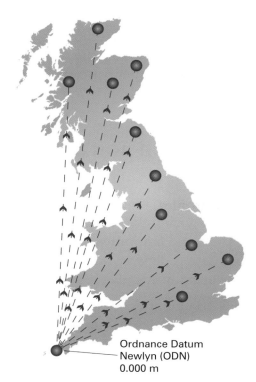

Ordnance Datum
Newlyn (ODN)
0.000 m

Figure 7.1 Ordnance Datum Newlyn (ODN)

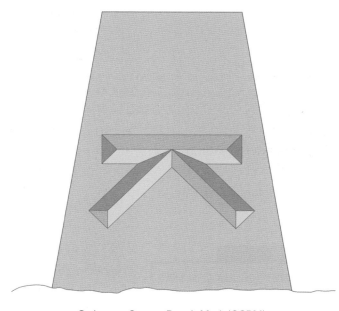

Ordnance Survey Bench Mark (OSBM)

Figure 7.2 Example of a bench mark

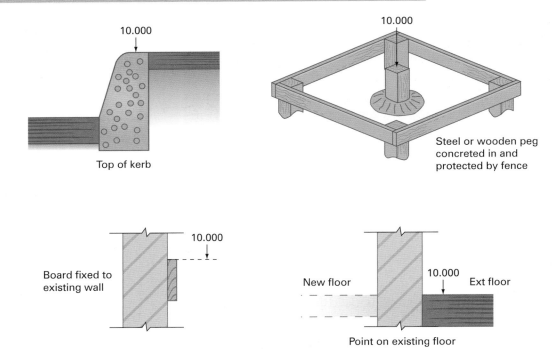

10.000
Top of kerb

10.000
Steel or wooden peg concreted in and protected by fence

10.000
Board fixed to existing wall

New floor   10.000   Ext floor

Point on existing floor

Figure 7.3 Some points that could be used for datums

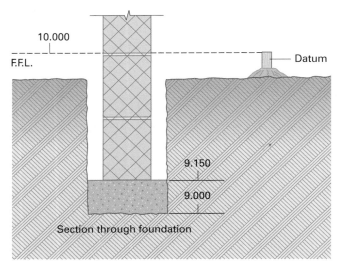

10.000
F.F.L.
Datum

9.150
9.000

Section through foundation

Figure 7.4 Datum with levels

Figure 7.4 shows a datum with an 'assumed' level of 10.000 m. The floor level is 10.000 m so the floor level is the same as the datum. The bottom of the excavation is 9.000 m, so the excavation is 1.000 m below the datum peg. The top of the foundation concrete is 9.150 m, so the thickness of the foundation concrete is 9.150 – 9.000 = 0.150 m.

Site clearance and health and safety

Many things need to be taken into consideration during the stages of setting out, from the tools and equipment required, to the actual foundation digging, whether being dug by hand or using heavy plant equipment.

The area where the structure is to be built could have been **barren** for a long time, and may have become a tipping ground for all kinds of rubbish such as glass, metal objects, even hypodermic needles. Therefore, great care should be taken when clearing the area ready to commence setting out.

When putting pegs into the ground, remember that objects can be buried out of sight such as underground pipes and cables.

Key term

Barren – land not looked after or used, maybe wasteland

Methane gas can also be a problem if the ground has been used previously for material excavation, such as sand or gravel, and then backfilled over the course of time for house construction. Some of these considerations would probably have been checked for at an earlier stage, but you should always be aware and take precautions such as wearing appropriate personal protective equipment (PPE; see pages 63–66).

Working life

Steven is clearing a newly acquired site when he comes across a pipe sticking out of the ground. There is a sort of open top to it.

- What do you think this pipe could be?
- What should Steven do next?
- Who should he tell?

Steven will have to make sure that the pipe is not delivering a service to the building site – damaging the pipe could have serious effects for the site and the neighbourhood.

How should he make the pipe's presence clear? How could he find out what the pipe is for? What impact will the appearance of the pipe have on any work that will be carried out on the site? Steven will need to make sure that the pipe's presence is known about, as well as working out what it is used to supply.

Locating existing services

Before any excavations take place, whether it is digging out foundations or trenches for new drains, etc., a survey of the area must be carried out. This is done to find out whether there are any underground services in the area. These services could be:

- gas pipes
- water pipes
- electricity cables
- telephone cables
- drainage pipes.

If a mechanical digger is carrying out the excavation, then damage to the service can happen extremely quickly. The digger bucket can go through the ground and the service without much effort. This can cause delays to the work due to the time it may take to carry out repairs to the damage, which will add extra cost to the project.

There will also be a great deal of inconvenience to the people in the surrounding area, who may be left with no electricity, gas, water, etc. for a long period of time while the service is being repaired. Service providers can't always send out a repair crew immediately, and this inconvenience may go on for several days.

Functional skills

When carrying out site inspections you may encounter problems with the site. When this happens, it is best to ask for advice on what to do. By doing this you are practising the following functional skills:

FE 1.2.1–1.2.3 – Reading and understanding information including different texts and taking appropriate action, e.g. responding to advice/instructions.

Did you know?

Previous checks would be carried out by ground survey before site commencement

Remember

Causing inconvenience to people will create a bad image for the company you work for. This may have an effect on the future business for the company

Remember

Incorrect measurements could mean digging out finished concrete

Did you know?

The North Point is the arrow on plans and drawings that shows the position of the North Pole, relative to a compass point. This gives the direction to establish the building correctly

Key terms

Building lines – an imaginary line set by the local authority to control the positioning of buildings

Boundary lines – lines that dictate ownership, for example lines between properties

Frontage line – the line of the front of the building

Several scan devices are available on the market that can be used to locate any services. These should also be used to survey the land before any excavation work begins.

K3. Assisting in the setting out and building of masonry structures to working drawings

Procedures for setting out

Setting out a building is an extremely important operation as mistakes at this stage would be very costly to put right later. Great care should be taken on reading the drawings and making sure that the correct measurements are used.

Setting out at the right place

Finding the right place to set out sounds like an obvious thing to state, but it is very important that this is done absolutely correctly. Buildings have sometimes had to be completely demolished for being put up in the wrong place! This is because **building lines** and **boundary lines** are often involved, and there are very strict regulations governing these.

The building line shows exactly where you have permission to set out and construct the building. If you set out the building outside

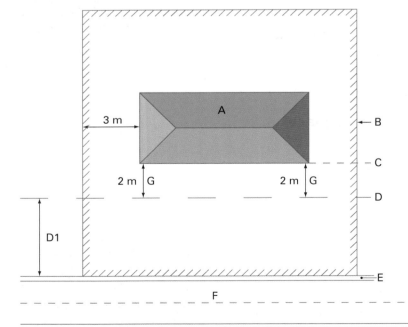

Key

A = Plan of proposed building
B = Boundary of site
C = **Frontage line**
D = Building line
D1 = Distance set by local authority (council)
E = Pavement
F = Road
G = Distance from building line to frontage line

Figure 7.5 Positioning a building in the right place (site plan not to scale)

of this line, you will be placing it an area where you don't have permission, or the right, to construct the building.

Dimensional accuracy

It is most important that a building has square (90°) corners. Therefore, the setting out of a building must be square to avoid construction problems later, for example the roof not fitting!

Site square

A site square is an optical instrument used to set out right angles simply and accurately. It is supported by a tripod. The body of the instrument contains two telescopes that are mounted at 90° to each other. The telescopes also pivot vertically so that various distances can be sighted.

A lock screw is located under the body of the instrument, and a fine adjustment screw enables accurate location of the target. The site square is plumbed by a bubble in a circular levelling device on top of the instrument.

Using a site square

Step 1 – set up datum rod A over corner nail and plumb instrument.

Step 2 – site nail in peg B using lower telescope.

Step 3 – position nail in peg C using upper telescope.

Builder's square

A builder's square is the most commonly used way of setting out a corner if no optical square is available on the site. It is made of timber, is usually made on site, and obviously has to be practical enough to be easily carried and held in place for checking corners.

How to set out a right angle using a builder's square

Step 1 – set out frontage line peg A to peg B.

Step 2 – position square parallel with frontage line C.

Step 3 – adjust line at D to make a right angle at the corner.

Step 4 – when the line is to the side of the square, the corner is square (90°).

The 3:4:5 method

A building can also be set out using the 3:4:5 method, which is a way of forming right angles using **trigonometry**. It may sound tricky, but the 3:4:5 rule is not very difficult to understand.

> **Remember**
>
> The building shown in Figure 7.5 is 3 m from the left-hand boundary and 2 m behind the building line – it is most important that a building is accurately positioned

> **Find out**
>
> Some buildings do not have square corners, as in a circular building or a building on an awkwardly shaped site. Search the Internet for pictures of famous buildings that do not have square corners and those that do

> **Remember**
>
> The manufacturer's instructions will explain in more detail how to use equipment and check for accuracy

> **Key term**
>
> **Trigonometry** – the part of mathematics concerned with triangles and angles

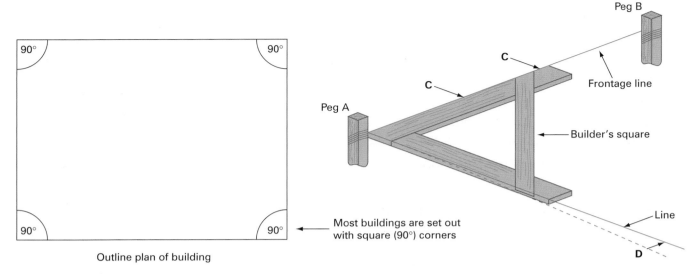

Figure 7.6 Right angle set out with a builder's square

If you take three straight lines, one 3 cm long, one 4 cm long and one 5 cm long, and then join them together to make a triangle, the angle opposite the longest line will always be a right angle.

How to set out a right angle using the 3:4:5 method

Step 1 – set up frontage line from peg A.

Step 2 – position peg B.

Step 3 – set up peg C.

Step 4 – right angle is formed as shown.

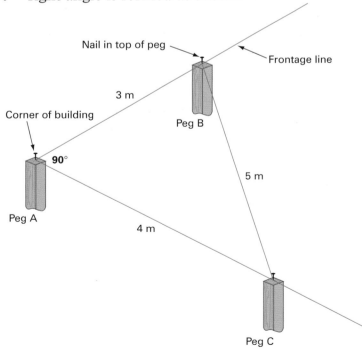

Figure 7.7 Right angle set out using 3:4:5 method

Jack has been asked to recheck a corner to make sure it is at the right angle. He finds out that the optical square and the builder's square are being used at another site.

- Should Jack continue working without these tools?
- Could he check the corner without them?
- What could he use to check the corner instead?

Jack should be confident that the method he is using to check the corner will give him a correct answer.

- Which one would be best for checking the corner?
- Should Jack consider using the tools to check any calculations he makes before digging?
- What problems should Jack keep in mind when using replacement tools?
- Should Jack let anyone know about the fact the tools have been taken to another site?

Jack should make sure that tools are not regularly being removed from the site, as this could have an effect on how the site works.

Functional skills

When taking measurements for corners, you must make sure that you are following the correct method and that your calculations are correct. When you are doing this you will be practising the following functional skills:

FE 1.2.1 – 1.2.3 – Reading and understanding information including different texts and taking appropriate action, e.g. responding to advice/instructions.

FM 1.1.1 – Identifying and selecting mathematical procedures.

FM 1.2.1a – Using appropriate mathematical procedures.

Methods for transferring levels

Transferring levels by spirit level and straight edge

This is a very basic method of transferring a level (see Figure 7.8). Peg B is levelled from peg A (the datum) and then peg C is levelled from peg B. The straight edge and level are rotated 180° at each levelling point to eliminate any error in the level or straight edge.

Remember

A level can go out of true or a straight edge can be bent – check first

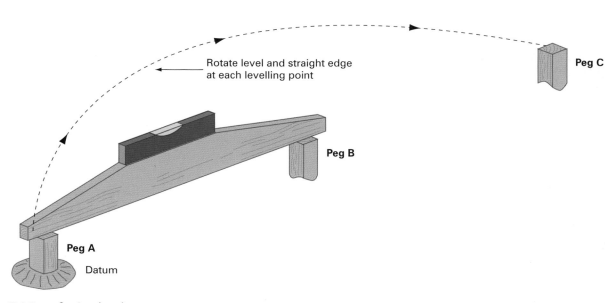

Rotate level and straight edge at each levelling point

Peg C

Peg B

Peg A

Datum

Figure 7.8 Transferring levels

Figure 7.9 An optical level

Optical level

An optical level is a levelling device that comprises a camera, a tripod and a staff or grade rod. The camera swivels on a pin projecting from the top of the tripod. There are many different models currently on the market and their accuracy differs over varying distances. The average optical level is accurate to within 6 mm over a distance of approximately 30–40 m.

Once placed in position on the tripod and adjusted for level, the optical level projects a level line across the distance between the datum peg and the point to which this datum level is to be transferred.

Most common procedure for transferring levels with an optical level

Step 1 – securely position tripod and lower level onto pin.

Step 2 – adjust optical level using the adjustment knobs at the base of the level. Ensure that the bubble is accurately positioned within the vial on the top of the level.

Step 3 – position staff or grade rod on top of the datum peg and adjust focus on optical level until a clear reading can be made.

Step 4 – take reading at the point where the crosshair of the viewfinder crosses the staff or grade rod.

Step 5 – get a second person to move staff to new location to where level is to be transferred. This location is identified by a peg driven into the ground and slightly extended in height to that of the original datum peg.

Remember

The tripod should not be disturbed during levelling. To avoid internal damage to the camera, never carry the level while it is on the tripod

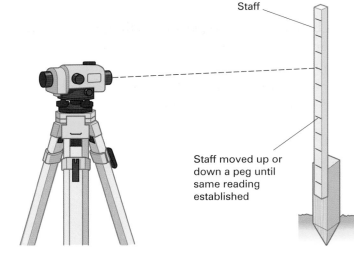

Initial reading taken with staff positioned on top of datum peg

Datum peg

Staff

Staff moved up or down a peg until same reading established

Figure 7.10 Transferring level line using an optical level

Step 6 – second person holds staff or grade rod against the peg, with its markings or gradings facing the optical level.

Step 7 – second person moves staff up or down on the instructions of the person using the optical level, until the same reading is established.

Step 8 – second person marks base of the staff or grade rod on the peg.

Step 9 – a timber rail can be fixed at this point to maintain the mark. The top of the timber rail will be lined across this mark to show the height of the transferred datum level.

Transit level

Transit levels are also used for the purpose of transferring levels. They can also provide vertical plumb lines and checking verticals for plumb.

Laser level

Laser levels are the latest technology in construction, taking over from the Cowley and dumpy levels. They are very accurate and easy to set up. The level is fixed to a tripod. Press the button and it automatically finds level, shooting a red dot that can be picked up on the staff giving the reading.

Laser levels can be used for all types of levelling throughout the course of the work, from setting foundations and floor heights, to suspended ceiling levels or even putting in straight plumbing pipework. Some are accurate up to 100 m and, if the level is knocked, it gives notification of movement.

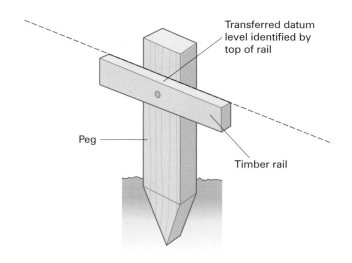

Figure 7.11 Timber rail in position

Figure 7.12 A transit level

Figure 7.13 Laser level

Step-by-step guide to setting out a building

Here are a few golden rules you should always observe during the setting out process:

1. Make sure you know where the building line and boundaries are.
2. Check your equipment before commencing.
3. Establish a datum where it will not be disturbed.
4. Always use measurements given and avoid scaling.
5. Set out a base line (for example, front of a house). Make sure that you do not infringe on or over the building line.
6. Be aware of any underground pipes, etc.
7. Check the drawings for errors.
8. Take all measurements with care and accuracy.
9. Check and double check setting out after completion.

Step 1 – Establish frontage line

1. Peg A to Peg B.
2. Nails indicate corners of building.
3. Pegs reasonably level with each other.
4. Pegs must be secure and not move.

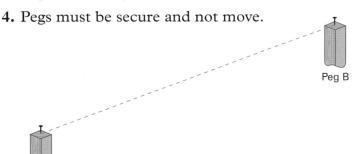

Figure 7.14 Step 1 – Establish frontage line (front base)

Step 2 – Establish peg C (Figure 7.16)

Assume sizes are

4 m × 2 m:

$X^2 = 4^2 + 2^2$
$X^2 = 16 + 4$
$X^2 = 20$
$X = \sqrt{20}$
$X = 4.472$ m

Two tapes can be used now from A and B to find C.

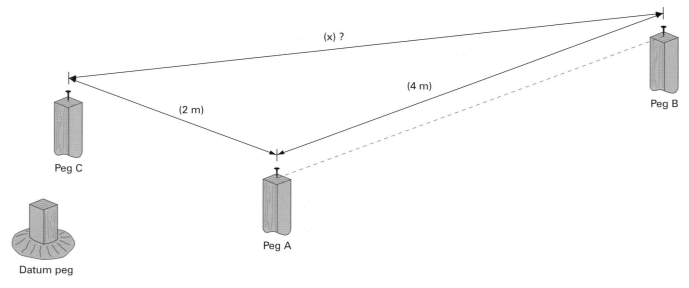

Figure 7.15 Step 2 – Establish peg C (using a site square, builder's square or the 3:4:5 method)

Step 3 – Establish peg D

1. Use two tapes and measure from pegs C and B.

2. Check diagonals A–D and C–B.

3. Building is square if the diagonals are the same length.

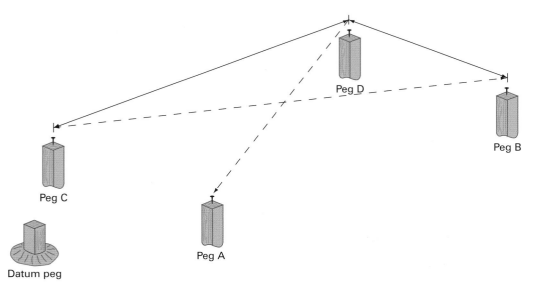

Figure 7.16 Step 3 – Establish peg D

Step 4 – Erect profiles at E and F

1. Project line from nails in pegs A and B.

2. Mark profiles with nail or saw cut.

3. Profiles should be 1 m minimum away from face – further if machine digging.

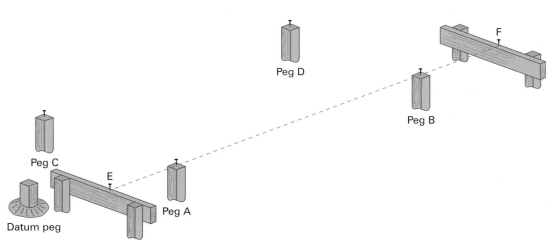

Figure 7.17 Step 4 – Erect profiles at E and F

Key term

Profile – a support for a line outside the working area

Step 5 – repeat step 3

The **profile** at peg D showing alternative corner set out.

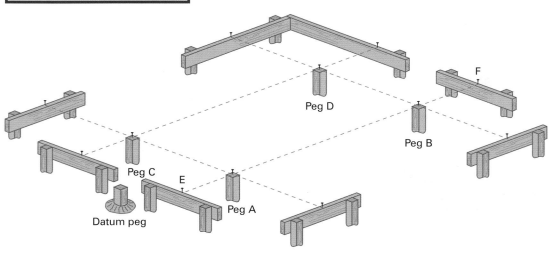

Figure 7.18 Step 5 – Repeat step 3 for remaining profiles

Step 6 – Remove corner pegs

1. Attach continuous line as shown.

2. Line represents face line(s).

3. Line should not 'bind' on crossing.

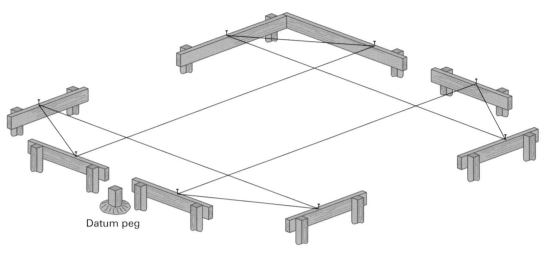

Datum peg

Figure 7.19 Step 6 – Remove corner pegs

Step 7 – Edges of foundations marked on profiles

1. Line attached – plumbed down and marked on ground with sand (shown dotted).

2. Trenches excavated.

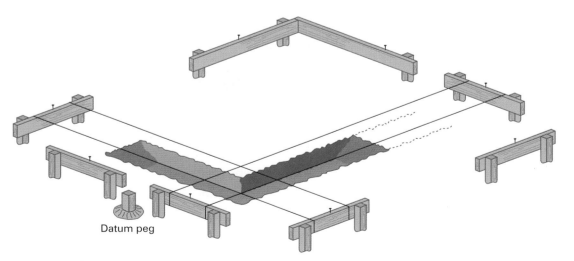

Datum peg

Figure 7.20 Step 7 – Edges of foundations marked on profiles

Single wall and corner type profiles

Corner profiles are used for setting out the main corners. Corners can be joined together to make a strong profile. This means that there is less chance of pulling when lines are attached.

Pulling occurs when the lines are attached to a single wooden profile and the line is then stretched too tightly; it can start to pull the pegs that the profile rail is attached to. This can give a distorted or false line. A good way of avoiding this is to have two profiles joined together. This gives more strength to the line and the profiles.

However, sometimes machinery may be used to dig out the correct positions of trenches and other similar tasks. The area needed for the machine to move may mean that single profiles have to be used. Single profiles would also need to be used for the marking out of any internal wall foundations.

Figure 7.21 A marked profile showing wall and trench positions

Locating walling and trench positions

As part of setting out, you must accurately locate walling and trench positions onto both single wall and corner type profiles.

Once the centre lines have been established onto the profiles, the trench positions and wall positions can be marked onto them, using the drawing and specification to determine the cavity size, wall thicknesses and foundation width.

These measurements can then be added to the profile by the use of nails or saw cuts.

Did you know?

Digging foundations by hand is now less common, as this method is often time-consuming and costly

Key term

Spoil – waste material excavated from a trench

Space between profiles and excavations

The working space required between profiles depends on the method of excavation. When machines are used in excavations, there needs to be space to allow the machines to move.

If trenches are to be dug out by machine, the **spoil** either has to be put into piles within reach of the bucket arm or carried away using a dumper. In this case, if the profiles are too close together they may be damaged or run over by the machines. If the foundation is going to be dug by hand, less room will be needed as the spoil is removed by wheelbarrow.

If profiles are moved in any way, the measurements on them will be altered. Once concreted, walls may not fit onto the foundation. This will be very expensive to correct.

Reasons for carrying out regular checks

Regular checks of measurements should be carried out while setting out. This is to ensure that all walls, trenches and other constructions are in the correct positions and square, before any excavations are carried out. Once these are dug out it is very difficult to change them other than to carry out extra digging work which will cost extra money.

There are a number of problems that can be caused by incorrectly placed setting out, for example walls not sitting on the foundations.

Transferring setting out information onto foundation concrete

Once the foundation concrete has been laid, the wall positions are now ready to be marked onto the concrete. This can be done using spray paint, chalk or by using mortar by marking position lines. The lines used for marking out the trenches should be positioned onto the nails/saw cuts marked on the profiles for the walls. These should be set on the external positions so that the lines cross to show the external corner positions.

Depending on what you are building, this should now give you the outline of that building with the four corner points clearly visible. Use a level to plumb down onto the concrete foundation, with the top of the level just about touching the line. Be careful not to push the line as this will give an incorrect position when marked. If the level will not reach to the line, a straight edge can be used to gain the height required. The level is then placed against the straight edge to plumb.

Once the position is achieved, mark the bottom of the level or straight edge on the side that is against the line. Repeat against the other corner line. It is also better to mark a position approximately 900 mm along the line from the corner each way. You can now draw or mark two lines that should meet at the corner. Repeat this for all external corners.

At this point, from these marking, you can mark the internal wall positions knowing the cavity size etc., or taking account of the measurements marked on the profiles. The corners can now be set out and built to the gauge required.

As the walls are built, the positions can be checked by the lines pulled through on the profiles to ensure that they are in the right position.

Did you know?

To help stop movement when plumbing, hold a piece of batten against the level or straight edge at a 45° angle so that one end touches the ground or foundation. This should steady it

FAQ

With so many different types of level available, which is the best type to use when setting out?

A laser level is probably the best type of level available as they are very accurate and easy to set up. They can also be used for all types of levelling throughout the course of the work, from setting foundations to fixing ceiling levels. However, you may be limited by the technology on site. A transit level is probably the next best type of levelling equipment available. Whatever you use, make sure that you check it first and use it correctly.

Why do you set brickwork out dry before building a wall?

The reason for setting out a wall dry is to see if the measurement will work to full bricks or if it needs to be adjusted to fit. This is a very quick way of checking that the work is accurate and correct.

How will I know where to set out a building?

The exact location of the building and any parts of it will be outlined in the specification. The local authority will also provide the building line, indicating the boundaries that the building will need to stay within when setting out.

Check it out

1. Draw a sketch of a corner profile.
2. Explain why care must be taken when digging foundation trenches, showing what may happen if the foundations are not dug correctly.
3. Explain what an optical site square is and where it would be used. What advantages does this type of square have over other similar tools?
4. Explain how to check a spirit level for accuracy. Write a method statement showing how to check that this tool is accurate.
5. Name six pieces of equipment or tools used when setting out, and describe exactly what each of these is used for.
6. Explain what the building line is and who sets it.
7. Explain what barren land is. What are the problems that might exist when working on barren land?
8. Explain why adequate space must be left between profiles and trench positions. Use diagrams to show what this is used for and prepare a sample risk assessment of the dangers that might exist if this space was not left.

Getting ready for assessment

At the end of studying this unit you will need to carry out a synoptic test on basic setting out. To prepare for this you will need to use the information contained in this unit and your practical experience. You should be given the opportunity to gain this and practise these skills by your college or training centre. These should provide you with the opportunity to practise and prepare for this test.

You will need to be familiar with:

- understanding and working to drawings
- setting out corners using different methods
- carrying out checks on measurements and why this is important
- the materials and equipment required for setting out
- finding and transferring different levels.

The skills in this unit will not only be useful here, but will also be needed when you are carrying out any practical tasks involving brickwork or blockwork. Remember to always take your time and ensure that this stage is correct before you continue work building your test pieces.

This unit has introduced the facts that help you to make decisions in your practical work. In your synoptic test you will need to use the knowledge that you have gained from this unit to carry out the practical task.

For learning outcome 4 you have seen why buildings must be set out in the correct location and to the building line. This knowledge will make clear why it is so important to check these stages when carrying out the initial setting out. The theory and practice behind the setting out of buildings, and the methods that will be used, have also been explained. Again, using this knowledge will make your work accurate and correct.

Before you start work, think of a plan of action that will tell you the order you need to do things in. This will help you to avoid making mistakes. Your tolerances must be correct on plumbing, gauge and level as you work. Without checking this, you could make serious mistakes in your construction that will have a big impact on the final construction.

Your speed in carrying out these tasks in a practice setting will also help to prepare you for the time set for the test. However, you must never rush the test! Always make sure that you are working safely. Make sure throughout the test that you are wearing appropriate and correct PPE and using tools correctly.

Good luck!

Knowledge check

1 Why must care be taken when excavating with a digger?

a) So as to dig in a straight line.

b) So as not to dig too deep.

c) So as not to damage services.

d) So as not to dig in the wrong place.

2 If you used the 3:4:5 method, what would you achieve?

a) Set out a level line.

b) Set out a right angle.

c) Set out a building.

d) Set out a foundation.

3 Where is the average sea level point taken for ordnance bench marks?

a) Newquay

b) Margate

c) Newlyn

d) Bristol

4 What optical instrument is used to set out a right angle?

a) Builder's square

b) Site square

c) Dumpy level

d) Set square

5 What is 'spoil'?

a) A mistake.

b) Rough concrete.

c) Excavated material.

d) A type of foundation.

6 What is 'barren land'?

a) Waste land

b) Landfill area

c) Reclaimed land

d) Constructed land

7 What does TDM stand for?

a) Traditional Bench Mark

b) Trade Bench Mark

c) To Be Made

d) Temporary Bench Mark

8 What type of level shoots a red dot to give a reading onto a staff?

a) Transit level

b) Laser level

c) Site square

d) Set square

9 What is the main consequence of setting a building outside of the building line?

a) It will cause problems when laying foundations.

b) The area might not have been properly checked for existing services.

c) You won't have permission to build in this area.

d) The ground might not be suitable for building on.

10 When using a corner profile, what is the best way to avoid pulling?

a) By joining two profiles together.

b) By checking your equipment before use.

c) By using a spirit level.

d) By checking your work with an optical level.

Common Scottish bricklaying terms compared to English terms

England	Scotland
Half bats	Half bricks
Right-angled quoin	Right-angled corner
Large spirit level	Large bead
Club or lump hammer	Mash hammer
Mixed mortar	Comp
Gable end	Pein end
Footings	Foundations
Queen closer	Pup or closure
Wall ties	Kit ties
English Garden Wall Bond	Scottish Bond
Flush joint finish	Bag rubbed finish

Index

Index